THE
BOXER'S
HEART

THE BOXER'S HEART

A Woman Fighting

Kate Sekules

Overlook Duckworth
New York & London

This edition published in paperback in the United States in 2012 by

Overlook Duckworth, Peter Mayer Publishers, Inc.
NEW YORK:
141 Wooster Street
New York, NY 10012
www.overlookpress.com
For bulk and special sales, please contact sales@overlookny.com
LONDON:
Gerald Duckworth & Co.
90-93 Cowcross Street
London EC1M 6BF
www.ducknet.co.uk
info@duckworth-publishers.co.uk

Previously published in 2000 by Villiard Books and in 2002 by Seal Press

Cataloging-in-Publication Data is available from the Library of Congress
A catalogue record for this book is available from the British Library

Typeset by Jouve
Manufactured in the United States of America
US ISBN 978-1-59020-811-3
UK ISBN 978-0-71564-369-3

FOR SCOTT

All life lies in the movement resulting
from the clash between the two polar forces,
love and conflict.

—Empedocles

CONTENTS

Prefight   1

1. How Did I Get Here?   11

2. From A to B (Aerobics to Boxing)   25

3. Here We Are Now   39

4. Let Her Come Forward   63

5. The Punch That Counts   86

6. I Spar How You Spar   105

7. I Am a Contender   125

8. Fight Time   146

9. Big Belts   170

10. My Heart   194

Postfight   224

Afterword   231

THE
BOXER'S
HEART

PREFIGHT

HELLO my name is: BOXER/HANDLER. That is what my chest reads tonight, the night before Valentine's Day 1997. I am not feeling romantic, because in about four hours' time I'm going to become a professional fighter, the first woman—well, one of a pair—to step through the ropes at Philadelphia's Blue Horizon. Tonight's card is titled the St. Valentine's Day Massacre. I hope I'm the side with the guns, but I have no idea what arsenal I might be holding, since I've never done this before. This is not only my professional boxing debut, this is going to be my first fight. Ever. As they slap the decal on my coat, I'm having serious and pointless second thoughts. Perhaps I was a little too blithe. Perhaps it wasn't so clever to sign that contract, the one from which one phrase echoes in my brain: "I understand and appreciate," it goes, "that participation carries a risk to me of serious injury including permanent paralysis or death. . . ."

Perhaps my opponent is better than I've been led to believe. She does, after all, look like a tree. Perhaps I have done something quite stupid in agreeing to fight a six-foot-three Division A basketball player with a six-win, three-knockout record. One who weighs twenty-five pounds more than I, is thirteen years younger, and whose reach extends eight inches farther than mine. Oh—and whose manager is the St. Valentine's Day Massacre promoter.

Such thoughts are crowding in, but I refuse to dwell on them. I can't afford to. Instead, I take refuge in a brand of gallows humor that, fortunately, is coming naturally, with an assist from the surroundings. The Blue Horizon is the oldest prizefighting venue in the land, as its full name—the Legendary Blue Horizon—suggests. Those serious Philadelphia fight fans are legendary, too: they love their boxing, and the bloodier the better. The Blue's part of North Philly is never going to be gentrified, I think. Maybe it's my circumstances, but all I notice on the drive from the Best Western (by cab, no limo for *my* corner) is barbed wire, broken glass, and ripped pavement, all bathed in jaundiced streetlight.

I have two handlers—my trainer and my corner. They know me pretty well, the Boxer Me at least, but I wonder if they know exactly how hard I'm leaning on them, experts in prefight choreography though they be. My trainer must know, since I've spent the last ten hours peppering him with questions: Am I ready? Can I handle this? What if I'm not mean enough? How do you know I'll know what to do? What if she's better than we think? What if I get really hurt? What if I forget everything/freeze up/cry? Only the other week, there was a dreadful little news item where a well-known heavyweight collapsed in tears on the canvas, and this guy was a veteran with a record as long as his reach. I'd have assumed these crazy nerves get blunted over time, but maybe the opposite is true, since every fight shortens the odds of your receiving the punch that counts. Everything that's happening is novel but also familiar, as if my immersion in gym life had prepared me for a night like this one, in which I am an essential player, but in a minor role. I watched *Rocky* for the first time this week (so that's why everybody's telling me to run up the Art Museum steps), and the temptation to identify with the boxing cliché of our time is strong; yet I'm resisting.

My dressing room is suitably vile. I've even had to bring my own makeup and costume guys because the directors provided only a very basic trailer without staff. It is up two flights of creaking mildewed stairs, a roughly partitioned doorless closet furnished with a wooden table. An embarrassed scuffle follows our arrival, as a filthy sheet is procured and secured to protect my modesty, at the orders of the local boxing commissioner, who needs visual evidence that I really am female.

————————

It is four hours until the first fight, and I learn that my bout is scheduled fourth out of nine, a prime place on the undercard, billed thus on account of my opponent, Raging Belle, who has a large dressing room with lackeys and bouquets. Her manager, the promoter, whom my trainer calls the "Big-Nose Guy," keeps doing the rounds of the dressing rooms, spending long minutes in hers, bouncing along the row of contenders, finally poking his nose behind my sheet wearing a terribly worried expression and asking if I'm okay. Of course I'm bloody okay. *Shouldn't* I be okay? Does he think I'm going to back out now? He should save his concern for his skyscraper girl, Raging. Illogically, Raging wants to become a model after she's finished with pugilism, and the Big-Nose Guy is not above exploiting her pretty face for his purposes, billing her as "the cover girl of women's boxing," and attempting to preserve her pulchritude by permitting her to fight in headgear. When I signed the contract, he and his sidekick shared a joke: since her face is his fortune, they decided, they'd be sure to stop the fight at the first sign of her blood. I digested that grim information, both sides of it—evidently, my face can bleed and bruise all it likes; but all I need do for the TKO (technical knockout) is smash up the Raging Belle's nose. Curiously, the shabby treatment feels good tonight. I am comfortable assuming the underdog position, or as comfortable as I can be with a helter-skelter of raging butterflies trapped inside me.

The past two weeks have been the least comfortable of my life. I had no precedent for the scale of those nerves, nerves with teeth and claws that never left me alone except to sleep the sleep of the brave—a phrase I suppose I understand now—and to train. The effects of my gym work have alternated between soothing my anxiety and pouring gas on the fires of my fears, depending on whether I had a good day, with everything coming together and my bravado high, or a bad day of imposter syndrome. One of the latter accounted for my busted nose and the pair of black eyes I'm still sporting at the Blue, a little faded, but noticeable. When the fight physician examined me this morning at the weigh-in, he paused over those.

"Hmmm. Is this discoloration normal for you?" he asked.

"Yes." I lied. Luckily, Pennsylvania is notorious for its perfunctory medicals. More disturbing to me than my dodgy nose was how a big part of my heart leaped when I had that fleeting shot at disqualification.

The physician now appears again for the prefight routine, with its special new component: I have to prove I am not going to be a mother any time soon. Tonight's good doctor is dapper, in a long black Nehru-collared jacket that makes him look half downtown hip, half undertaker, so, needless to say, we dub him Dr. Death. It makes a surreal picture, Dr. Death and me poring over a pink plastic stick I just peed on, as men at their testosterone zeniths mill about, snorting air humid with warm-up sweat. Raging Belle and I are not pregnant.

The day has consisted mostly of what I would normally call wasted time. I spent it in my room, failing to nap, watching *The Hudsucker Proxy* on HBO, getting one of my trainer's famous rubdowns with the green embrocation he concocts from Ben-Gay, eucalyptus oil, and rubbing alcohol, and reciting my litany of questions. After the lurid tension of the week, this day has been the eye of the storm. I woke up and wrote in my journal: "Today I can't be bothered to be nervous. If I don't know it now, it's too late. . . . Like cramming for exams."

Consequently, the weigh-in was fun. In a downtown high-rise, next to the Office of Mental Health and Substance Abuse Services, the Athletic Commission was crawling with officials, trainers, managers, and their half-dressed charges, most of them getting their first look at the guy who'd soon be inches away, trying to bury his glove in their face. The loudest things in there were the jackets—SMOKIN' JOE, PRINCE CHARLES WORLD CHAMP, Tommy Hilfiger—until the Big-Nose Guy arrived, escorting Raging Belle, and a muffled commotion ensued as she was installed in a private room to insulate her from the effects of her outfit, a ridiculous short lime-green tank dress and high heels. As far as I could see, the attention Raging reaped was more resentful than lascivious. None of the other St. Valentine's Day Massacre fighters has an HBO crew on their tail like she does, or a private waiting room, or a paycheck from the promoter, or a generous purse balanced on a minuscule record. They have paid their dues. The stupid girl! Haughty poseuse—acting like a starlet, giving women a bad name! I wanted to beat her up.

The weigh-in business done, lunch at a backstreet diner with the two other fighters from my gym and all our corners was a simple fueling pit stop, but for me the tang of solidarity was pungent. Eating chicken in my leather coat, I felt special, marked out for something. Then came the afternoon, the loose time folding itself away, carrying in the fight, incipient panic. An hour before we left, the phone started to ring. Would I mind the HBO cameras in my dressing room? They need "B-roll." Could I be interviewed by the local news channel before the fight? When? Just before? I don't know. I don't know how I'll be feeling. Oh, okay, but be gentle with me.

Channel 6 has set up its camera in the arena, so three hours before fight time we are paraded ringside, where I get a preview of the battleground. The Blue is a gorgeous cliché. It looks just like the oldest fight venue in America should, like a bombed-out church, with the ring where the altar used to be, pews of folding metal chairs, and a peanut-gallery choir.

"There isn't another sports arena in the country remotely like the Blue Horizon," wrote Bill Barich in a *Sports Illustrated* paean to the place. "It's the sort of raw and smoky tavern that George Bellows painted early this century, a throwback to the era of straw hats, stogies and dime beers. Only 1,500 fans can be crammed inside for an event, but the crowd compensates for its lack of size with its animal howling. . . . Indeed, if boxing has a soul, it might well be located in the City of Brotherly Love."

I sit on the stage, the ring in back of me, a klieg light in my eyes.

"Are you ready for this?" asks the reporter.

"Oh yes, I'm ready," I lie, silently recounting the times I've asked my trainer the very same question. Now the reporter turns to him.

"How do you rate Kate's chances?" she asks. "She's facing an experienced opponent. Is she ready?"

He nods, shrugs, never a man of many words. She persists.

"What would you say is her style?"

"Unorthodox," says my trainer. *Unorthodox?* That's news to me. What the hell has he been letting me get away with? The reporter, desperate for a usable sound bite, turns to me, which is futile, since I am not going to betray feelings, in case they breed doubt.

"How does it feel in the ring, fighting another woman?" she asks.

"I don't know." Now it's my turn to shrug. "It's my first time, remember? Ask me in three hours."

"So, how are you feeling? Are you nervous?" she persists. I shrug again.

"No. I've just got a job to do."

Man, did I *say* that? So that's why athletes spout such appalling banalities. These questions have nothing to do with *me*, or with what

I'm about to do. I feel fraudulent, too, being interviewed before my first fight ever as if I were a contender, but it's still hard to resist the attention.

Back in my closet, it's time for the rituals of preparation. I am left alone to don my battle dress—my black trunks with white stripe, two sports bras, the plastic breastplate, the black satin robe borrowed from my trainer's best young fighter, my black mouth-guard in the pocket. My hands are encased in the gauze bandages used for fights in place of canvas handwraps—over and over and round and round, through the fingers, round and round, a full half-inch thick. They are little mummies. Then the wrap is repeated in coach tape, and we await the commissioner's approval. The commissioner is what they call a "jobsworth" back in England, an inflexible type who can be depended upon to intone: "Oh no, I can't do that, mate. It's more than my job's worth." He's sure the wraps protrude a millimeter too far above my knuckles; he imagines a frayed edge; but eventually he is satisfied, and signs my hands with a Magic Marker; then my corner takes his crooked scissors and carves the palms out. Normally I wrap my own hands; this is a whole other level of wrapping. They feel snug and compact. These are professional fists. After tonight, it will be illegal for me to use them on the street. Imagine! My own little scarred knuckles, lethal weapons in the eyes of the law. I have been boxing just long enough now for that to seem plausible, yet absurd, much like this entire escapade. Even now as I'm laced into a pair of scarlet fight gloves, a full four ounces lighter than my sparring gloves, I am half-expecting some deus ex machina to intervene and prevent the fight. I am not exactly ready to rumble. My heart rate has slowed back down. I feel lethargic and pale and weak.

Some friends of mine have made the trek to Philly to witness my debut, and I have never been so happy to see them. Do I want to be alone? they wonder. No, I do not. I need their normalcy. And here's

Jill Matthews from Gleason's, who went down in history as the first female Golden Gloves champion, who, at this point, has started amassing a string of wins that will soon lead to two championship belts in her weight, and whose current manager is the St. Valentine's Day promoter's son. She's been spying on Raging Belle.

"She's a wreck! She's quaking in her boots!" screams Jill. "You've got it in the bag, Kate. Go get her!"

Time passes and time passes and I toy with my emotions, trying them on like outfits—a suit of humility (no), a coat of cockiness (perhaps), a sensible sweater (keep it), fear (necessary)—but soon it dawns on me that my state of mind is now irrelevant. In about an hour I will finally live the eleven minutes I've been preliving over and over and over again. It dawns on me that this is it, my cue to unleash the dogs of war held back my whole life long. How are they? I wonder. Are they asleep? Crippled? Do they, in fact, exist? And in case they don't, where's the cutman?

Now there is a racket outside my closet, a cheering and clattering and somebody yelling, "First knockout!" Two to go, then it's me. When the third bout goes in, my trainer dons the focus mitts—flat gloves used for target practice.

"Come on," he says, and leads me into the blue corner room next to my closet. Like me, the guys in here are tonight's away team, required to provide a good spectacle and then, it is hoped, lose. The mood is somber, the guys are tense, slumped sweating in towels, ignoring this intrusion. I get my first real hit of fight juice from the suspicion that they dismiss me as a gimmick, the mere opponent of the cover girl of—puh*leeze*—women's boxing.

We try some combinations, very tight, to warm me up, and we go over the plan, which is this: throw the first punch. That's it, the entire plan. Slam a big right into her face and "knock her thoughts out," as my trainer puts it. But what then? I keep asking him. How do I fight someone so big? How? You'll know what to do, he says, don't worry. And I'm hitting the pads—jab-jab-right, slip, slip, left-right uppercut, hook—and I'm asking, but what *next*? After the big right hand, what then? And he's saying, I told you, you'll know what to do. Fighting is easier than training, you'll see. And I'm yelling back—SLAP-SLAP-BOOM! BANG, BANG-BOOOM!—But what if I *don't know*? What if? What—ba-DA-BAM!—then? And now I stop asking because I'm busy hitting and I see that he's right and I will know what to do. I already do know. My trainer lowers the pads and I grin at him, and when I look around, I catch some ten pair of eyes.

"Hey," says one boxer. "You can hit."

"You're fighting that girl, right?" says another. "Well, she big. You fight a big guy before?"

"No," I say. "You know, this is my first fight in fact."

"Overhead rights," he says, seriously. "Overhead rights and body shots."

"Yeah, git inside and attack the body," says another guy. We do another round of padwork and I feel the boxers' eyes and I feel good. By the time I have to go, I have the opponents on my side. I am ready. My trainer helps me into the robe, with his fighter's name stripped out with a triangle of coach tape, and buckles on my headgear (useless thing, but *she's* wearing it, so I must, too). Opponents high-five me. They rally round.

"You get her, you hear?" they say.

———————

My ring walk is lined with wise guys and well-wishers, but the packed house is a blur. I step through the ropes and pace the ring, counting the steps, one, two, three, four, four and a half, that's how far it is to the middle of the ring, the ground to cover for the first punch. Carefully I fail to note my friends' locations and take my corner, shifting foot to foot, loosening out my arms, shadowboxing. I have to remind myself to breathe. An age later, she arrives, a giantess in a pristine scarlet satin outfit, her robe lettered RAGING BELLE.

The crowd gives voice, about equal parts cheers and boos. I hear wolf whistles, catcalls as if from under water; I don't care. Now the tuxedoed ring announcer takes center stage, pulling the mike lead like a tail.

"Boxing fans, this next bout . . ." At the mention of the referee's name, the crowd yawls.

". . . a ladies' bout scheduled for four rounds in the middleweight division . . ." I cringe at that reminder of her weight advantage. I am two divisions lighter.

"First, out of the blue corner, from across the pond, in London, England . . ."

I catch the words "international restaurant critic" and the names of some of the magazines I write for, and cringe afresh.

". . . let's welcome again from London, England, Kate Sekules! Sekules!" How in hell did my parents' name get to the Legendary Blue Horizon? Absurdly, the Talking Heads song "Once in a Life-time" starts playing in my head: "*And I ask myself, how did I get here?* . . ." Now, this is beyond strange. This is for real. My trainer prods me in the back and hisses at me to walk out and greet the crowd, and though I have done nothing to deserve a cheer, I do so, cringing at this too (after all, I come from the land of embarrass-ment), and there arises a medium hurrah, I suspect from my friends. He next announces the contender, lists her record of six wins, three by way of knockout, and no losses. She punches the air and there's a fat hurrah, I suspect because she is pretty.

She and I and the ref meet in the middle. I look up at her, a reach away at last, and I (at five eight and a half) feel very short. She won't look me in the eye, but I do look into hers, and there I see fear—unmistakable, undiluted fear. I like that. The ref speaks:

"No holding, no hitting on the break, no illegal punches, no low blows. Protect yourselves at all times. If I give the eight count, go to a neutral corner and stay there until I give the word. Now touch gloves, go to your corners, and come out fighting. Good luck, ladies."

My robe comes off, my mouthguard goes in, my seconds climb out. And now here it comes. Here's the bell . . .

1

How Did I Get Here?

When did you start boxing? I am asked. Depends, I say. Do you mean when I first threw a jab in the first aerobic boxing class at Crosby Street Studios where it all began—both women's boxing and my boxing—in New York? Or do you mean when Lonnie "Lightning" Smith got in the ring with me, and me oh-so-cool and thinking, Hey, I've got the boxing thing down, except Lonnie was water, and I could not land a finger? Or do you mean when I first sparred with a girl? Or when I first got hit so bad that it hurt, or when I saw the black dots in my eyes, or when my knees buckled, or when my nose broke, or when I was first afraid of what I had set in motion? Or do you mean when I first stepped through the ropes for money, or back when Stephan Johnson and Juan La Porte taught me my first footwork and I felt the hunger in my body to know this thing, to be this thing, an actual boxer?

It began in 1992. There were no women boxing in 1992. There had once been women boxers, but the world and I were not aware of them. Even the boxing community (I use the term approximately) barely bothered remembering Cat Davis or Marion "The Lady

Tyger" Trimiar or Jackie "The Female Ali" Tonawanda (who was briefly the male Ali's bodyguard), or even, say, the Webber twins, Dora and Cora, even though the twins were still *in* the boxing community, and, it turned out, would fight again—and win—after turning forty. I had given not a moment's thought to the existence of female boxers, because I did not like boxing. When the Scorsese movie *Raging Bull* played on television, in about '85, I switched it off. I couldn't stomach the sound of the punches, not only in the ring but also in the apartment—the male-bull, the wife-victim, the violence ...

I dislike violence. Nevertheless, the first time ever I threw a punch, I was hooked. Nowadays, thousands and thousands of women who work out know how that feels, since the boxing class is a fixture on every city gym schedule. When she hears I box, a stranger usually counters with her own experience: "I took a boxing class at my gym," she might say. "I loved it! I hurt for days! And I run thirty miles a week." She usually has a friend who boxes, though doesn't spar, is hazy about the difference between kickboxing and the straight-up sort, and probably changed her own allegiance to Tae-Bo in 1998. Yes, the concept of the aerobic boxing class long ago became pretty unsurprising, verging on dull, but the fact of women fighting for real has teetered on the edge of the mainstream since 1995.

That was the year the Golden Gloves—the principal amateur boxing competition in the United States—created the first female divisions. The Gloves is not the only route into the sport for men in this country, but it is the popular and sensible one. Success there wins a fighter a shot at the Nationals, and at international competition leading to the Olympics, or, for the impatient, better management for a professional debut. A woman boxer's path is less clear, and as polymorphic as the athletes themselves. Even now, with the sport having taken off to some extent, the 2004 Olympics may or may not sprout a distaff ring, and a Gloves entrant in, say, Portland, Oregon, may or may not find an opponent in her weight class, and could conceivably win a coveted pair of diamond-studded twenty-four-karat-gold-plated boxing gloves on a walkover. In other words, there are female Golden Gloves champions who have never fought. Even odder, there are professional female boxers who enter the ring without having fought—a reckless leap, like going straight from the bunny slopes to a ski-jumping competition. I am one of these.

Let's get clear from the start that this is no champ's "as told to" autobiography. My record is small. The story of how I acquired it is better. If I have cared too little for the fight itself and too much for dissecting how boxing makes me feel, how it changes and challenges me, and what my gender means in this context, I'm happy. I fought to shake things up, to play with the world. And if I—sometime bookworm, singer in a band, Londoner, magazine editor, fiction writer, travel and food critic, softball addict, Caucasian of mixed heritage, pony-mad child, expatriate—could become a convincing pugilist, then anything under the sun is possible.

I wonder myself what set this obsession in motion. I suppose it's rooted in childhood, in growing up a tomboy; and it must have something to do with following a decidedly nonlinear career in which I rarely felt I quite fitted in the world. I have to assume I am playing with my damaged parts. If I had stopped, as the majority of women do, at training, I would not think that. Training to box is one of the toughest physical challenges you can set yourself, and it is clean. But once you step through the ropes, a dimension rears up that is not pure at all. To compete as a runner, a swimmer, a player of tennis, golf, basketball, football—any noncombat sport—what you do is an extension of what you did in training, only more intense; but to compete as a boxer, your aims are suddenly quite distinct from those of your training sessions. You hope to inflict so much pain on your opponents that they fall over and can't get up.

Nobody boxes who doesn't have to, goes the adage, but what does "have to" mean? I used to assume the obvious, that it's about fighting your way out of the ghetto, until I found that nothing was more alive for me than fighting my way with all my heart *into* one particular ghetto. I didn't have to box for the money, but I did "have to" box, and I'm not the only one. All the boxers who appear in these pages have to, and yet the best female boxers I know all had other fish to fry. Jill Matthews (12-1-2), holder of the unified featherweight belt, is a rabbi's daughter, hairdresser, and singer. She is a hyperkinetic motormouth who hammers out self-deprecating one-liners that Sandra Bernhardt would envy and claims to hate half the world, although everyone loves her. Veronica Simmons (22-0-0), the middleweight world amateur champion, is sleek, big, taciturn, and unfathomable—not unfriendly, not warm. She is a federal corrections officer and was an all-state college basketball champion. Lucia Rijker (14-0-0), often called the best female boxer in the world, is the charismatic life-and-soul anywhere she goes. You'd think her absolutely ego-driven, except that she's a devoted Buddhist. Rijker was already the world kickboxing champion, and now she's being courted for major Hollywood roles, like the lead in *The Matrix*, which she turned down because the filming would have coincided with her first world-title fight. Aside from boxing, it doesn't matter what these three and I have in common, there is an affinity, a fellowship. I believe the common theme, the hunger to box, is hidden deep and can be located only by its owner. I believe the fuel for the fight derives not from what we have done, but from how we ourselves view what we have done, and from hidden things we can't talk about easily. I believe it is related to the drive found in all athletes but that it has a distinctive flavor, and that it may not be so different in a man, except that women share discrete areas of additional pressure in this culture. When I look into my own past and heart, I see clues that suggest how *any* woman might understand the need to fight.

Show me a female boxer who wasn't a tomboy and I'll show you a liar. Not that tomboyhood is restricted to embryo pugilists; far from it. Tomboys are everywhere, and they are normal, and they are expected to grow out of it, though many, like me, never quite do. It is not the same for little boys, for whom displaying feminine behavior (not to mention wearing girls' clothes) is taboo. This contradiction implies that qualities customarily associated with masculinity (aggression, drive, forthrightness, ebullience) are useful, whereas those generally tagged feminine (gentleness, kindness, self-deprecation, concern with appearance) are dispensable, verging on undesirable. But that notion is way outdated. A girl child today has role models—rock chicks, Xena, Oprah, Venus and Serena—who synthesize tomboyhood and femininity. Girlpower wasn't available to my generation. For women my age and a decade on either side, being a tomboy was a rebellion against what seemed the weak position; it was a brand of defiance. Personally, I have not finished kicking against a prescribed female role that restricts us. Doors have opened, sure, but what makes me mad is that it's still okay for girls to grow up believing what they weigh and wear is more important than what they know and read, say and do. Sports can cure that. I am fighting stereotypes.

I cannot speak for all female boxers. Often, the reasons for fighting remain unconscious, and since a boxer with doubts makes a fighter with flaws, it's probably better that way. Women who fight do so in the boxing world—a pretty reactionary microcosm. At its worst, it is an organized crime syndicate founded on a mercenary and fear-based power structure, in which women are usually found half-naked in stilettos, displaying the round number. Women who enter this world in boxing boots are not necessarily fighting for anything more than attention. Take Christy Martin, for instance, the first famous female professional boxer, who signed with Don King and appeared in satin trunks, not a swimsuit, on the cover of *Sports Illustrated* after fighting on a nationally televised Mike Tyson undercard. She flatly rejects feminism: "I'm not out to make a statement about women in boxing, or even women in sports . . ." she said in that *SI* piece (titled "Gritty Woman"). "This is about Christy Martin."

Some women who run the show don't want to mess with the status quo either, like boxing publicist Kathy Duva, widow of the famous promoter Dan Duva (whose father was the legendary trainer

Lou Duva). She has said: "I don't want to deny any woman the right to do what she wants, but I don't really want to promote it. Maleness is a vital component of boxing. To do it, you have to act like a guy, and that bothers me."

But what, exactly, is "acting like a guy"? It is not a question of mere aggression, although that's what Kathy Duva presumably means. It is not about clothes, although Christy Martin hedges her bets on that one, sporting pink trunks in the ring and leather miniskirts to meet the press. In fact, clothes are potent symbols, as well as sexual signifiers. For me they have always been a litmus test, signaling my comfort level in any situation (and who has not felt the misery of being dressed wrongly?). When I was a child, I dressed like a boy in order to play like a boy. As a teenager, when not wearing school uniform, I tried on different identities. In my twenties, conscious of sexual politics, experiments became deliberate. How I looked and the shape of my body seemed to shape my experience rather than the other way around. Some seeds of fighting lie there.

As far as I was concerned, I wasn't a girl. I hated dolls and pink, climbed trees, and coveted my cousin's toy guns. I crocheted well but swam better; I could throw but not dance. My first best friend was Candy, who would get sent home from nursery school for wearing trousers under her dress. She was an athletic genius who won horse shows *and* piano competitions. I envied her prowess. Then my best friend was Cha, who had fourteen guinea pigs and could paint but not read. We were inseperable until wrenched apart at eleven, when she was kept back and I was sent to an academic girls' high school in a Jacobean mansion in Hammersmith. There my best friend for a couple of years was Fiona. She was a Cockney with a foul mouth, spiderleg eyelashes, orange feathercut hair, and a boyfriend named Shane. She told me about oral sex. "It tastes like ice cream," she claimed. I hadn't a clue what she meant. I was still mad about ponies, and had a crush on Donny Osmond. My journal recorded my moods in code, and, in obsessive detail, the scores of the intramural games in which I was team captain. Moods and scores were linked.

At school we wore a uniform topped by a gray flannel blazer adorned with the school motto: *Francha Leale Toge*, Old Cornish for "Loyal and free go I." Loyal to what? Free from what? I wondered. Certainly not from the restraints of fashion, especially not after ninth grade, when we dropped uniform and met boys, when having a thin body in the right jeans became the key to success. Uniforms have their uses; they delay the time when clothes become a divisive source of anxiety. On the other hand, it was a uniform that helped me form a low opinion of sports that persisted for years and did me no good. It was what we wore for the eurhythmics called "Dance" we endured in sixth grade. That uniform consisted of baggy gray knickers—British panties—and white vests, or tank tops. Since some of us, including me, were sprouting little breasts and menstruating, this state of undress was humiliating, and however satirically Fiona and I pranced, I felt painfully exposed and thigh-conscious among child bodies and fat girls (was I one?). "Dance" was supposed to teach little girls form and grace (thanks a bunch, Isadora Duncan), through movements like *wringing*, where we twisted our arms wrist over wrist like baby housewives squeezing water from wet clothes, and *dabbing*, where we prodded the air, plink, plink, plink, as if bursting tiny fairy bubbles. This was what we got instead of gym, Little League, basketball, track, swim team. I regret that. I regret that to my seventies teenage tomboy mind, sports were more about "Dance" than anything cool, and I therefore dropped them one by one. First went the ice skating, my mother's only sport. She who grew up in Silesia, skiing to school and skating along the river. (It was so cold then, she says, they would cry because of it, and the tears would freeze.) Then my parents, worrying about homework, made me quit my extracurricular swim team. Hockey went south next, and volleyball, netball (sad basketball), and rounders, an anemic version of softball played by British girls that is nowadays being replaced in Britain by true softball—the game that would bring me back to sports, rescuing me from aerobics a decade later.

Ninth grade marked a big change, not so much because we

dropped sports and all uniforms but because we discovered our brother school. From then on, that neighboring all-boys school joined ours for after-hours dramatic activities, like murdering Shakespeare's comedies and getting sick on cheap white wine at parties and making out. The boys were glamorous. They played rugby and rowed crew on the Thames. We wore rugby shirts as fashion. I wondered why we didn't get to row, since our school was almost as near to the Thames. Of course we did not compete with the boys. I say "we," but I did not belong to any of the cliques at the cliquiest school in London. They were different from the American high school sort—no cheerleaders and homecoming queens, no jocks, no geeks, no stoners and freaks. Instead, there was the drama clique (one of those boys was Hugh Grant); the art room clique; the trio known as Charlie's Angels because they were simply perfect; the debutante set; the boy magnets; and the rest of us. The rest of us didn't gel. Fiona was expelled. I was lonely. I read all the time. I became an amateur anthropologist and watched my classmates jockeying for status, resenting and hugging my outsiderhood.

The summer term of ninth grade a new girl arrived.

"You must all be kind to her," said the teacher. "She will seem strange because she had a serious accident and her brain was damaged. She nearly died and is healing very slowly."

The new girl was Candy. She had been thrown from her horse and her hat had fallen off, which was presented to us as a morality tale, as if being properly dressed were the necessary prophylactic against harm (which does not obtain, I later learned, in the boxing ring). This Candy was a stranger. Her motor skills had returned before her intellect, and I would glimpse her on the playing fields, captaining the hockey team, serving aces, skinny and childlike with legs that bowed backwards like parentheses. We never spoke again.

Meanwhile, Cha had been sent to a progressive, coed school

where bullies had knives, where she outgrew our rolled-up Levis and backyard menagerie and games of Chinese jump rope and leap-frog. After my first trip to Europe sans parents, at age sixteen, joining Cha and her new stepfamily for one perfect week on the Peloponnesus, watching the sunrise wrapped in our bedsheets, drinking tea (I have a photograph); after my seventeenth summer, when my father died; after I had left for college and embarked on a three-year voyage over the edge—I got a phone call. Cha had killed herself. She was found by her mother one morning, hanging. I didn't go to the funeral.

It left an odd impression, all my friends dematerializing. Nothing seemed solid, least of all identity. I could be anybody. I had a virulent strain of the soul disease endemic among teenagers—that *nobody understands* feeling—and assumed the trendy girls at school found me boring. I decided I was fat, and that this disqualified me from participating in the punk wave that hit London in 1977. To be a punk you had to look wasted and not go to a good school, so I compromised: I listened religiously to alternative DJ-god John Peel's late show under the covers every night and scoured Portobello Market for peculiar vintage clothes. Privately, I aligned myself with Siouxsie Sioux and Poly Styrene of X-Ray Spex, but I was stuck indoors, with my expatriate parents, a good girl with bad thoughts and an encyclopedic knowledge of the oeuvre of Stiff Little Fingers and XTC. I went to parties with the glamorous boys and occasionally "got off with" one of them, and cycled precariously home at two A.M., back to the sanctuary of home, and remained a virgin and went to Stranglers and Ian Drury and Clash gigs and Rock Against Racism festivals and waited for my life to start.

I was not a boxing fan, but I do remember being aware and in awe of several boxers, I think because my mother never resisted making disparaging comments when Ali was mouthing off on some chat show, or when 'Enry Cooper appeared on the aftershave adverts, endorsing the "grea' smell uv Brut." Henry Cooper was a British hero, though mainly remembered elsewhere for flooring Cassius Clay in the fourth in Wembley Stadium in '64 (then losing, by TKO, in the fifth). John Conteh had less charisma but won more, a lot more. He held the WBA light heavyweight belt from 1968 to '74, and the WBC belt from '75 to '77, and was therefore on TV a good deal. I remember being impressed by how nice he seemed, and even discussing this with my mother. Ali's jubilant arrogance was beyond the pale for her, so I rooted automatically for him. I wasn't against my mother, just the way she mistrusted anyone arrogant and physical— and Ali was proudly, almost cartoonishly, both. Though it's hard to credit now, many people despised the most famous of boxers, especially in England, including in my home, where humility was a loud virtue. My father didn't despise Ali. He was, in fact, immune to him, as he was to all athletes because he was blind to sports. He preferred opera, history, and wine. Boxers were the furthest possible people from my people at this point. I do have a sister eleven years my senior whom I worshiped, but did so from the other side of London, because she had moved out when I was seven. She didn't like sports either and, as she recently told me, thinks boxers are "belligerent and nasty."

I didn't think that. I thought Ali and Conteh and Cooper were fascinating, yet I failed to watch their actual bouts. Had there been female combatants, it might have been different, but in the mid-seventies, I suppose women were too busy fighting for rights to fight in rings. In the U.S., there was Gloria Steinem and *Ms.* magazine; in the U.K., we had Germaine Greer and the far more radical (and inaccessible to teens) *Spare Rib*. The early-seventies hippie, free sex, marijuana thing gave way to a politicized piety that presaged the dour political correctness of the eighties, while the Beatles and Stones gave way to Led Zeppelin and Pink Floyd and other grandiose white bands for white boys. Instead of Dylan and Bowie, I listened to Top 20 hits on the radio ("Seasons in the Sun"! "Crocodile Rock"!); and, tragically, instead of *Spare Rib*, I listened to *Cosmopolitan*. That was where my first impression of the adult female world came from. I believed *Cosmopolitan* had my best interests at heart and I believed everything it said about how orgasms and diets are extremely important and easy to succeed in. The latter became my hobby. It caused me to gain weight and learn a style of self-loathing that today's increasingly sophisticated magazine industry, its putative ideals ever compromised by its advertisers' desires, still disseminates—if anything, more so on this side of the Atlantic. By the time I'd traded *Cosmo* for the *New Musical Express*, and the Top 20 for the New Wave, and Laura Ashley dresses for drainpipe jeans and vast men's shirts and ties (a fashion moment nobody wants to revive), damage had been done. I did not enjoy the high school years.

What I learned in school: to be a good sport. To swallow my pride. Not to speak up. French, German, Spanish, Eng. Lit., Math. To count calories under my breath, all day long. To watch. That this was not my prime. Optimism.

Fall 1979, everything changed. My father had a heart attack and died that summer, just before my eighteenth birthday. By then he was skin and bone, his flesh the color of iodine and covered in an infernal itching rash from pancreatic cancer. The doctors had lied to us, telling us that he would make it, or had at least advised my mother to lie to me, at least during A Levels—the big exams that would decide my future. I loved him so much I believed the lie, despite the evidence that he was wasting away. My father had always been overweight and was forever being put on thousand-calorie diets that I watched with interest, and later joined, devouring his calorie charts while he groused and counted days to the return of cheese. To me, he was gentle, self-contained, and lenient, and it is because of him that I trust men. I got special treatment. With my mother he was demanding and condescending, which drove her to hysterics. Rather than fight back, she would blame herself for everything, and I learned to parrot my father and sister and accuse her of martyrdom, which would cause high-decibel shouting storms in the apartment, and conflict in me.

Five years after he died, I learned my father had been Jewish. I knew some of his biography—born rich in Vienna, emigrated at age fifteen, went to technical school instead of university, fought for England in World War II—but there were gaping holes in the story that, when filled in, made some sense of the war-zone aspect of home that led to my habits of solitude. When my father was thirteen, it turned out, his father had killed himself. Not because of Kristallnacht, which hadn't happened yet, but because the economic depression had killed his hat-trimmings business and he despaired. My father had heard the news from "friends" at school who'd taunted him—*Your father's dead!*—just as they'd taunted him about being a "Jew boy." In 1935 his mother managed to get his younger sister to London on a Kindertransport. Two months later, by the skin of his teeth (after a bout of appendicitis and the eventual intercession of an uncle already in England), he was sent too, with his mother following shortly afterwards. His twelve-year-old sister was sent to boarding school, but since there was absolutely no money, he, at just fifteen, had to make his own way. So he learned English and trained as an electrician. Soon, he took communion in secret in the Methodist Church. My mother was raised Lutheran in Germany. Her father was a Nazi sympathizer. Her brother trained—reluctantly—as an officer in the Kriegsmarine. When my mother was seventeen, her father abandoned her mother and ran off with his secretary, her brother drowned in his first U-boat operation, and her mother, defeated, killed herself.

A lot was repressed at home. There was much love, but it was not until I was fighting that I could feel any link between my parents' pasts and my childhood and me now. The operative word here is "feel." I'd figured out that to have as parents a converted, ashamed Jew and a Nazi-once-removed (though she herself was anything but a fascist) living in postwar, German-hating Britain, each carrying the grief and guilt of parental suicide, was a shaky foundation, but there is a gulf between knowing and understanding. When my father died, I went crazy. I left home for Manchester University, joined a band, dropped out of school, and discovered sex. I didn't see a connection between my bereavement (double, if you count Cha) and my behavior, though for three years I didn't cry, didn't sleep (much), and medicated myself in and out of extreme moods via every street drug up to and including heroin. I never shot up, but did cut my arms experimentally, to see how I'd feel. I felt nothing.

But I was getting kicks at last. The rebel I'd been training since tomboy days, who'd gone to ground for years, surfaced. My secret music dream came true and my band was big around town. I still listened to the New Wave godfather, John Peel, but now we did sessions for him, and he loved us, and I often sat with him as he broadcast the show. My Portobello Road clothes looked great with my half-bleached hair and everyone knew me, and I got thin from amphetamines. My mother was distraught. My sister found me sullen and delinquent. However I spun it, that didn't sit well with me, and I had the sensation of falling, and of unreality, and beneath the high times I was depressed. In '81, I moved back to London with the band. We set up a record company, recorded a single, did another Peel Session, and a year later, just as four hip alternative labels (they still existed) were courting us, we split up.

And I moved to a big house with friends I still have, and I went back to school and got a degree and stopped the drugs, and lived with my boyfriend, then with the next, and I swam laps every day and started to write and gained weight, and got mired in that obsession again, and read *Fat Is a Feminist Issue*, and discovered a thing called an "aerobics class," very new to London, and I liked it. Once, I went to a jazz club with my boyfriend and a bully stole my seat. He didn't really want the seat; he was cruising for a bruising with my big boyfriend, who, contrary to his appearance, had never had a fight in his life. The arrogance of the bully got my goat, but what really killed me was the way he ignored me, though it was my seat he took, assuming that my man would do my fighting. Now, I was fit and I was big and strong, and I was angry. My heart was pounding, so badly did I want to sock the guy. I wanted him to think women worthy of attention, to think again. But my boyfriend, a friendly sort, defused the situation and, before I knew it, was headed to the bar with the guy to bond over a beer, leaving me to admire him for his grace, but still fuming. From that moment, I ached to know whether I had what it takes to have hurt the guy. I was muscular (a mixed blessing, though one I was now enjoying intermittently), but I didn't know if I could *use* my strength. In the back of my mind, from then on, was always the question: Can I throw a good punch?

2

From A to B
(Aerobics to Boxing)

Three skeletons doing the lambada. *IEs Mi Estudio!* they grin. That's the ad I pick from *The Village Voice* for the gym least likely to employ a standard pep team in thong leotards. It is 1992. I'm in New York—in a SoHo sublet, to be precise—and I need a place to sweat. Crosby Street Studio turns out to be as hip as its logo, just right for SoHo in the days when bohemians without trust funds still lived there and art galleries outnumbered Banana Republics. It consists of two huge, sunny loft studios with schizophrenia—graffiti art versus ballet barres; hip-hop versus yoga—and is run by a Canadian-born former actor and tennis player named Leslie Howe, whom I could no sooner imagine going "*Whooo!*" in the high-impact section than I could see Queen Elizabeth sparring.

I hate aerobics. Let me count the ways: the mirror; the rat-on-a-treadmill aspect; ridiculous moves with the arm-waving and the twirling; tedious *boom-chick-boom-chick* disco music in four-four time. But Leslie's class features sounds mixed by her DJ friend Vincent, moves inspired by sports and African dance, and not a headset microphone in sight. It is all right. It keeps me fit as I perform the steps in a half-trance, my thoughts elsewhere.

One day, we're about to do the limbo-dance, slapping-the-floor part, when a great thing happens. Suddenly, Leslie puts her left foot forward, points her shoulder at the class, folds her forearms up to her chin, and throws a punch. We class members look at each other, dubious. Leslie takes up the position again, rocks back onto her right foot and punches from the other side, then steps on her left and throws another jab, then a right, then a jab, all in time to the Vincent groove. Gradually, each in her own time, we all awake from the torpor born of mindless repetition, adopt various simulacra of the boxer's stance, and follow suit. Bam! The punch that matters. I must look like a chicken trying to hit a golf ball, but I fall in love with myself throwing that fist, head over heels, right there, bam! Unlike my years of submission to aerobics, this punch feels like me. It satisfies the tomboy. After five minutes of shadowboxing, I am happy and drenched. What a lark! Boxing! How mad.

Well, pretty soon, on the schedule sheet at Crosby Street, this notice appears:

Gleason's Gym Boxing Workout

Learn boxing skills from professional fighters
Juan La Porte and Stephen Johnson.
Hit heavy bag, speed bag, double-end bag,
jump rope and padwork.
Get the best workout in town!

"You should try it, Kate," Leslie says.

"Ooh, no, I don't think so. Isn't it very serious?" I whine. I have never met a boxer. In my mind, John Conteh notwithstanding, a boxer is a growling bully, a boot-camp sergeant, a cruel misogynist. That class must be for the guys who work out here. I fail to perceive the hypocrisy of this opinion.

"No, the class is real laid-back, and boxing's a blast. I've been doing it a while now."

"What—at Gleason's?" I gasp. I know about Gleason's. Gleason's is the most famous boxing gym in the world. The name has forever languished in my internal lexicon, unused. "Is that in New York?"

"Sure," she says. "In Brooklyn. I've been going every morning." I resolve to try the Crosby Street version of a Gleason's Gym workout. What can it do to me? I can leave. I need never go back. And I do so like this shadowboxing in class.

It takes me a couple of weeks to get around to it—in other words, to screw up my courage—but one October evening, pretending it's no big deal, I take the elevator to Juan La Porte and Stephan Johnson's Boxing Workout. It's been a while since I've been in the dancers' domain of the lower studio with its barre and rosin box, and it has changed. From the tall ceiling, on two fat chains, hang two canvas heavybags. Attached to the only mirror-free, windowless wall is a pair of platforms with teardrop-shaped red leather bags depended beneath. The place is nearly empty. There are no people with limbs at funny angles or yogis with pretzel legs. Just two muscley men in tanks and sweatpants, one short and thick, the other my height and wiry. I do a nervous smile.

"Hi! Is this the boxing class?"

"No," says the short guy. "*You're* the boxing class."

We laugh. Bugger, I'm thinking. I can't leave now. Then another body shows up, a slip of a Japanese girl, and we begin by jumping some rope, something I last did with Cha, but an adhesive skill, apparently. I can do this. Then we start the lesson, and I'm feeling millionaire-ish from the one-on-one teaching ratio, not realizing it's the norm at boxing gyms.

I get Stephan, the wiry one. He has a soft voice, he is diffident, and very patient, carefully teaching me the most fundamental of fundamentals. The first thing he does is wrap my hands in cream bandages, hooking a loop over my thumb and passing the canvas repeatedly around my knuckles while I splay my fingers, then looping it across my wrist, around my thumb, wrist, knuckles, and fastening it with Velcro at the wrist. I love the feel of these hands, snugly parceled, and the way they look, sort of important and foreign. Stephan shows me how to stand with my left foot forward, pointing at the mirror but a bit pigeon-toed, my right foot shoulder-width behind at a forty-five-degree angle to it. Don't lock your knees; bend them, he says, and don't have your feet flat on the floor. Keep your weight evenly distributed, he says. Try transferring it from foot to foot, keeping on your toes. There. Now have your left shoulder in, over the foot, toward the mirror, he says, and angle your upper body to the right. That's to make a smaller target. Now put up your fists, pressing your elbows over your ribs. Your hands should be by your chin, the left hand in front and a bit higher, so you're looking over it.

As kids, we used to play that game Twister, where a spin of a wheel dictates which colored circles you must place your extremities upon, and you end up contorted, precariously balanced, and locked in place. This boxing stance reminds me of Twister. When Stephan puts me into position, it looks right, but how I'm supposed to achieve any mobility from here is beyond me. Still, I warm to it a little, weaving from foot to foot, bending my knees deep and bouncing back up. Now, says Stephan, there are four punches, and all of boxing is those four punches: jab, right, hook, and uppercut. He explains how the jab is the first thing, the lead-off, the punch that sets up a combination. Extend your left arm straight out in front, he instructs, stepping in with your left foot at the same time, then bring it back. That's all there is to it, the cornerstone of boxing, easy. Easy like copying out *War and Peace* in the Cyrillic alphabet. I throw my first jab. It looks okay to me.

"Not bad," says Stephan, "but your arm's gotta be straight. Don't bend your elbow like that, keep your wrist firm and try to turn your fist at the end, so it's flat to the floor. You gotta snap it out, and snap it back, right to where you started, in close to the body, like this . . ." He sends out a pair of jabs so fast, I miss them, then repeats it in slow motion. I copy, he corrects, I try and try, again and again. My left arm, previously used only for catching softballs, is getting tired. When I bring it back in, I find I can't wrap my elbows in tight like I'm supposed to. My breasts are in the way. I recall what the Amazons did about this.

After an hour, we join Juan and the Japanese woman for speed bag and calisthenics. Juan is a joker and a flirt, and is built, as the English say, like a brick shithouse. The speed bag is his party trick. It's good for your reactions, he says, saturating the room with rhythmic thunder, his hands a blur—*digada-digada-digada-drrrrum, diddly-diddly DA!* When I try it, the air-filled leather bag bounces off the platform and I just keep on missing the rebound. It seems the harder I try, the more elusive the bag becomes. Juan finds this hilarious. Stephan says not to worry, I'll get it. Abdominal work is full sit-ups and other moves the fitness industry has renounced as evil. In the end, I'm dripping with sweat and I feel wonderful, and idiotic to have been afraid, and hooked. And I didn't even hit anything. I try the other boxing class, Michael Olajidé Jr.'s Aerobox, in which we incessantly jump rope and speed-box to a rabid techno soundtrack. It's so impossible, I get defensively furious at the guy, until he comes up afterwards and shakes my hand and says I did great and, by the way, he just took the New York Jets through it and it defeated them. Olajidé is plyometric like Tigger and wears a glamorous eye patch— which, I later learn, covers a torn retina he got in an uninspired (his opinion) bout with Thomas Hearns. He sees half of everything. I keep doing his class. Before long, I'm at every boxing class on the schedule.

To my shame, I remember going on to friends about how sweet the boxers were, showing off that I knew real pugilists. It seemed radical to scrape against that world, and I loved setting off the tiny social firework that I was boxing now. Or, rather, "boxing." I did not pretend that this was the real thing, but new acquaintances could always be counted on to respond with the same few lines—namely: "Bet your boyfriend's careful!" or "Oooh I'd better watch out!" or "Aren't you worried about your face?" The boxing classes were getting popular, and Crosby Street metamorphosed further into a faux fight gym, festooned with a tickertape parade of drying handwraps and a spaghetti of jump ropes. More boxer-teachers appeared: Lonnie "Lightning" Smith, 1985 WBC junior middleweight champ; Carlos Ferrer, who has his own white-collar boxing gym now; and my favorite, Terry "The Panther" Southerland, a gap-toothed ranked lightweight. Leslie Howe replaced half her aerobics sessions with "Boxers' Exercise." The dance classes stopped. A ring appeared. The canvas was a little loose, but it looked lovely. I was looking lovelier myself. Boxing was helping me like my image. The aerobics-class mirror had been my adversary, but the shadow-boxing mirror was there to use, not abuse.

Performing grapevines in Lycra shorts to "Can You Feel It?" had yielded benefits, but also a new way to watch myself critically. A few years back, circa 1988, the early aerobics classes in London had brought me back into my body, recalling the pure joy of movement that I'd barely felt since swinging on car tires in the adventure playground with Candy, but class remained an exercise in self-assessment, leading to joy or gloom according to the size I judged myself that day, compared to my neighbors. The challenge of the choreography was so faint that my mind would wander, often onto its tedious fat track. There were side tracks of resentment—resentment of my desire to conform and resentment of spending my entire fund of psychic energy on wishing I could lose ten pounds. On bad days, and they were legion, misery about weight blocked out the world. I tried to circumvent the compulsion—took the back row, put oomph into the steps, pretended I was dancing, boycotted classes with shitty music, dieted—but I couldn't lose myself in that infernal floor-to-ceiling fog-free mirror. It was "Dance" all over again, something degrading that girls were forced to do while boys learned sculling and cricket and rugby.

Apart from a couple of enlightened teachers, I felt alone in fighting the weight obsession as opposed to the weight. The camel's back broke when Dawn, my favorite instructor, read out a news clip about Karen Voigt, fitness queen of California.

"Says here she's five-eleven and weighs a hundred and twelve pounds," she said. "I don't *think* so." Derisive laughter, then silence.

"It's not true, is it?" one woman piped up.

"Probably not with all that muscle. She just wants to shame you into buying her videos."

Relieved laugh. Another woman spoke:

"But ... is that *possible*, five-eleven and a hundred and twelve pounds?"

"I suppose so, but you'd have to work out six hours a day and live on lettuce and supplements. It's not worth it, girls."

In exposing how the fitness industry propagates and then profits from our imagined inadequacies, Dawn was part of the solution, but I was part of the problem, submitting to the madness. I had to get out of estrogen-filled rooms full of career dieters. That was something else I resented: only women had eyes for this territory, the bond that divides, comparing with caliper eyes—*Is she thinner than me? Am I bigger than her?* If one more locker-room pal said, "Wow, you've lost weight," I would throw up. I was already sick on the empty calories of magazines and their toxic concepts like "model," "calorie chart," and "if you can hold a pencil under your breast, it's too droopy." Men seemed able to avoid the whole thing. My father, for one, thoroughly enjoyed cultivating his paunch (which probably killed him, but that's another issue). Men got to play free.

I left the studio and went exploring—tried weight training, Pilates, yoga, running, squash, flamenco, returned to tennis (I was no good) and swimming (chlorine hurt my eyes), found a circus school and learned the trapeze. In 1989, softball was just catching on in London. The band Madness had gotten hooked on it during U.S. tours and started a pick-up game in Regent's Park. I joined it. Three years later, I won the London "Ringer Award" (a bell on a stick) for being the player on the most teams, and sort of played for England in the Advertising Age Softball World Series in Dallas. (We came in last.) Softball hit the spot, being infinitely engrossing and also a coed sport. Not only was this more fun socially, it seemed an antidote to the syndrome described above. On the London diamonds, nobody could argue that men were better athletes than women, only that Americans were better than Brits. Well, except for one particularly fine player who did argue the former: my American boyfriend.

We met one Sunday during warm-up while I was running, glove up, for a fly ball and smashed heads with someone and was knocked out cold. Flat on my back, I saw stars, cobalt-blue dancing lights; then the stars cleared and I saw Sam. "He's cute," I thought. Later, he admitted he'd once shot hoops with an All-State girl player who trounced him, but that she was the only superior female athlete he'd ever encountered. I'll never be pussy-whipped, he said. *Pussy-whipped?* Bam. A custom-designed, call-to-arms, son-of-the-jazz-club incident. I was infuriated and attracted. I had to lock horns. An intimate relationship should be shelter, fellowship, love, not battle; but after two long bouts of living-with-someone, and many flings, I was fighting the very concept of settling down. I thought I had a new variety of femininity. I was roaring girl, predator, untamable creature. You can't pin *me* down, no. I will not submit. In men it's called commitment phobia; in me it was the very same, a mask for the terrifying desire to have exactly what I fought. Sam and I were well matched. He was a good opponent.

After a year, Sam returned to his native New York, which gave me an extra excuse for going there in 1989. The next three years, I was a yo-yo across the Atlantic. I lived in sublets, wrote guide books, travel articles, restaurant reviews, took aerobics classes, played softball—but not in New York. Here the ball game was not the cutting-edge craze I knew, and I was unhappy playing three innings in right field (at best) on a competitive yuppie team, or being tolerated at Sam's all-male league champs' practices. I felt a sharper gender divide in the U.S. Itinerant and sportless, my body became my adversary again—a protean and recalcitrant "it"—and I sought alternative ways to get into my body, in every sense: acupuncture (the Chinese *stop* paying their physician when they're sick), herbs, the chakras, visualization. I began to view the body as a vital energy system fused with mind, heart, and soul. I grasped that the thoughts in my mind don't merely influence, they literally *create* my world—bad body thoughts more than blocked out the scenery, they wrote the script. I quit reading magazines—evil influence.

Then boxing. Boxing brought it all together. It was purely athletic. It suited my frame. I looked more authentic doing it than beanpole women, even in my own critical eyes. The "blindsight," where I could not recognize reality, where one day I'd see myself as a hulking brute and the next as normal, even slim and graceful, abated. (Any woman who has asked the masochistic question "Do I look fat in this?" shares this affliction of blindsight—my misappropriation of a neurological term for believing you are blind though you are not. Oliver Sacks, famous chronicler of the outer reaches of perception, describes watching a sufferer: "[H]e manifestly responded to objects, could locate them, was seeing, and yet denied any consciousness of seeing." Or, my version: *I am manifestly slim, am told I am slim, have proof I am slim, yet deny any consciousness of being slim.* Models and actors and dancers and other women with perfect bodies are just as prone to blindsight, as are supersuccessful, high-powered women, no matter what their size or shape. I remember Oprah Winfrey's poignant admission that when she was fat, all pleasure in her accomplishments, her wealth, her life, was obscured by her self-loathing, so locked in misery was she about not fitting the acceptable mold. And let's not even start on Princess Diana. Blindsight means blind to your own qualities, as if it were wrong to approve of yourself unless you conform precisely.)

I was better at hitting bags than softballs—heavybags, double-end bags (the air-filled ball suspended at eye level on elastic ropes), and I'd got the hang of speed bags. I was so engrossed, I didn't even notice my body reducing and tightening. Crosby Street, however, was still a girly gym. Fashion was having a flirtation with boxing around this time, as clips faxed by friends proved. "The female boxer is the icon of the moment!" gushed *Vogue*, beneath a picture of a kangaroo "sparring" with a sticklike Shalom Harlow. The bloody (not literally) supermodels appeared in a Revlon ad, wearing scarlet boxing gloves to match the lipstick on their expensive pouts. On the West Coast, Michelle Pfeiffer and Jody Foster were "executive boxing" in the hit class of Hollywood. Women were flocking to SoHo, and the TV cameras followed. They didn't care whether the boxing babes they'd come to shoot could throw an effective uppercut. Neither did most of the babes. Flirting with Juan was a better sport. Someone pinned a crayon cartoon of a dog inside a heart on the notice board. "*Juan La Porte, Love Puppy,*" it said.

Leslie Howe remained enigmatic. Thanks to her Gleason's forays she looked like a boxer, her muscles cut, her gear street—sky-blue Adidas sweats and a T-shirt she'd pull up at the front and tuck behind her head during the abs section. She was living with Lonnie "Lightning" Smith and occasionally worked his corner. She was featured in several magazine spreads pinned on the notice board next to the Love Puppy. I felt awe and envy.

"Are those your *own gloves*?" I asked her. I didn't even have my own handwraps. "When are you going to fight?" I asked.

"I don't know," she said, "but I'm sparring."

She didn't explain what sparring was. Nor that she couldn't fight if she wanted to, because women weren't doing that then. I was restless in the fake ring. I wanted to graduate to Gleason's too, but as my teacher, the boss of boxers, and a fitness professional, Leslie resided in a lofty category where I didn't belong.

––––––

In March 1994, I returned from an extended visit to England (where Dawn was now teaching an aerobic boxing class) to find Crosby Street was gone. The rent, I heard months later, had doubled and Leslie had dismantled the ring, packed up the bags, and moved the circus uptown to the new Barneys store, to be director of a gym that never opened. Desultorily, I searched for bearable classes and wrote articles about fitness for the magazines I despised, my secret mission: to help explode the size-two conspiracy. For *Vogue*, I wrote about the mutated eating disorder of exercise obsession, and about the coming trend of mindful fitness. That one was never printed. Too weird, they said. Of course, now every gym has yoga, qi gong, Pilates, even meditation classes (not to mention boxing), but at that time it was all about treadmills. The trendy Crunch chain was taking off, pushing the envelope with live gospel choirs, African drummers, drag queen instructors, but it was a case of *plus ça change*—same moves, same miseries, different clothes. I figured I should take further action and went to New York University to get my Fitness Instruction Certificate.

The course was excellent, though it toed the party line of the moment—low-fat, high-carb diet, moderate, consistent exercise— and I had them rolling in the aisles at my nutrition show-and-tell when I presented Diets of the Seventies. It was all about low carbohydrates, I explained. Steak, but no baked potato; salad dressing, but no pasta. How absurd that sounded. The diametric opposite of what we knew to work. Not I. The seventies diet books I'd brought were mine. I was still able to drop weight when I dropped carbs, even at the height of pasta-bagel mania. My weight problem had never been about willpower; my problem lay in being told I had a problem in the first place, in blind obedience to the dogma of dieting. I would retain extra pounds to be perverse. It made me uncomfortable, but someone had to do it. Big is better, I insisted, not believing it for a second. See, I said to the class, the fitness and fashion industries are twins. As soon as hemlines rise, they must fall, so there's something new to sell, and when carbs are high, they must drop, and—watch—they will. And they did. In 1995, the high-carb Zone cashed in, as did Dr. Atkins, a few years later.

Exercise trends are just the same. The early nineties was the Step era. Effective and beloved as it is, I loathe the Step. Like treadmill,

Stairclimber, VersaClimber, NordicTrack, and so on, it requires automaton movement, divorcing mind from body. Nevertheless, I spent hours at NYU designing Step workouts, and for *Vogue* I interviewed Gin Miller, the Step's inventor, a couple of times. Gin is fascinating, self-aware, questing, and is herself conflicted about the fitness industry, having suffered for her unfashionable "Welsh footballer's legs," as she put it. But when I watch a Step class, it looks like people grimly climbing stairs to nowhere, seeking the mythical fitness grail. Boxing was different, but in a studio setting it remained redolent of the industry's lying ways. (My favorite statistic: 60 percent of gym memberships are never used; in other words, gyms keep afloat on our guilt.) Studio boxing seemed to bear the same relationship to real boxing that UV lamps do to the sun. I missed Crosby Street, but I sensed something had been lacking there. I had reached the end of its rope.

As I learned their business, I roamed the clubs like the Flying Dutchman, finding no port. By now, boxing classes had started at all the big gyms—Equinox had Michael Olajidé Jr.'s Aerobox and Stephan Johnson's boxing circuit, and Crunch had Terry Southerland. My mindset was horrible. Here's a journal entry:

I did Michael's class, and what do you know? I had to go and have another fat fit. This time I saw toward the end how I wasn't really bigger than a lot of the women I'd perceived as skinny while I was huge and hulking. In fact, I saw I was thinner than some. There were a bunch of models in the front row—Michael's acolytes—because ABC was filming. I just hope they didn't get me in the picture. It was awful feeling that the camera would need to keep away from the fat girl in the baggy tank in the back. Things improved a bit during the shadowboxing section, but what was irritating was that many of the front-row girls have obviously never boxed. No style, no form. In the locker room after, I saw one of the front-row people I couldn't help comparing myself to. She had defined abs and normal,

if a bit porky, shoulders, then a massive butt and great big cel-
lulite thighs. She didn't appear to mind or notice. That gets me
paranoid.

I was scared of liking my body in case it looked to others the way that
woman's body looked to me ... fat! And the *last* to know it! I was
quite aware how this preemptive strike of judging in the very way
I feared being judged was heinously hypocritical, but I found it
impossible to avoid that trap in a gym-with-mirrors, when I'd been
trying to find my true place on the good-body-scale since my first
bikini on the beach. "Do I look like her?" I'd ask my mother, pointing
out a flabby middle-aged person. In photos, I envy my own teenage
self, but I couldn't see straight in the mirrors I searched, and the same
was true now. I looked fine. More than that, I garnered frequent
and often extravagant compliments on my physique, which I accepted
hungrily and disbelieved totally. My neighbor Kyle, a choreographer
who used to take classes at Crosby Street, recently told me how all
the dancers there felt inadequate compared to us boxer types with
our amazing muscular bodies. Needless to say, we (well, I, at least) felt
inadequate compared to the dancers with their amazing lithe bodies.
But blindsight is like that.

Fleeing Equinox, I found a gym I liked well enough, with boxing
classes led by Luke "Mad Dog" Massey, a freckled, gold-toothed
model and amateur boxer from London with a lightning mind and a
filthy fast mouth. His boxing record was crap, he said, but his street-
fighting record was unblemished. He'd killed a guy, he said. Luke
taught enthusiastically, painting the sport dark to enhance his image,
teaching me dirty tricks like elbowing, and letting me move around
in the ring with him while he dodged my punches. It wasn't real sparring. The gym did a Crosby Street, opening an entire new floor for
boxing, but something was missing—the sun, perhaps.

Then in August, just before my thirty-third birthday, I ran into
Terry Southerland at Crunch.

"Terry, I'm sick of these play gyms," I complained. "I want to learn to fight." As I spoke I realized I meant it. Terry looked serious, then nodded.

"We can do that," he said.

"What? You're kidding!"

"No, I mean it. You know what you're doing. We'll take you to Gleason's."

In one sentence my horizon had stretched to . . . to where? Suddenly I had a ticket to the fabulous Gleason's, place of Leslie Howe, home of Juan La Porte, Stephan Johnson, Terry, et al. Though I'd been working up to it for well over a year, this was all a bit sudden. Cousins to the fears I'd felt before my first class accosted me now, and a new idea occurred—I wanted to go to the next level, but I had no reason or desire to fight my sisters. The notion, now that it was within range, was as foreign as owning a gun, rather horrible. I felt like paraphrasing Muhammad Ali's famous declaration: *I ain't got no quarrel with no women.* Instead, after the split second those thoughts took, I heard myself saying something quite idiotic.

"I want to fight a guy."

"Um . . . sure, baby."

"No really. I don't think I want to fight women. Can I do that?"

"Yeah, I guess I can clear it with the commissioner," said Terry, laughing in his boots.

3

Here We Are Now

Now, whoever has courage
and a strong and collected spirit in his breast,
let him come forward, lace on the gloves
and put up his hands.

—Virgil

I have never been to DUMBO, a place so named by Realtors to redeem the grotty area "Down Under the Manhattan Bridge Overpass," and as a sophomore New Yorker, I feel pretty hip knowing about it. Tell the truth, I have barely been to Brooklyn. My second day here, I got confused on the subway and whizzed under the East River to—maybe Borough Hall—and the sound of that word "Brooklyn," straight from murders in the news and horror stories people love relating when you're about to move to New York, chilled me rigid. I was scared of the subway platform. Silly me. DUMBO, mind you, is not as cuddly as its name. Take the F train to the first stop in Brooklyn; that's York Street, Terry said. Walk two blocks and turn right. That's Gleason's, on the second floor. Number 75 Front Street. It is the eve of my birthday, a dog day. I love the wet hot air and no sleeves because London would be sixty degrees at best today. I go under the bridge, past barbed wire, vagrant grass in the sidewalks, derelict factory buildings, a broken bar called Between the Bridges, no deli, no lofts, no people. Terry is meeting me up there.

Here it is, in an industrial block called the Gair Building, the letters *G, L, E,* and so on pasted on the windows, those windows open and leaking the familiar speed-bag *digada-digada* like a steel stamping machine. Okay, I'm nervous, I'm nervous all over again. Stephan and Juan at Crosby Street, they were visitors in girlworld. Now I'm the imposter in guyworld. I still don't quite believe that it's cool for me to go there, that nobody will mind. In fact, I sort of want them to mind. Then I'll have something to fight. I'm ready for a battle either way.

Up concrete stairs, a heavy heavy door. Opposite the door, an NYPD recruitment poster and the Virgil stanza, surprising, though it speaks in the masculine. On the left, a snack bar papered with centerfolds from boxing magazines. Smell of hot dogs, armpit musk, a treble of liniment. Ahead, a ring, a yard up off the floor, nothing like the futon rings at the Manhattan studios. This place is huge, swarming with bodies, loud with leather thumps, barbells clanging like trolley bells, hisses of boxers exhaling into a forest of bags, a lot of shouting, the bell. In relative silence, two guys spar in the first ring. There are other rings. On the right, there's a spacious black man sitting at a table. I smile at him.

"And what can I do for you, young lady?" he starts, but then Terry appears and grabs my arm.

"Hey, Calvin, this is Kate," he says. "Kate, this is Calvin. Calvin is the most important person at Gleason's. You don't get past this door if Cal says so." Calvin is laughing. I love Calvin. Terry says let's go meet the boss, and I'm going no no no, let's not bother the *owner*, but he's pulling me across the floor past another ring, empty, and to the corner, where there's a big, shabby office with a scale outside and a sign on the open door—IF YOU CAME HERE TO BITCH YOU HAVE ALREADY USED UP 98% OF YOUR TIME—and an avuncular, forty-something, apple-cheeked white man juggling phones. He makes the international signal for "be right with you," and I nod and smile and look at the walls. The walls are incredible.

In the center is a huge impressionistic oil in acid primaries of two fighters in a clinch, and all around it, floor to ceiling, is a gallery of every boxer I've ever heard of and tons I haven't (but will)—black-and-white group shots of spiffy men in zoot suits, their names hand-written in white ink; Jersey Joe Walcott and Jack Dempsey in comical woollen trunks; Joe Louis, handsome and mournful; Roberto Duran; Sonny Liston; Joe Frazier looking fierce; Jake "Raging Bull" LaMotta grinning; Floyd Patterson doing his peek-a-boo; that famous Neil Leifer bird's-eye shot of Ali and a prone Cleveland Williams. Mug shots are signed: "To Bruce. My man. Carlos Ortiz." "To Ira and all at Gleason's. José Torres." I peer into every frame. I think if I look hard enough, they will tell me how to box. Terry is beaming. He knew I'd like this. The owner stands, winding up the call.

"Yes, Dave, I do ..." His accent is Brooklyn-Jewish. He speaks slowly and has fun in his voice. "What is he? Seven-and-five? Okay, uh-huh. Then I need an eight-rounder for Ledoux and that's it. . . . Yup. Yup. He'll be about twenty-five. . . . Two grand. Okay, Dave, I gotta go, I got people here. . . . Ha ha ha. Okay, bye."

"Kate, this is Bruce Silverglade. Bruce, Kate. Bruce is the boss-man. Bruce," says Terry, "*is* Gleason's."

"Very pleased to meet you," says Bruce. "What d'you think of our place?"

"I love this place," I say. It's the truth. In ten minutes I have fallen head over heels.

"You here to work, or just looking?"

"I want to work."

"You know it," adds Terry.

"Well, I have quite a few ladies who work out here," says Bruce. "We were the first gym to have women. Since 1986."

"Really?" I'm wondering what took me so long.

"So you let me know if you need anything, won't you?"

Terry points me to the sign LADIES ROOM—*LADIES ONLY*. In here are no shampoo dispensers or hair dryers, just a pipe the size of a redwood trunk raining onto a mildewed carpet and paint falling off the walls in sheets. There are about two dozen lockers with names handwritten on strips of tape: Katya Bankowsky, Lisa Long, JoEllen

VanOuwerkerk, Dee Hamaguchi, someone called Sky's the Limit, and, yes, Leslie Howe. So she has company. Who are they? Are they tough? *Where* are they? I go out and lean against one of the rings and start wrapping my hands, acting nonchalant, like I do this every day. Well, I do. By now I own lots of Everlast handwraps and have already replaced my first bag gloves, a red vinyl Lonsdale pair I got in London, with some black leather twelve-ounce Ringside gloves. I have passed some rites of passage. I no longer get the shoulder pain or the shinsplints, but I still scrape raw patches off my knuckles. For some time now, I have been working on the focus mitts, but I can't do on them what the fighter in the ring is doing. He's slamming the leather into those pads in four-, five-, six-punch combinations, and bobbing and weaving, ducking and dancing to the gunshot of his glove connecting and the hiss hiss hiss of his breath, he and his trainer sharing a trance, no words. I want to do that. Terry comes over, tells me to start jumping rope, he's got to speak with his trainer. Who? I ask. There he is, says Terry, over there, that's his ring. Victor Valle. He says his trainer's name with pride and with love. Yes, love, I think.

When I got obsessed with softball, I read baseball books; then, my first day in New York, at the doubleheader in Yankee Stadium, though the Yanks were atrocious and the place was so empty it echoed, I was transported. The word made flesh. Now it was boxing books. I would scan their indexes for the names of men I had met. So far, I'd found Juan La Porte, Lonnie Smith, Michael Olajidé, Jr., and his father, Sr., and now Valle was there, training Lou Costello and Gerry Cooney. As I jump rope, I sneak looks at Terry in conference with Victor Valle, frowning, then smiling, punching his arm, shrugging. Until now I have seen Terry and Lonnie and Juan and Stephan only in play clothes, off duty; but here Terry is at work—like on the T-shirt with the picture of a door opening onto an empty ring, and the inscription: "Step Into My Office." Over there by the far ring, and in the one beside me, I get my first glimpses of the particular trainer-fighter relationship, and it moves me. I want that. It seems to contain the best of masculinity, the fraternal respect that exists between men when the hierarchy is clear, a paternal-filial bond based on an alternative blood tie. In books, on TV, fighters use the first person plural—he is not an "I," he is a "we": "We cut off the corners so he had nowhere to run." The trainer does it too: "We fought hard, but it wasn't enough tonight." Trainer and fighter are the most intimate team. All coaches help their athlete to fight fears, to focus, but come second in the triathlon and you go home with a silver medal; come second in a fight, and you leave cut and bruised, humiliated. A trainer shares in that. Here's Angelo Dundee on the aftermath of Ali's March 1973 loss to Ken Norton: "Going twelve rounds with that busted jaw, Muhammad had so much courage. . . . But when we got to the hospital, he's consoling me. I felt so bad, I was practically crying. But he's saying, 'Don't worry, we'll be back.'"

I'm sure Terry chose this picturesque time of day deliberately—prime pro training time, before the amateurs and "white-collar boxers" get here. In the shadowboxing mirror, I see me jumping rope surrounded by trainers with their fighters, fighters with their trainers, and I feel at home, forgetting that I am different and that maybe I can't have that. Presently, I'll find out where the boxer-trainer frame warps and where it remains solid when the boxer is me; but just now, I'm enjoying the new sights, new possibilities. I never imagined there'd be palpable love here.

Everyone is wobbly, because the mirror, far from being fog-free top-to-toe, is the Mylar funhouse kind, has dried sweat on it, and is duct-taped to the wall in sections, so in this one I'm giraffe, in that one, elephant. Having a fat fit in this thing is impossible. Anyhow, I'm already away on an I'm-a-real-boxer-now trip, since I'm good at jumping rope, turning it with flicks of the wrist, alternating feet, crossing arms, in a loose rope-in-front style I copied from a skinny Rasta who trains at Allstars, the amateur gym I attend in London. Boxers glance my way. Someone says, "You done that before." I'm glad when

Terry reappears and we go into the old Crosby Street routine, which seems inferior now to the boxers' training sessions, though the gist of it differs not at all.

Like Stephan said, all of boxing is four punches, jab, right, hook, and uppercut. And chess is six pieces, and computing is two digits, one and zero. It's what you do with them. I shadowbox. Shadowboxing relies on imagination. Your reflection is your opponent, or when you do it in the ring, you raise a phantom opponent to dance in front of you. The boxers whip their torsos side to side, have their heads on springs, catch a punch with a glove, make a rib shield of their elbows, fold themselves down, wrap themselves up, eat the whole ring in one shuffle and step. It looks beautiful. I, by contrast, have glue on my soles and lead in my arms. I feel exposed, the only person here with no clue what an opponent is like. Padwork is better. Terry brings the mitt down for each strike so I sound major, as loud as the guys. I've got my guard up, ready to defend against ridicule, but instead a man with an early Beatles moptop comes over and watches intently.

"She notta sa bad," he tells Terry.

"Kate's cool," he agrees, holding the pads for another one-two.

"She gonna fight?"

"We'll see."

"I want to," I add between combinations.

"She oughdda fight. She hit hard."

I love this guy. He is maybe five-foot-three. His hands, encased in silver tape, look like they're wearing badly forged medieval armor and he has deep crow's-feet from his sole facial expression—a smile to melt winter.

"Yeah, woman! You godda *fight*." We continue padwork to the bell, but Terry doesn't introduce us.

The bell is king. At the Manhattan gyms, it was a door-buzzer sound from a red box with little flashing bulbs like a lie detector. Here it's a bigger box mounted on an iron pillar with a piercing electronic *bweep bweep bweep*, and three traffic signal lights: green for work, amber for thirty seconds to go, and red heralding the one-minute rest. Everything, but everything, in professional boxing occurs in three-minute increments. Everything, that is, except women's bouts, where the bell goes after two minutes. (Amateur boxing also differs—from one-minute rounds for juniors to three minutes for the open category.) After three rounds of padwork, I move on to the heavybag, or I try to. They are all in use, pummeled till they swing like corpses on their chains, half a dozen slim leather cylinders, a fat canvas one, and an obese black one called SuperBag. When my turn comes, Terry stands beside me and tells me what punches to throw in what order, and again I feel uncomfortably green. Hey, I scold myself, these are pro boxers, not competition; learn from them. I use them as patterns on the double-end bag and the speed bag, getting more from them than from Terry. He's training me a little differently now, the emphasis more on form than aerobic conditioning, and I am grateful for the close attention and proud to be the first and only female he's brought to Gleason's, but I can't help noticing he is distracted. What he is here, after all, is a boxer.

"Terry, will I be able to spar soon?" I ask.

"I think we can do that," he says.

"Who will I spar with?"

"We'll find you someone."

I can't admit this to Terry, but I still don't fully understand what sparring is. At least I know it's practice fighting, but I don't get how you gauge how far to go, how hard to hit, or how the trainers regulate the action, and the action here isn't making it any clearer. Three rings—the fourth belongs to Johnny Rodz's Unpredictable School of Pro Wrestling—are alive with the sounds of sparring: guttural exhalations, slapped leather, stentorian admonitions from the ropes. It's the first time I've seen fighting up close, and the noises are squishy and snuffly, nothing like the clear metallic cracks on movie soundtracks. When someone connects with an uppercut, there's a muted splash. A blow to the head clicks on the headgear, or is a wet rag on the face. Patterns form in the breath whenever a punch derails it from the engine regularity—whiffle begets snort, *pchew-pchew* begets *hmph*—and their

satin trunks swish and their boots bang through the canvas and make
a blunt drum of the hollow ring. "Get him back, Jemique!" "Body!
Body! BODEEE!" Trainers are furious spouses, taking it personally
when their fighter does a dumb move. Then one session will suddenly pull the whole gym around it like a birthday cake, and the
yelling keeps climbing to higher registers, the pace escalates, every
punch spraying a sweat fountain; someone bleeds; everyone screams
advice; until a Latino guy with a walking stick—his name is Sinbad—
just lets rip, topping out the racket: "*Ayeeeee! Ayeeeee! Ayeeeee!*"

When a session is done, the combatants embrace. Even if it
looked like war, they do this, and the pack dissolves and the next pair
steps in. I am thrilled by the whole thing. It doesn't strike me as violent. I see it as an abstruse language that I know slightly, as if I were
in Tokyo after a year of Japanese lessons—my accent is convincing,
I smile and nod, but, frankly, I haven't a clue what they're going on
about. It is clear that the only way to get the subtleties of sparring is
to spar, but even then, the rules may bend for me. I want no special
treatment. In London, I learned to play pool to burst the ennui of
pub blokes when a girl stepped up to the table—the way they wouldn't
even bother watching a girl's shots. I thought beating them at their
own game struck a blow for all women, and I thought so all over
again with Sam and my softball swing, and with Sam not wanting to
be "pussy-whipped." Now I'm thinking it again. Let me spar, let me
learn, let me show what women can do. This is funny, because
nobody's telling me I can't.

Gleason's is the oldest continuously operating fight gym in the
United States, which—along with the fact that it has produced
eighty-eight champions (and counting)—qualifies it to stand here as
envoy for today's boxing world. Other places may be slummier (Front
Street, Philly), flashier (Blue Velvet, Manhattan), smaller (the Kronk,
Detroit), larger (L.A. Boxing Gym), but Gleason's is the most famous,

certainly in the States, and probably in the world. Gleason's knows this, and Bruce Silverglade is friendly to all media. Since running a fight gym, even the world's most famous, doesn't pay, Bruce has other irons in the fire. He owns two more Gleason's, in Amsterdam and Liverpool (and in 1996, he would open a third, a Gleason's "lite" at the Chelsea Piers Sports Center in Manhattan, catering, as he put it, "to the business person"). He is also an international boxing agent, a matchmaker—that's what he was doing on the phone the day I arrived, and what he has done on the phone every day since. Bruce books the opponents. In other words, he finds the loser. When film crews need the famous fight gym for atmosphere, he collects a location fee, and in my first few weeks here, I see HBO interviewing Kevin Kelley; LL Cool J shooting a video; a dozen photography students (they get in free); an infomercial crew with Christie Brinkley and Chuck Norris; and a shoot for Cartier diamond jewelry. What they all want is gorgeous grit. And apart from cash, that's what everyone wants from boxing.

I suppose that includes me. There is no doubt that part of what I'm falling in love with is the thing my very presence here will help subvert; that is, boxing as it used to seem—an arcane testosterone ghetto, photogenic and romantic, adoringly treated in black-and-white by Scorsese in *Raging Bull* or Bruce Weber in *Broken Noses*. I'm basking in the glamorous idea of myself in concert with the peeling walls, the ancient equipment, the intensity and ritual of this place, because I haven't yet fully entered it. My first weeks here remind me of how I felt when I was briefly the "phone girl" in a highclass Manhattan brothel, a job I took because I thought it would be interesting to get to know the girls. Instead, I felt a sort of shame for not doing *it*, for seeming to hold myself above the whores, for being the one who gave out their rates and rules on the phone ("Yes, we have wrestling mats." "No, no fisting"), vetted clients via entry video and buzzed them in ("Dude coming!"), but didn't get my hands dirty ("Yes, I am British. No, I'm not available"). Even my overdeveloped sense of curiosity gave me no wish to discover how selling my body might feel. Here at Gleason's, though, I do want to pay my dues. Into *this* society of outsiders, I—congenital outsider myself—want to be accepted. No straight man would desire to penetrate the ritual of a whorehouse, to be brought into the fold without special rules. His masculinity would be mocked. My wish to sink deep into the fight gym, however, does not threaten my femininity at all; it might even enhance it. What this says about the polarity of the genders, I am not yet sure, nor am I clear about what it means that boxing, the proto-typically male sport, seems primed to germinate a female division.

The seeds of the distaff division—of this round, at least—were planted in 1986, when Bruce Silverglade allowed women through the doors for the first time three evenings a week. That year, the Mets won the World Series, and Michael Jordan became the first player since Wilt Chamberlain to top 3,000 points, in his third NBA season. Boxing was holding its own—Larry Holmes and Roberto Duran were among the world's champions, and Cus D'Amato was training a promising teenaged protégé named Mike Tyson—but it was hardly having its heyday. Yet back in 1937, when cab driver and fight man-ager Bobby Gagliardi founded Gleason's in the Bronx, boxing mat-tered. The sport was run by the Irish then, which is why Gagliardi eschewed his own name—ironic, because the mob was taking over, and the first two champs to come out of Gleason's were as Italian as linguini: Phil Terranova and Jake LaMotta. At that time, there was a far more famous boxing gym (itself founded in 1920 to rival Grupp's Gym in Harlem), the legendary Stillman's, at 919 Eighth Avenue, where every champion trained, retired champs hung out—Jack John-son was always there—and crowds paid a quarter to gawk at the show and at the movie stars who sat among them. In the forties, every weekday had its fight night somewhere in New York, culminating in the Bronx Coliseum Fridays and Madison Square Garden Saturdays. Boxing was huge. Then, in 1959, the professionally bad-tempered Lou Stillman sold the gym, an event that made the front page of *The New York Times*.

"There's no more tough guys around, not enough slums," Stillman

told the *Times*. "That's why I'm getting out of the business. The racket's dead. These fighters today are all sissies." Well, not all—that
year, Cassius Clay from Louisville became the national 178-pound
amateur champion—but perhaps the neighborhood "flatnosed, tough
kids, prideful as hell" (as trainer Ted Walker described the sparring
hopefuls), were getting thin on the ground.

The sissies and champs decamped to Gleason's. It became the
hot New York gym, raising its profile higher when it moved from the
Bronx to near the old Madison Square Garden in 1975. The price of
a spectator's ticket was a dollar now, and that dollar bought ringside
seats for the sparring sessions of Emile Griffith, Roberto Duran, Vito
Antuofermo, and Larry Holmes. By the time Tim Witherspoon,
Hector Camacho, and Michael Spinks were working in the two rings
a decade or so later, boxing's star had dipped. The lease expired, the
rent skyrocketed, and Gleason's crossed the East River to Brooklyn.

In 1985, Bruce Silverglade needed a change. His marriage over,
sick of his job, he had been introduced to the beloved owner of Gleason's, Ira Becker, through his extracuricular work as president of the
Metropolitan Amateur Boxing Federation, and through his father,
who was the Olympic boxing team's manager. Becker was looking
for a partner to buy the gym, so Bruce bought it—on credit cards
("I wasn't credit manager at Sears for ten years for nothing"). So
audacious was this method of financing in the early eighties, *Fortune*
magazine ran a profile on him. These were heady days, a minirevival.
When the gym moved to Brooklyn, Becker and Silverglade staged
popular monthly cards, featuring sparring as well as amateur and
exhibition bouts in Gleason's Arena, a ring they installed in a parking
lot down the block. Bob Jackson and Al Gavin's famous Gramercy
Gym, where Rocky Marciano, José Torres, and Floyd Patterson
trained, closed up shop and moved into Gleason's (where it still lives).
While it was still in Manhattan, the door marked LADIES ROOM—
LADIES ONLY attracted an interesting little crowd, including choreographer Twyla Tharpe, who based her next season's work on the
sweet science, society fashion designer Diane von Furstenberg, who

did the famous wrap dress (not inspired by handwraps but by boxers' robes, remembers Bruce), and prolific author Joyce Carol Oates, who did much of the research for her still-in-print *On Boxing* there.

Oates's book has been criticized as pretentious, and maybe it is, but I have my own particular quarrel with it. Oates, who acquired her taste for boxing from her father, claims that "Life *is* like boxing in many unsettling respects"—except for the fact that life is lived by people of two genders. Oates's seat by the ring at Gleason's (she didn't train) offered a grandstand view of a handful of pioneering female fighters, and yet she considers herself uniquely immune to what she terms "women's characteristic repugnance for boxing."

"Boxing is a purely masculine activity and it inhabits a purely masculine world," she claims in *On Boxing*.

> Men fighting men to determine worth (i.e., masculinity) excludes women as completely as the female experience of childbirth excludes men. And is there, perhaps, some connection?
>
> In any case, raw aggression is thought to be the peculiar province of men, as nurturing is the peculiar province of women. (The female boxer violates this stereotype and cannot be taken seriously—she is parody, she is cartoon, she is monstrous. Had she an ideology, she is likely to be a feminist.) . . . Boxing is for men, and is about men, and *is* men. . . .

Even then, nine years before the first sanctioned amateur female bout, Oates was (dismissively) snubbing a small but determined coterie of female professional boxers. Most of these sparred in the rings at Gleason's, and at least one trained there every day: Marion "The Lady Tyger" Trimiar, who, along with Cathy "Cat" Davis, and Jackie "The Female Ali" Tonawanda, dragged the New York State Athletic Commission to court to win the right to fight at home. (In the end, it was Gladys "Bam Bam" Smith and Toni "Leatherneck" Tucker who fought the first professional bout, duking it out on a Manhattan undercard in

July 1979, for a female promoter.) The three New York boxers fought hard all through the seventies, winning far more notoriety than purses, since the competition was thin and the public skeptical. Tonawanda racked up a 35-1 record, fought two men, knocked one out, and landed a job as Muhammad Ali's bodyguard. Tyger Trimiar broke the ban in several states, and sparred with the soon-to-be middleweight champ Vito Antuofermo in a ring outside a Little Italy café during the Feast of San Gennaro. Evidently, Oates-style distaste was the prevailing attitude at the time, and Cat Davis, the most public relations–savvy of the fighters, got a slating in *The Village Voice:*

"Cat Davis is a kinky media phenomenon, a product of the Great American Hype Machine," wrote Jack Newfield in October 1978. "Her manager-boyfriend stands accused of trying to fix her fights, of controlling a fake 'commission' that regulates boxing, and of using phoney names for her opponents. ..."

All true, probably all true. But whether or not the scene was corrupt, it staggered on, fending off "foxy boxing" associations set up by the porn industry in the seventies (although the cause wasn't helped by fighters with names like Squeaky Bayardo, Cha Cha Wright, Gumdrop Miller, Flory "Nonstop" Goldberg, and Shirley Temple). By the mid-eighties, the sport was running out of steam.

"There was nobody to fight back then, nothing going on," remembers Dora Webber, who, after turning pro in 1985, racked up eight wins and promptly ran out of opponents. But women's boxing had merely gone underground, where it would gather strength for the main event yet to come. Down in West Virginia in 1987, "The Coal Miner's Daughter," Christy Martin, inadvertently fought her pro debut by entering a "toughwoman contest," where she beat up some chain-smoking barflies and won a thousand bucks. She liked it so much, she did it again the next two years, then learned to box, and did it some more. In 1993, she signed to Don King and three years later brought women's boxing its largest audience ever by decisioning the talented Deirdre Gogarty on the Tyson-Bruno undercard.

Underground is where the entire history of female boxing has unfolded—and there *is* a history. Women have been boxing in public since the eighteenth century (discounting probable ancient Greek action), and my hometown, London, is where it all began. The *London Daily Post* of October 7, 1728, carried this reply by Elisabeth Stokes, "styled the European championess," to the challenge issued by Ann Field of Stoke Newington, an ass driver by trade: "As the famous Stoke Newington ass woman dares me to fight her for 10 pounds, I do assure her I will not fail meeting her for the said sum, and doubt not that the blows which I shall present her with will be more difficult for her to digest than any she ever gave her asses."

Six years before, claimed Elisabeth Stokes, she'd beaten "the famous boxing woman of Billingsgate" in nine minutes, making 1722 the earliest recorded girls' bout. Accounts also exist of the match between Elizabeth Wilkinson and Hannah Hyfield, who fought bare-fisted on Putney Heath in 1728, and there were, no doubt, many others who bled unrecorded. Remember, the very sport of boxing was in its infancy then, just beginning to be led out of the dark era of backroom bare-knuckle fighting by "the father of pugilism," James Figg. Male or female, there was nothing reputable about boxing.

By Victorian days, as you'd expect of that era, the tone of the commentators changed from an awestruck prurience to a hypocritical prurience: the London *Times* of March 24, 1807, noted that the sight of Betty Dyson and Mary Mahoney "hideously disfigured by hard blows ... afforded the most disgust," nor did it shrink from reporting how the Irish Martha Flaharty downed a pint of gin at dawn before beating Peg Carey to a bloody pulp. In fact, the Victorian British newspaper of record had far more comprehensive coverage of these girls' brawls than today's do, on either continent. It was not until 1888 that the first American women's fight was reported, when Mrs. Hattie Leslie (who claimed a record of 34-0; 29 KOs) met Miss Alice Leary (52-0; 47 by knockout) in Buffalo, New York, in what was, according to *Boxing Illustrated*, a fierce brawl. Leary broke Leslie's nose and floored her for two eight-counts; Leslie, her left eye almost closed, came back in the sixth to take Leary down twice, finally knocking her out in the seventh with a right to the jaw. For the Victorian woman, who couldn't even vote, merely being seen without her stays was quite risqué, so women's boxing would continue to masquerade as cheesecake through the nineteenth century, spending its final decade, says *Boxing Illustrated*, as "a popular form of entertainment in saloons, brothels, and a star attraction on the vaudeville circuit."

Women's boxing staggered on into the twentieth century. In the teens and twenties, Flint, Michigan, had its own subculture of stenographer-pugilists—the "Busters Club," banned from the YWCA—while in Europe, from the twenties to the forties, women's boxing lessons similar to today's aerobic classes were all the rage, and carnival boxing booths often featured a female challenger. A couple of these gained considerable fame, like the Irish girl Polly Burns (the subject of the documentary film *My Grandmother Was a Boxer*), and the French slugger Jeanne La Mar, who, in 1911, defeated the German champion, Steffi Bernet (who went on to form the Berlin Women's Boxing Club in 1928), then came to the U.S. in an unsuccessful search for challengers. A prefiguration of today's situation was available in Mexico during the twenties, when promoters were all but obliged to include a women's bout on the undercard, such was the public demand, and in Europe and the U.S., there was a vogue for girls' boxing troupes, like the one formed in 1935 by Mickey Walker ("The Toy Bulldog"), the crowd-pulling welterweight and middleweight champ from New Jersey, in his retirement.

Out of this half-sideshow, half-sport, one boxer stood out from the crowd, a tiny girl from a small town in Yorkshire, England, later the first woman to be inducted into the Boxing Hall of Fame: Barbara Buttrick. In 1945, fifteen years old and standing four-foot-six, Barbara liked to play cricket and soccer with the local lads, then beat them up. One day, wiping her muddy shoes with a sheet of newspaper after a soccer game, a story jumped out at her, headlined POLLY THE

CHAMP—a piece about the then-sixty-five-year-old Polly Burns. That was it. Barbara mounted a campaign to be a boxer that took her from Yorkshire to London and on to the boxing booths of southwest England and France. At twenty-two, the Brit, now ninety pounds and almost five feet tall, left Europe with her husband-trainer for the United States, where she metamorposed into the "The Mighty Atom," Battling Barbara Buttrick, Fly and Bantamweight Champion of the World, and improved her record to 30-1. Both in the U.S. and in her native land, Buttrick had a second career fighting laws and bans, though most who actually saw her box were converted.

"Mickey Riley, veteran Dallas fight manager and old-time boxer, said she was the neatest fighting machine he'd seen. He thought she could handle most men her weight in the ring," reported *The Dallas Morning News* when Buttrick arrived in town in 1955. Among the schemes that never came off were most exhibition bouts with male fighters, including an attempt to spar in public with the actor Richard Attenborough. Barbara had had to go solo for her boxing debut. The English Variety Artists' Federation having banned her, she topped the bill at a London music hall called the Kilburn Empire, where she skipped, shadowboxed, and hit a heavy-bag in a green spotlight, a weird idea that got very good reviews.

Photos of Buttrick's American bouts look like odd movie stills— the opponents resemble Jane Wyman and Veronica Lake trapped in a parallel universe, big blondes in full makeup with salon hair, startled at the attack of the small Barbara. The most surreal shot records her sole defeat, at the hands of the seven-inches-taller, thirty-pounds-heavier featherweight champion JoAnn Hagan from Indiana.

"In those days, women's boxing was frowned upon and ridiculed," JoAnn Hagan's then-boyfriend, a retired boxer himself, wrote me recently.

"It wasn't the boxers you got pressure from," says Buttrick, "it was mainly the commissioners. They didn't like to see it."

Twenty years later, they still didn't like to see it, except in Nevada, where the State Athletic Commission became the first to set the ball rolling in the modern era, by granting Caroline Svendsen a license to box in 1975.

"I felt like it was Christmas day," said Svendsen at the time. "I could hardly wait to open my presents."

Twenty years later, the twenty-two women who entered the first New York Golden Gloves would feel the same way.

———————

At first, the owners of the lockers in the ladies' room are as invisible to me as Svendsen, Buttrick, Trimiar, and Tonawanda, but since Terry and I converge at Gleason's at a variety of times, they soon start to materialize, a motley collection of every color, size, and class. What I'm seeking among them is kindred attitude. Katharine Dunn, the boxing writer and novelist, has characterized the timbre of the fight game backstage as: "men being kind to each other"—and the female version is what I hope to find in the locker room, as relief from the look-you-up-and-down rivalry of the Manhattan gyms. I am, of course, a hypocrite, because my own heart is none too generous. I judge the women I see here: Is she a talent or a dilettante? Is she here to box or to flirt? I am suspicious of the uncoordinated evening women in tight shorts and little bra tops. I scowl at them and align myself with the boxers, wearing what they wear—baggy shorts, a tank top with the straps taped together in back, a bandanna—and working as hard as they. I wonder if the men discern any difference between me and the dilettantes, or whether none of us is taken seriously.

Perhaps to deflect criticism, my first locker-room pal fails to take herself seriously. Sky Hosoya trains over lunchtime, when Terry and I often converge after his morning session (he's training hard for a bout) and before my classes at NYU. "Sky's the Limit" was the wrestling handle of this gravel-voiced glamourpuss who recently defected from Johnny Rodz's ring, and who possesses grand Hollywood muscles. She looks thoroughly pugilistic, but Sky is correct in claiming that she moves like Godzilla ("We're both from Tokyo," she points out), and she's on the receiving end of a lot of bitchy criticism, something I refuse to partake in—insurance against it being directed back my way. There is a vast discrepancy between Sky's boxing ability and her popularity. "She can't box," say the men, smiling condescendingly. But I, too, am being watched. I feel the eyes all the time. I see Terry over there, talking about me with someone, I'm sure—with the small smiling man, whose name is Domenico Menacho, and who is becoming my fast friend, and with John Toliaferro, a friendly young trainer, good with beginners, and Sky's trainer, Reggie Forde, a top-ranked middleweight in his day, and even Victor Valle and Hector Roca, the most famous trainers here. I tell myself it's more flattering to be derided than ignored, in case that's the word on me. Half pleased, half embarrassed by my half skills, I'm probably my own harshest critic, slotting myself low down in the athletes' pecking order I've drawn up. It goes: 1, Champions; 2, Professionals; 3, Amateurs; 4, Black and Latino Boxers; 5, White Boxers; 6, People Who Spar; 7, Good Fitness Boxers; 8, Bad Fitness Boxers. I believe it is my own inner list, not one that really exists, but if it does exist for others, I truly hope they've not added a ninth category: Women.

There are additional women I see rarely or not at all, lurking around corners of time—in the morning, I hear, there's Leslie Howe, Lisa Long from Staten Island, Dee Hamaguchi, who has a black belt in judo, and Bruce Silverglade's girlfriend (now his wife), JoEllen VanOuwerkerk. Sometimes the impressive and friendly Tanya Dean drops in from Bed-Stuy Gym looking for sparring, and there's the mysterious Katya Bankowsky, whom I haven't met but who—so Bruce tells me—is my weight and wants to spar. Sparring is still a mystery. We women don't do it, not with each other. Sky, Dee, Tanya, they do it with guys their trainers procure, usually someone under his tuition, and then there's Dennis, a keen, pudgy "white-collar boxer" who gets in with any girl, and always gets his nose bloodied, but among ourselves, there's a stand-off. Like at a bad singles mixer, none of us quite matches another; if we're here at the same time, our weights diverge too far, or our abilities don't mesh. The fitness boxers, uninterested in and unequipped for sparring, are not even in the running.

One of those is Terry's girlfriend. I know her from SoHo Training, a lovely person in perfect shape, but no boxer. When Terry's fight comes around, I meet her at the Westbury Music Fair, on Long Island, where the bout is taking place. It's my first live fight. (I do watch on TV. With Sam, I saw Stephan Johnson win a decision without using his right hand. I don't know which of us was more impressed by the fact that I knew him.) Terry has no nerves. In the gym lately he's been gently cocky, shrugging, saying, "I don't think he'll give us any trouble." I guess he knows something about the opponent, picked by Bruce in tandem with Dennis Rappaport, a Long Island promoter with a strong resemblance to Hugh Hefner. The bout is a ten-rounder, two before the main event, which is Melvin Foster versus Trevor Berbick, and he's billed as a prospect to watch. Unlike Terry, I have nerves, but as soon as he steps in the ring, disrobes, dances, flashing his gaptoothed smile, they quiet down. He owns the ring. His opponent, a thickset brawler named Kenny Baysmore, charges him like a bull, grasping him in too many clinches, while Terry snatches himself away, zapping round the ropes like a crab on amphetamines, smooth as his moniker ("The Panther"). In round six he fells the bull with a flurry of uppercuts and a hook to the head. Afterwards, he shines in his red tracksuit, modestly accepting congratulations. He is so gracious he even introduces me to people ("Kate's my female boxer"). If Terry's mother were here, she could not be prouder than I.

Back in the gym, my itch to spar is now unignorable. What's the point in perfecting combinations I'm never going to throw at a human? Maybe Terry just likes the *idea* of training me. He has, after all, taught me no defense. Ritchie, his only other student here, has recently started sparring. He is a guy. (And is there not, Joyce Carol Oates might ask, perhaps some connection?) Outside Gleason's, Terry trains James Truman, editorial director of Condé Nast, the publishers of *Vogue* and other insidious dictators of female thought, and the running joke between us, that I'm going to beat him up, is getting stale. What if Terry's holding me off from sparring forever, like he held off the bull opponent, sidestepping to avoid getting caught? So I ask again:

"Terry," I say, "when can I spar?"

"I think we're ready."

"*Really* this time?"

"You know it."

"Who with?"

"Dennis." The pudgy white-collar guy.

"But I don't want charity sparring," I whine.

"Nah! Dennis is good. He goes hard. We'll start there, then we'll see."

The next day, I take out my plastic mouthguard, long since boiled and formed to my top teeth, but still a virgin. Terry is ready with headgear and Vaseline, which he smears all over my face—to help blows slide off. I'm a kid with a birthday, but a big exam on the birthday. Ritchie, when he came out panting and happy after his inaugural three rounds, said he wished he hadn't been so hyped and gone in so fast and run out of gas. He said I shouldn't do that. There's a lot more time in there than you think, he said. This was my most concrete advice.

Terry laces me tight into his own sparring gloves and tapes the laces.

"How far do we go, Terry? Is this a fight?"

"No, you just working."

"Working how?"

"You'll see."

"How will I see?"

"You'll know when you're in there."

"But what do I do?"

"You work"

"Is that like fighting?"

"Just get in there, girl."

And I take the corner, my first corner, and wait for the bell. It goes. I stride across the ring, but slowly, heeding Ritchie, and there's little Dennis, crouched up behind his fists, frowning, looking as fierce as the mild-mannered can. I poke out a jab, stopping short of his face, and another, landing slack on his padded forehead. Shit, I'm supposed to hit him. Weird. I step to the right, as if he were holding up focus mitts, and I guess I look down, because—slap-bam!—I'm hit, twice, on the bone above my eye. It doesn't hurt, but my neck was snapped back and I'm appalled, simply shocked. He hit me! He bloody hit me. But of course he did. *That is what we are doing here.*

"Git to work, Kate," says Terry, laughing. Laughing! I'll show him. I run in on Dennis, his fierce face, and stick a jab in there, on his nose, and another and another, but he doesn't counter, so I get confused and back off.

"Git back, Kate," says Terry, and I get back and jab again (set the combination up with the jab, Terry says—as Stephan said, as Juan said—everything behind the jab), and I intend a right hand, but Dennis's in first with a glove in my face. It's soft, dammit. He's pulling his punches. That annoys me. I can take this, don't you *know*? Adrenaline kicks in. I want to show them all, even in the full knowledge that this sparring is pretend. So he's not going to hit me, huh? Well, that gives me license to hit him. So he thinks I'm delicate, huh? I'll show him. He seems incapable of fielding my punches, and this annoys me further. Does he *want* to be hit? Okay, fine, I'll hit. But the three minutes is felling me, my lungs start to rasp, Terry's gloves feel like lead. Dennis keeps going *ptew-ptew* with the left in my face like a fly that I swat away, the only defense I know. When the bell goes, I turn to Terry with a bunch of feelings I've never kept in one place before: furious humiliation at the certitude that men are humoring me; exhilaration because this is FUN; humility at having so much to learn; pride at this being, so far, so very, very easy; and, above all, relief that I have broken the ban. I have made it to the ring.

In the second round, I hit more and harder, and I bloody Dennis's nose. I back off, gloves out questioningly, and he nods his head, so I keep hitting. His flabby belly yields spongily when I connect, feeling revoltingly human, so I concentrate on the nose, which is nice and solid. The blood upsets me not at all. I'm rather proud of my handiwork. By the end of three rounds, I am speckled with scarlet, drenched in sweat, and cock-a-hoop.

"You see?" says Terry. "That wa'nt so bad."

"Well, of course not. He wasn't hitting me." Dennis comes round, wet, stained T-shirt stuck to his convex midriff, and I ask myself who looks more like a boxer and who won.

"I wasn't holding back, you know," he says, unbuckling his headgear. "You did really well."

"You know it. You did good, girl," adds Terry.

"Yeah, well, I guess it was okay for the first time," I mutter, angry and pleased. If he's not lying about holding back, I must be pretty good at this, but I reckon he is lying in a habitual, kind-to-the-little-lady way. Now I've had a taste of sparring—or "sparring"—I see I'm starting all over again, and I'm hungry to learn. But who at Gleason's is man enough to hit me? Maybe a real boxer; maybe only a woman.

In the locker room we keep away from the subject of sparring, and the gap left by that silence is wide. I know what I think: that we are all scared to admit we're not yet *gen-you-wine* boxers. We've got to keep up appearances. I try to protect even myself from the knowledge that what I do is Disney sparring, and I find my tiny social firework goes off with a bigger bang when I come over all mysterious at dinner, saying, as Leslie did, *I don't know about fighting. But I spar.* And I do spar most days now—with Dennis and his bloody nose, with Domenico Menacho and his medieval duct tape, or with Terry, on whom I can't lay a glove. Domenico is by far the most satisfying because he coaches me, underscoring my mistakes by whacking me—hard. A lot of sparring is counterintuitive. My natural response to being punched in the eye, for instance, is to turn my face away, which of course leaves me blind. Dennis will pause if I do that, and Terry will tell me not to turn away, but Domenico will keep popping me until I manage to compose myself and hit back. I'm learning.

Some three weeks later, Terry is all smiles. He's got a surprise for me, he says. He's found a girl for me to spar. Cool! I say, catching my breath. A jolt in my stomach informs me how my desire to progress has not been entirely sincere. I've been enjoying the boasting opportunities of this complacent, easy sparring, as well as its other side effect: Sam has developed a brand-new crush on me. It dates from one night when I showed him a jab. "You just stopped it half an inch from my face," he keeps saying. "You would have knocked me down. I thought your boxing was cute until then." This sudden admiration has brought interesting repercussions in bed, and I am drinking it in, a victory in my fight to prove that women are not inferior athletes. Yet, I secretly know, it is undeserved. Well, now I have to put my money where my mouth is, and face a woman, someone who will not hold back, who is the same as me, yet who might wish to crush me, or whom I might wish to crush. I can't predict how this will be. The prospect looks very different than it did before Gleason's. Denuded now of personal and horrible subtexts, it has become simply the real thing.

"Who is it, Terry?"

"You'll see."

"No, tell me. Is she my weight? Is she good?"

"Yeah, I'd say you're about the same."

"What? Both?"

"Yeah, she's a good match."

"But who is she? Do I know her?"

"Yeah, you know her." He's been grinning throughout. I suspect foul play.

"Why won't you tell me who she is, then?"

"You'll see soon enough."

So the next day, I turn up early, and I'm all warmed up, mouth-guard in pocket, my new Reyes sparring gloves Terry helped me select already laced up, shadowboxing in excited anticipation, trepidation, even elation, when she walks in with her trainer.

4

Let Her Come Forward

"Hey," says Leslie Howe.

"Oh my God," I reply.

"Told you you'd know her," says Terry, as delighted as a yenta matchmaker. Leslie's trainer, a compact Latino guy, starts to wrap her hands, and I start to feel shaky. Leslie has at least two years' more sparring under her belt and I have usurped her sport. This is not Crosby Street. She has not come to teach me.

"I'm amazed I never run into you here," I say, reaching for contact.

"Oh, no, I left a while ago. This place is so fake. I'm training up in the Bronx. With the Lady Tyger—you know?"

"She's a trainer?"

"Yeah, she's intense. She couldn't make it today, though."

"She fight still?"

Leslie laughs.

"Oh, no. She gained about a hundred pounds."

Her hands wrapped, Leslie goes to warm up, and I ask Terry the same questions as before: How far do we go? What if it gets out of

hand? He says relax. Since I started sparring, Terry is more interested
in me, even though he has a way of being completely charming, then
disappearing abruptly behind a scrim. On insecure days, I imagine
him silently ridiculing me, stupid white girl, but as I get better at
boxing, and with all these men asking when am I going to fight and
saying shame to put all that talent to waste, I'm beginning to trust
that he's engaged, and I'm beginning to need to, because I think I
might fight soon. Terry teaches in fits and starts, watching and watching and then imparting some small gem that repairs a fault or leads to
a quartz moment of understanding. He shows me a feint and a roll.
"You never do this without a reason," he says. "You do something at
the end," and I *get* what the pretty move is for, how you pop up with
your weight distributed differently, ready to surprise the guy with a
hook perhaps. With every new piece in my repertoire, I wonder how
many more there can be. I love that this sport made of nothing but
four punches—jab, right, hook, uppercut—is layered like the rock of
a mountain. I feel the moves being tamped down inside me, one on
top of another, learned, fixed, and owned. Like food into flesh, I consume a move, chew, and digest it until it, too, becomes part of me.

Leslie returns to Victor Valle's ring and we take our corners.
Now I'm more curious than nervous since Leslie is not a vicious
gangsta streetfighter, and because I am cocky. At the bell, we advance
and circle for what seems a long time, until one of us—I forget
which—essays a jab and the other counters. The softness of her glove
is irritating, until I realize that my jab, too, is pulled. I'm a bit relieved,
but more disappointed. I don't want to be polite. When Leslie taught
me the speed bag, she said if you think, you can't do it, but I bet she's
thinking now. I know I am. I remember Leslie's jab in aerobics over a
year ago, and that phrase "But I'm sparring," and I remember wondering who she was sparring with and how it felt and—well, now
I know. She's sparring with me.

Nothing, however, happens. Between rounds, I ask Terry if it's
okay to go harder, and he says keep it steady. It's confusing, because
what we seem to be doing is dancing. I'm no masochist, but I crave

the hit to make this real, I want a little chaos. What I'm feeling like is a big cat in a circus, primed to pounce yet sparing the prey, until at last, in the third round, Leslie gets one in, a beautiful hook that catches me on the cheekbone. I feel it sharply without pain and I love how it feels—or rather, I love how I can take it so easily.

"Thorry," she lisps through the mouthguard.

"No," I say, annoyed, "'s fine."

"You okay?"

"Course I am. Box."

My cheek stings but, unlike with Dennis, being hit doesn't make me want to retaliate. I seem to have some overriding sister reflex, and the rules of sparring are opaque as ever. Surely I should hit her now? But the brakes on my fists stay locked. The notion that I might not be able to get a shot in doesn't occur to me.

———

After four rounds we call it quits. I'm tired, and unsatisfied like I didn't come. Terry unlaces my gloves, says I did fine, the bored little crowd peels off, and Leslie and her trainer depart. That evening, I'm examining the mouse under my eye, my very first, very own battle bruise, when the phone rings. It's Leslie.

"That was cool," she says. "Let's definitely spar some more."

"Sure," I say, surprised that she wants to.

"I like the controlled sparring," she explains. "I sparred with this woman up in the Bronx the other week. It was horrible. She was this huge brute. She just got me in the corner and laid into me. I couldn't get out."

"Why didn't you stop the sparring?" I ask.

"I don't know. I guess I didn't believe it was happening. It was like I was standing outside the ring watching myself getting beat up."

Although that hasn't happened to me, I understand how it would be; how I might also submit to the mismatch. In my spurious gym hierarchy, the huge vicious woman would have more right to the

Bronx ring. But in the same system, Leslie and I have equal claim to the ring, even though she has been boxing longer; and, therefore, being cast in the role of teddy bear is an irritation. Leslie proceeds to rub salt in the wound.

"You know, I'm really sorry about that shot," she says. "Are you okay?"

"Like I said. Of course. It's nothing," I snap, sounding like I'm putting on a brave face.

"No, 'cause I really wasn't trying to hit hard, you know."

"Look, it's sparring. Don't worry about it."

We chat for a while, about the rumor that the Golden Gloves is taking girls next year, about her new job as director of Barneys Gym, and after I put the phone down I notice I am fuming. Was she crowing? Why did I hold back? Now she thinks I'm easy. Maybe the coiled-power thing was mere delusion. I've got to get back in the ring; I've got to find out more.

I'm alternating Gleason's with Terry's other place, SoHo Training, where he's been hired because he is now the Manhattan boxing trainer du moment. He has also gone into business as Panther Fitness, manufacturing speed ropes in beautiful packages with sexy graphics. More and more, I only like Gleason's. At SoHo Training I see Mad Dog Luke, he of the gold tooth, and he rants about how Terry's a crap trainer and Gleason's is a pussy gym and women can't box, and yet I laugh—he's just sore I ditched him. When he adds that Terry told him he doesn't give a shit about training people but doesn't mind taking their money, I laugh more feebly. Terry doesn't seem mercenary at all, but Luke has given voice to the very thing I've been fearing, and the words reverberate on the days I'm feeling inept and slow. One of those days, I speak up.

"Terry, I want you to tell me if I'm wasting my time and yours wanting to fight. I want you to be honest."

"I am," he says, and explains how he wouldn't even bring me to Gleason's if I wasn't serious because it would reflect badly on him. He says there are plenty of people who beg him to take them here, people he wouldn't bring even once, and that nobody would talk to me if I wasn't any good, and haven't I seen women here getting completely blanked? He wouldn't have put me in with Leslie, he says, if I wasn't up to it. Leslie, he tells me, was really nervous about sparring. She thought I might be too strong. I think of the big Bronx woman and understand that I wasn't cast in the warm and cuddly role after all, and I feel better. Victor Valle, Terry continues, would certainly not have taken the trouble to watch me on the bag and give his thoughts. That's really something, he swears.

"Here's what we'll do," he says. "We spar on a regular basis. Then, in February, the Gloves start. So in late December, we decide if you want to enter."

"The Gloves? So there *are* women's Golden Gloves?"

"Well, sure there are."

And he is right, as a headline in the *Daily News*, the newspaper that has staged the famous tournament for sixty-seven years, soon affirms: NEW KIND OF RING FOR LITTLE WOMAN. The article below quotes Pete Brodsky, president of USA Boxing Metro, the New York arm of amateur boxing's governing body, who claims: "We thought there would be women competing last year, but apparently there wasn't that much interest." But "Interest certainly exists this year," the article's author continues. "Bruce Silverglade of Gleason's Gym said yesterday there are already seven women working out at his gym and he expects the number to increase." Then Bruce speaks up: "The women we've seen are all highly motivated, well conditioned athletes who are looking for competition. They have the right to compete."

Well, all the women except me and Leslie Howe do. A rumor is afoot: USA Boxing and the *Daily News* might be lowering the age limit for the first women's Gloves—to thirty-two and under instead of the men's limit of thirty-four. Leslie, at thirty-six, is out in any case, but I, four months into my thirty-third year, am borderline. Lying is out of the question, because since that talk with Terry, I have become the proud possessor of a brand-new official USA Boxing license. Still, I am optimistic. It's not as if there was a line round the block of thirty-two- to thirty-three-year-old female boxers. Actually, I believe I'm the only woman in New York whom the extra two years would affect.

Just in case, I'm hedging my bets with another scheme, a fight involving my mysterious potential sparring partner, Katya Bankowsky, whom I finally meet in the locker room. She is indeed about my size, if an inch smaller in every direction except biceps, a feminine Dolph Lundgren with a Yale degree, a career as a freelance producer of commercials, and a dry wit. We hit it off the day we meet, but not in the ring, because—and I'm not clear how this happens—we immediately get caught up in one of Bruce's, as Katya puts it, hare-brained schemes and consent to meet each other in a December undercard bout in Georgetown, Guyana. If this were a professional bout, we'd be disbarred from the Gloves and all amateur competition, so Bruce is trying to get it demoted to an exhibition; but in my mind it's already fake, because Katya has been training here way longer than I, is a supercoordinated athlete who packs a punch like an ox, and she's someone whom I like enormously. I have nil desire kill her, nor she me (I think). But nothing is quite clear.

"You know," Katya says to me, "I'm not so sure about this. Perhaps we shouldn't fight."

"Oh go on, let's do it," I counter. "We needn't go all out."

"Well, that's easy to say, but whatever we think, it can get out of hand in there."

"Look, all we need do is decide to hold back."

"But then you'll hit me and I'll get mad, and I'll hit harder and then . . . You can't necessarily control it. It could get ugly."

Katya knows more than I about actual combat, since she recently took a fight I balked at, a last-minute substitution for a non-sanctioned amateur four-rounder at the Police versus Firefighters annual smoker for charity (the firefighter dropped out). I was there with Sam. Bruce Silverglade and Domenico Menacho were there. Katya's cameraman was there. The reason was the same for all of us: to witness the first Gleason's female fight outside the gym. The camera would record it for the inaugural scene of Katya's movie, a feature-length documentary to be shot on expensive celluloid and financed on credit cards (just like Gleason's). It already had a title, *Shadow Boxers*, and was about women's boxing, whatever that might turn out to be. *Shadow Boxers* would consume five years, six figures, and half its director-producer's sanity, as it metamorphosed into several different animals, ending up—well, you'll see. But tonight's shoot carried an irresistible "Hey, kids, let's do the show right here" spirit, a good match for the hall throbbing with loud, partisan cops and firefighters, awash with beer. I was nervous, far more so than I had been for Terry; after all, Katya was my surrogate. Now, backstage in the opponents' room, she was poker-faced but twitchy as Bruce stood by, avuncular, apprehensive, stoical.

"I've seen the police girl," I said. "She's small."

"No problem, woman!" said Domenico, wrapping Katya's hands. "You beat her easy!"

"It doesn't matter what she's like," said Bruce. "You'll do great." I had lied. The cop had the strut of a bodybuilder and was spotted by Sam slapping large men on the back. When she stepped through the ropes and revealed the arms of Popeye, my heart both sank and sang. This was no walkover. I'd get to see my opponent, or co-boxer, in an all-action preview. Since I'd passed up the opportunity to get in the ring myself, I was secretly glad she wouldn't have it too easy, and that I had a ringside seat.

Katya was magnificent. Never losing her head, she countered everything the cop threw, stalking her and sticking her with stiff jabs, working the body, doing it all by the book. The cop was too muscle-bound to move much or hit hard, but she was well trained and could take a punch. When the announcer declared Katya the winner and the girls' bout the fight of the night, five hundred drunken law enforcers rose to their feet and cheered. Bruce and Domenico were proud as new dads.

At Gleason's, Terry is all ears about the fight. He has taken to spying on Katya, leaching information for when he'll work my corner in Guyana. He thinks it's hilarious the way Katya and I are hanging out, "philosophizing." He says he's fought a lot of friends and that they keep their distance from the moment they know until the decision. When I tell him it's different for girls and that this was why I'd wanted to fight men, he gets suddenly serious and says, What do you mean? Why? I say I'm more competitive with men, but that's not quite right. Really, I'm not all that clear about my attitude toward fighting Katya. Watching the cop bout told me all I needed to know about her performance in the ring; now what I want to know is how it *felt*.

———

When the date is set for December 27 and I learn we'll have to be in Georgetown over Christmas, I call it off. I couldn't do that to my mother. As soon as the pressure's released, I see there would have been no faking the fight, and the idea of beating up my new friend seems all the more absurd. I make friends fast, try to remain open-hearted, believe nobody on earth is a stranger—so where is the line to be drawn? Who *could* I hurt? Not Katya, and not Leslie. I wonder about boundaries. Is there a grain of truth in Joyce Carol Oates's ravings? Does the fact that my body can integrate another body during sex or pregnancy make me more permeable, and therefore more vulnerable, than a man? Or have my qualms nothing to do with antique gender assumptions? This so-called noble art requires suspension of normal rules of etiquette and respect, so that in the gym, honor is attached to something I would normally find abhorrent. Had I hurt Leslie, the spectators would have been impressed, but I might have found it a Pyrrhic victory. On the other hand, I might have found it liberating in some unforeseeable way. From closer up, fighting is frightening me in different places than I thought it would, and this makes me want to do it all the more. Go into what you fear, I say.

The Guyana fight canned, I load my hopes back onto the Gloves for the five minutes it takes for the age rumor to prove true. The *Daily News* is intractable, despite pleading phone calls from me and from Bruce, and despite the article—entitled GOLDEN GIRLS WILL LACE UP GLOVES—that I read on the plane to London for Christmas. Its two photos are captioned: "STRIKING FIGHTING POSE: Kate Sekules works with trainer Terry Southerland" and "IN THIS CORNER is Kate Sekules of Manhattan, who will be on Golden Gloves team representing Gleason's Gym."

"Everyone here is very excited," Katya has told the reporter. "Let's face it, the Golden Gloves is a major event."

But not for me.

———————

After a Christmas marinating in chocolate and naps, I stayed in London on and off through April, writing a travel guide to the city. In the wrong place at the wrong time, I trained, with a sinking feeling of regression, at Allstars, an amateur gym in a deconsecrated church. In my hometown, women's boxing was nowhere, despite Allstars' pioneering two-hour Boxer's Workout—led by the gym's boss, Isola Akay—which was popular with Sunday soccer players and cool Notting Hill girls who played in bands and wore vintage sweats. It would be almost another three years before the Amateur Boxing Association of England sanctioned female amateurs, and an additional year before welterweight Jane Couch would take the British Boxing Board of Control to court and win the right to fight professionally on her home turf—a victory that the British Medical Association called "a demented extension of equal opportunities." Now, in early 1995, the ABA would have closed down Akay's gym if it had found me training there alongside the guys, an antifeminist sentiment the boxers seemed to share. In deep contrast with the scene at Gleason's, I was persona non grata, weathering scowls from the laconic trainer as we worked the bags and he corrected everyone but me. But I kept going, and Akay continued to champion my illegal presence and give me padwork, and I sparred with the Scottish heavyweight pro, and the chilly climate gradually warmed up, and by the time I shipped myself back to New York, I had another second home in Allstars. Yet, as I was more tolerated there as an eccentric than accepted as an equal, I was feeling less like a bona fide boxer than ever.

———————

Meanwhile, Katya Bankowsky, Dee Hamaguchi, and Lisa Long had undergone the rite of passage and become real combatants: the Golden Gloves finals had just finished at Madison Square Garden's Paramount, the arena that (as the Felt Forum) had once been the fight game's epicenter. I got back to the gym just in time for the victory party, at which Bruce made a speech and a vast cake with *Congratulations Golden Gloves Champs* in green icing was devoured. Only Dee had made it out of the first round—and all the way to the finals, which is only fitting, seeing as it was Dee who worked with the ACLU Women's Rights Project to compel USA Boxing to sanction female amateurs in the first place. Her final-round vanquisher, Jill Matthews, the hairdresser and mature student, punkrock singer and rabbi's daughter, child gymnast and hyperkinetic Roadrunner boxer, left the ring to face a phalanx of cameras, including that of Katya Bankowsky, who was filming the news crews filming Jill for a scene in *Shadow Boxers*.

"D'you realize you just made history, and if so, how d'you feel? Were you thinking of that going in the ring?" the CBS reporter asks her.

"Of course," shrugs Jill.

"The question most men have, and I have," he continues, "is . . . why?"

"Why d'you want to be part of history in the making?" mugs Jill. "Err. Figure it out."

"What did you do to prepare?" another reporter asks.

"Got a manicure and a pedicure," she explains.

"The men here," continues the CBS reporter, "they fight Golden Gloves because they have dreams of being world champion one day and making big money. Where do you go from here?"

Jill pauses a beat.

"To a bar."

———————

Katya was free to shoot, having lost in the first round to twenty-three-year-old Long Islander Kathy Collins, who had taken up boxing to lose weight, lost 104 pounds in six months, lost the Gloves to Denise Lutrick, and immediately announced she intended to turn pro. That fight was weird, said Katya. Unlike in her cop bout, she had felt detached in the ring, and had allowed Collins to hit her almost without retaliating. She wasn't sure why this had happened. Lisa Long, the world champion in escrima, a Philippine martial art, had also lost—in the first-ever round of female boxing in the Gloves—but her fight had been a shock of a more literal, visceral kind. It was horrible, she said, really nightmarish to be caught in an all-out brawl with Taneasha Harris, a tenth-grader form Mount Vernon High School, when she'd come prepared to box. Not hearing the crowd screaming for her—*yell-ow, yell-ow*—not by name but by the color she wore, she had nodded at the ref when he wanted to stop the bout in the third round, and she could not forgive herself. Years later, Lisa showed me a photo of what Harris had wrought that night; it was a mug shot of a torture victim, both eyes closed, her face covered in blood and welts. Yet the shame of quitting still haunted her. Of the four Gleason's women, only Sky Hosoya was wearing a pair of gold, diamond-studded gloves to the party. She had won them without fighting, being the sole welterweight among twenty-two

female entrants. Had the age limit not been lowered for women, Sky
would have found an opponent: me. I expect my congratulations rang
hollow.

Not that I would have been in any shape to fight. It wasn't physical condition I lacked—my Allstars routine had kept the muscles and
cardio system in good order—but desire. As Bruce likes to say, boxing
is 90 percent mental, and in England my mental picture of me-the-
boxer had slid further into fiction. This spring I was dragging my
carcass into the gym, where I would desultorily punch bags and
Dennis, roundly bemoaning my ineptitude, as if Gleason's were a
sentence I was serving. Terry, though cheerful as ever, was losing
patience. "Don't worry about the work," he said sympathetically one
day, as I beat myself up, "people all over the world are starving to
death." Terry was increasingly hard to pin down. As president of Panther Fitness, he was branching out all over, into health club consulta-
tion and bigger "boxercise" ventures, not to mention further fights of
his own. At the same time, I was craving a deeper trainer relationship.
I wanted someone to be there more, both literally and in spirit. My
relationship with boxing itself had gone stale—like that point in any
relationship when you need a damn good fight and a heart-to-heart
to clear the air and begin a new phase. As I had sometimes done with
boyfriends, I resisted the shake-up, preferring, I suppose, to take
umbrage with boxing.

So when Bruce offered me my second opportunity to fight professionally, I passed. The bout was to be billed as the first female pro
fight in New York. The challenger was Katya's Gloves opponent, the
winner of the runner-up ruby-studded silver gloves in the 139-pound
weight class that she'd worked so hard to join, Kathy Collins. It was
in an arena I knew, Long Island's Westbury Music Fair, the place
where Terry Southerland had beaten Kevin the bull. It was Collins's
home turf. She had wasted no time in making good her vow to be the
first female professional out of the Gloves gate—the fight was in
three weeks' time. Nor did it take Bruce long to find a woman to step

into the breach, another superannuated distaff boxer banned from the Gloves and curious to know how a fight felt: Leslie Howe.

The day of the fight, *The New York Times* printed a piece by Robert Lipsyte under the heading: FOR THESE WOMEN, A HEAVY RIGHT IS MORE POWERFUL THAN SISTERHOOD.

"It's a few rounds early to declare a trend beyond the recent upsurge of upscale women aerobicizing through bloodless sparring," wrote Lipsyte, "but it's never too early to pontificate on gender matters." Lipsyte had interviewed both Howe and Collins, and Leslie's quote about tonight's fight opened the piece:

"Some people will find it evil and weird, and some will find it a turn-on," she said. "It's a subjective reaction. There are ramifications. . . . Boxing feeds your ego, your sense of grandiosity." ("Howe tends to intellectualize her sport," opines Lipsyte). Kathy Collins recalled how she felt during her bout with Katya Bankowsky: "Everything worked, I was slipping punches, my jab. . . . I felt so empowered. I felt like a machine. And not a bump on me." She told him that in her three Gloves fights "I learned a lot about aggression. . . . Women think of themselves as ladies, there's the whole friendship and sisterhood thing. If boxing is going to work for us, we have to have the eye of the tiger." How right she is, I thought, having been caught up in versions of the friendship and sisterhood thing with the very same two opponents. Of tonight's fight, Collins said, "I don't want to be part of some kind of novelty. If this is a sexual freak show, I'm out of here."

Arriving early for "The War at Westbury II: Guys and Dolls"— another spectacle staged by Dennis Rappaport, the tuxedoed Hugh Hefner of Long Island who could milk razzmatazz from a greenmarket—it looked like Collins's worry about the "sexual freak show" may have been on the money. Rappaport was busy living up to his own hype ("Where Boxing Meets Broadway"), posing outside with a chorus line of blondes in satin shorts and big red gloves. "While many boxing promoters make empty promises, Dennis Rappaport turns promises into accomplished realities," it said in the program. "Tonight Long Island will enjoy the excitement of ladies professional boxing at the Westbury Music Fair. History in the making!"

History was going to be made at the lowest spot on the under-card, six bouts before the main event, and four before "Electrifying Lightweight" Terry Southerland would try to improve his 18-2 record. This time I was not there for Terry. At 7:30 P.M., the crowd still sparse, I took a seat alone in front of a pocket of beer-swilling fight fans in acid-washed jeans. They rated the parade of card girls accord-ing to breast size. I composed withering ripostes for when they did the same to Howe and Collins and, by the time the female four-rounder was announced, I was ready to try out my new fists on these guys—like I hadn't in the jazz club ten years ago. I also had the "coulda bin me" feeling again, stronger than when Katya had fought. Now here came Leslie, dressed in a leopard-print hooded robe and matching trunks, head bowed, trotting the gangway with her gloves on the Lady Tyger's shoulders, her cut man following with bucket and stool. She climbed into the ring and as she shuffled and shadow-boxed in her corner I thought I'd throw up with nerves. It *couldn't* have been me! No way could I stand this. Leslie looked so cool, her inscrutable face, her sculpted legs. I was so proud of her—and at the same time, despite my vicarious terror, envious as hell. Then, after several hours it seemed, the announcer welcomed the local girl, Kathy Collins, making a big deal of her, as if she'd won belts and belts, not forgetting to mention (neither did the program) how she was fat a year ago, then took up boxing and lost over a hundred pounds. And in she came, jogging with intent, climbed through the ropes, took her corner, and raised her fists as if she'd already won. This was the one who Katya said had been a crazy person in the ring, flying at her, winging relentlessly, the one who, presumably, had learned to watch through the eye of the tiger. Sure enough, I could see her glaring at Leslie as if she hated her when they met in the middle for the referee's talk, and I wondered how my former teacher would deal with that, knowing only her dignified side, remembering her polite sparring, the way she "tends to intellectualize her sport." My heart was in my throat. Was she up to this?

At the bell, Collins cocked her fists, sprinted across the ring, and started in, tripling her jab, throwing wild roundhouse rights and bunches of uppercuts in a flurry more suited to the closing seconds of the final round. Howe, thank goodness, kept her head, stepping away, looking for openings. A counterpunching style looked natural on her (not that she had any choice), her defense was elegant, and I thought those punches that connected didn't look too loaded. Still, the action was relentless, and the two-minute round seemed to last an eon. In the break, it occurred to me that none of my startling insults had been needed, so I snuck a look behind me and there sat the good old boys, meek as churchgoers, passively awaiting the next round in silence.

The bell went for the second round, and again Collins roared out of her corner, windmilling arms, fists everywhere, and again Leslie dealt with it, threw shots when she could, blocked a lot of potential damage. Who was winning was anyone's guess. If this had been an amateur bout, Collins would have been ahead by sheer punch quantity. Amateur fights are scored on a points system. Each legal blow landed counts as one-third of a point and there is no extra merit in a hard blow. Each boxer starts each round with twenty points and at the end of each round, the blows are tallied up and the difference is deducted from the weaker performer's score. But this was not the amateurs; this was a professional bout, and those are scored quite differently. Four criteria are taken into account by judges in a pro fight: clean hitting, effective aggressiveness, defense, and "ring generalship." At the end of each round, the dominant boxer gets ten points, and the weaker fighter nine, eight, or seven, according to how great the discrepancy. Clearly, Kathy was way up on the aggressiveness scale tonight, and the shots of hers that landed landed clean, but Leslie certainly had the edge in defense (well, she was the only one who had any), and her ring generalship (meaning coping with situations, taking advantage of opportunities, adapting quickly to a style, neutralizing the opponent's attack—in short, smart behavior) was impressive.

Since nothing changed in the second half of the bout—neither fighter tired or changed tactics, neither threw anything staggering or backed down—my scorecard was one big question mark. However, after the final bell, when the half-capacity crowd stood up and applauded nicely as if for an enjoyable Broadway musical, I knew who had won. Kathy Collins was the home team, the fiery fun fighter, the hungry one. I thought on aggression alone, especially since this was the "first ladies fight," she had got it. The way she was hugging her trainer and grinning and pumping the air, she knew she had won too. The ref gathered the pair into the middle and held their arms and we waited for the announcer to come on and—hell, I was wrong. Since both ladies put in such a strong performance, he said, the judges had scored it equally. The fight was a draw.

Clearly, Kathy Collins would have taken the rematch right there. While Leslie hugged the Lady Tyger and beamed, Kathy stalked off, her face a mask of fury. I thought, *Damn, you didn't lose, what's the fuss about?* But this woman was on the warpath (literally, as it soon transpired). The mood in the arena seemed subdued, as if nobody had exactly understood the plot of the good Broadway musical. Behind me the boys exhaled. "That was okay," said one. "They can *fight*," said another. Two hours later, Terry Southerland won again.

After the excitement of the Gloves and Westbury—other people's excitement—I, too, lost the plot. Someone in Gleason's locker room told me a story about Dennis, how he had offered her a stipend to spar with him in private because he enjoyed being beaten up by women, and how she'd said she was flattered but had to decline. She said he was so gracious and honest that it didn't seem gross. But I thought of Dennis's ineffectual defense all those times I'd sparred with him, the way his blood was always showing, and I felt queasy. We'd been duped, all of us, inadvertently getting him off in the name of sport. I felt more foolish that I hadn't caught on than angry at our misuse. Of *course* someone was bound to eroticize male-female sparring; how strenuously I'd ignored that scenario. What denial. I'd auditioned as an athlete and won the part of an S&M porn star. Worse, the matching masochistic drive in Sam, awakened by the feint I'd jokingly thrown at him, was getting stronger. It was exacerbated by distance, since he moved to L.A. in April and we were no longer officially together, but he still had a "thing" about my "physicality," as he called it. He was ashamed, appalled, and entranced by it. Though he used to be my boyfriend, Sam's new fetishization of me felt strangely like Dennis's. This whole business was unclean. To adopt willingly the dominant position is one thing, but to be placed there against one's will is abuse. I began to think that what I wanted was to relinquish control, to capitulate completely—in bed, yes, but also in general to a man who was strong enough—even though capitulation was precisely what I had always fought. And, obviously, in the ring capitulation is catastrophic.

Instead of working it all out in the gym, I went traveling for three months and lost boxing. I was doing the opposite of boxing: assessing the top hotels and restaurants in the western half of the United States for their Mobil five-star ratings. It was the reward for my conscientious, underpaid guidebook efforts, and anybody's idea of a dream job. I came a bit unglued that summer, visiting friends and borrowing others' friends in Santa Fe, L.A., San Francisco, New Orleans, Oregon, Arizona, Vancouver. In L.A., my proximity made Sam so angry I couldn't deal with him and broke off all contact. On my privileged travels, all the confusion about sex and power I'd sublimated into the daily work of boxing resurfaced, so that by the time I returned I was hungry for the gym like never before.

———————

The women's locker room wears an aura of renewed vigor, and that isn't just my projection. There are new girls, good girls, especially

Bridgette Robinson and Veronica Simmons, and, fresh from her historic Gloves victory, Gleason's new female professional, Jill Matthews. If there had ever been a ninth category (women) in that athletes' pecking order, these three blow it away. You can tell, because the white noise of the gym commentators tunes into a definite signal from time to time, and I hear them criticized. I take this as a sign that we are being taken seriously, that the Dennis days are over. Merely watching Bridgette work the mitts with her trainer, Reggie Forde, would stop any fetish dead in its tracks. Her right hand, says Reggie, reminds him of Sonny Liston's; she hits harder than half the men here. Well, she's twice the size of half the men here, a big, bald brute of a woman in low-slung Levi's and a heavy key bunch on a D-ring on the belt. Bridgette, when she's done training, enthrones herself in the orange swivel chair in the locker room, dons her wire-rimmed specs, and gets the update on everyone's week. She drops her head and goes into spasms of laughter, stifling the sound like she's playing pranks at the back of the schoolroom. You want to hug her, which is something that would not occur to you out there in the ring.

Now, Veronica Simmons you would never hug. She is big, too, but in baskeball-player fashion, with long legs and sleek, cut muscles. She trains with the young and patient John Toliaferro and also hits like a truck, though I have heard it said that she is too static. Veronica never smiles. She is inscrutable, even in conversation, which she holds more readily with the black girls, whether or not by design I don't know. I wouldn't dare pursue personal issues with her, beyond asking what she does for a living (corrections officer) and what sport preceded boxing (basketball; she won a scholarship).

Small, sinewy Jill Matthews performs constantly—in the locker room; onstage fronting her band, Times Square (with her husband, David, on guitar); probably while cutting hair; and certainly during her childhood gymnastics career that nearly took her to the Olympics. She feels she failed at that sport, she says, and now she's getting a chance to redress it. Jill, despite her long strawberry blond mane and eyeliner, is a tomboy or—she insists—a gay man in a woman's body ("David *hates* it when I say that. *Eurgh*, he goes. *Don't!*"). About Jill it is said that she has no defense, something that I suspect is said of me, too, since it is true.

The biggest change for me is that I have a new trainer. When I came back, I didn't specifically leave Terry, he just melted back into his busy life and his morning sessions with Victor Valle, so I looked around for a Gleason's trainer, one of the guys who live here. I picked Angel Rivera, a thirtyish, brick-solid Puerto Rican whom I always liked. He wears baggy jeans, a white T-shirt, and a short Afro do, and seems to bring intense concentration to training his people; he always has an opinion and always laughs, flashing the whitest teeth I ever saw. Since I've been with Angel, I feel accepted into the fold, more a part of the gym and all who train in her. My technique has improved tenfold. I pick up my feet and acquire lateral movement, do a lot of drills where I catch a punch and counter, catch and counter, or step to the side, step in and throw, or drop down, pop up, and hook—nothing different, but it feels different. Where before I would string a bunch of moves laboriously together like beads, now they coalesce without my thinking about it. I am less awkward. Like most of the trainers, Angel has a small flock. He keeps us all on the go like a cabaret plate-spinner, cajoling one, jumping to the bag to keep that one's momentum going, throwing a quick yell to the shadowboxer. We range from sixteen-year-old Sechew Powell, who has won the Junior Olympics several times in several different weights and is now ranked the number-one lightweight in the country, to a middle-aged professional psychic. I spar with all of them. With Sechew it's excruciating at first, since I'm sure he must be crying with boredom, but he swears he learns something every single time, no matter who, and I, in turn, learn from his attitude. Naturally, he pulls everything, and I find it difficult to pretend it's real. When I manage to connect, I can't tell whether he's allowed me to do so or whether I earned it. He says I earned it, but I still don't know. With the psychic, the tables are turned. I am forbidden to hit her, while she tries to hit me as hard as she can. For a New Age person, she is remarkably violent. It helps me to make sense of my sparring sessions with Sechew and the others: I see how they really might get something from it, because to use defense alone is a whole lot harder than it looks.

The Golden Gloves was a milestone for women's boxing, but the news of it, frankly, reached few people. Now, almost a year after the Collins-Howe matchup, comes an event that thrusts the sport further into the limelight than it has ever been. On March 16, 1996, at the MGM Grand Garden in Las Vegas, Mike Tyson, fresh out of jail, is due to challenge the British heavyweight, Frank Bruno, for his WBA belt. So little is going on in the heavyweight ranks that this show, to be televised live on pay-per-view, is bound to be watched by every remaining boxing fan on the planet. And on the undercard, for the first time in a nationally broadcast event, there is to be a women's bout. It is going to be the TV debut of Christy "The Coal Miner's Daughter" Martin, who signed with Don King in October 1993 and has been racking up a 34-2-2 (25 KOs) record ever since, so far invisibly. She is to face an Irish fighter, "Dangerous" Deirdre Gogarty.

Tyson reaps the expected storm of attention—after all, this is his first attempt at a belt since his release from jail for rape, the perverse nineties corollary to Ali serving time for conscientious objection. Iron Mike is not my cup of tea. At this point, long before he chewed off Holyfield's ear, got a shrink, and seemed a bit more simpatico, he is just a bully with an ugly slugging ring style. Still, I wouldn't miss the Tyson-Bruno bout for the world. I'm rooting all the way for Frank, a hero back home along the George Foreman cute-and-cuddly axis. But, needless to say, the main event for me is Martin-Gogarty. This is far from true for the all-male crowd I'm watching with—a couple of them sometime sportswriters—in a Greenwich Village apartment. Women shouldn't box, they chorus, largely to get a rise out of me. This bout is going to be a joke. Bring on Mike.

Well, as the millions who watch tonight witness, it is Mike and Frank who are laughable; the main event is six minutes and fifty seconds of tedium. We are all embarrassed for boxing as Frank Bruno clings to Tyson like an orphan until Tyson pries him off and slaps him to the canvas in the third. But even as the big nonevent unrolls, talk in the apartment is still about the women, though nobody can bring himself to take them exactly seriously. "Bring back the chick fighters," they keep saying. "Lesbians fight best." Later, the reporters (whatever they might have said in private) will print genuine praise:

"The Gogarty-Martin bout was superior to most male fights," writes Steve Wulf in *Time* magazine. "It was crisp and clean and devoid of the arm holding, head butting and eye thumbing so prevalent in boxing."

"Not only was the bout ... more competitive than the typical prelim," concurs Richard Hoffer in *Sports Illustrated* (in the issue with Christy Martin on the cover), "it also had more action and better boxing than the main event." *Newsday*'s Greg Logan feels the same way: the fight was "the absolute hit of the Mike Tyson-Frank Bruno card. What began with a visceral squeamish feeling for many fans—men and women alike—ended in a cascade of cheers for two athletes who gave their all."

Whatever criticism has been thrown at Christy Martin since (and there is much of it, all concerning the way she ducks dangerous opponents), tonight in Las Vegas she is mind-blowing. Not even my opinionated companions can deny that she has perfect style. They react rather like the ringside crowd, as Tom Humphries describes it in the *Irish Times:* "it took five, maybe 10 seconds for the beery, testosterone charged crowd to realize they weren't watching a novelty act. ... The mixture of ferocity and serious boxing skills left the most chauvinistic ticket holders gapemouthed." "Martin is a model fighter, hardly ever throwing an incorrect punch and always pressing the action," Richard Hoffer expands later in the inaugural issue of *SI for Women*. "She, alone among King's fighters, has never produced one boring round."

And let's not forget the performance of Deirdre Gogarty. There is no doubt that Martin has the upper hand, but Gogarty, who appears about ten pounds lighter, fights back every inch of the way, bloodying Christy's nose early on (we'll get used to that sight, she has a faucet nose) and displaying a defense as impressive as the winner's attack. But, of course, defense doesn't win fights.

Every single boxer, trainer, and hanger-on at Gleason's has seen the fight. Overnight, the women here have emerged from behind the scenery, no longer spear carriers. There are roles for us! Speaking parts! Trainers scrutinize us with narrowed eyes. Could she beat Christy? I, as the only woman of approximately matching weight, am instantly cast as Christy's inevitable nemesis. "Hey, you could beat that girl" is something I hear more than once a day. Outside the gym, if the subject of boxing arises and I boast that I partake, someone always assumes I must be that girl on the Tyson card. Everyone has heard of her. For years, Christy Martin continues to be the sole female boxer to cross the average sports fan's radar.

When I ask Bruce what he thought of the fight, he admits to being more impressed than he believed possible—and he was already the chief proponent of women's boxing around here. (Angel, by contrast, pulls a face and says, "Not bad.") Take Gleason's pulse the day after the Tyson-Bruno bout and you'd think Christy Martin was the most interesting thing to happen to boxing in years. So when Bruce announces that the girl (the term she prefers) herself is going to make one of her many media appearances right here at Gleason's gym next week, there is quite some excitement. She will do interviews with several news crews that will tape her working out before they talk to her. When she sends word that she wants sparring partners, everyone looks the other way, has something else to do that day. I don't get it. Why don't they all—Veronica, Katya, Lisa, Sky (the others are too light or heavy)—leap at the chance? Do they know something I don't?

It doesn't matter. Aware I'm in over my head, I still want to know how it feels. Christy, after all, is the girl with the biggest slice of the pie. I decide to let my trainer be the judge.

"Angel," I beg. "May I?"

"Sure," he shrugs.

5

The Punch That Counts

Gleason's is Times Square, bustle bustle, crash crash. Cameras are rolling in—ABC, NBC, CBS, the *Shadow Boxers* crew—Christy Martin's publicist is fretting over protocol, a few of Don King's lesser people are clustered with Bruce in the office. I am lurking in the corner. For days I've been giving myself advice: I mustn't mind about Christy being better than me, I must just learn. And relax. Above all, relax. Recently I asked Reggie Forde, Bridgette's trainer, how to relax in the ring. He laughed.

"It's like making love," Reggie said. "When you're wit' a woman for the first time, she's not relaxed because she don't *know* you. You gotta play wit' her a little, let her know you're gonta have fun together." I laughed too. I saw exactly what he meant, although, by dint of my boxing, there seemed to be a role reversal—I'm not one of Reggie's skittish fillies, I'm a colt, I'm a Reggie. I should be relaxed already. There was a wistful old-fashioned appeal to the scene Reggie painted that eluded me in my machismo. He wasn't coming on to me; this was man-to-man ring advice, without agenda . . . or was I being the gull, like with Dennis? Boxing tips often arrive with an ambiguous gender spin.

Christy Martin's attitude toward knotty questions of gender is . . . there aren't any! Married to her trainer, Jim Martin, and identified by ring moniker as her father's daughter, Christy is keen to prove her femininity. The trunks that get speckled with blood are fringed powder-pink satin. Jim Martin supports his wife's chosen trade now, but he came the long way round. He has recently been joking to the press how, when Christy Salters appeared in his Tennessee gym in 1990—complete with mother and small dog—he was so mortified he "had it all set up to have her ribs broke." Now Jim Martin is glad his wife is tough, and equally glad she is not "a manly type woman." So is Christy, who favors miniskirts and lots of makeup, as if this drag proved she's not a lesbian. It galls me, but only mildly. Not even the most gauche of her antifeminist statements can override the image of her "ferocity and serious boxing skills." She's expanding perceptions of what women can do, albeit involuntarily, but her wish to be viewed as simply a boxer, not a female boxer, is completely bananas. If she were a he, he'd be just another lightweight with an okay record—and a papered one at that, since most pre-Gogarty opponents were tomato cans. ABC, NBC, et al. are only interested in her sex.

When Christy Martin arrives, her attitude and entourage underline her determined ignorance of this. We are sniggering behind her back like eighth-graders; the men, too. They wonder what the big fuss is about. As is the fashion around here, they have been shooting her down just as they do with guys who win, even those on the home team. And, as always, the criticism says more about its source than its object. Thus I find myself defending Christy Martin's boxing skills to Angel, even as I prepare to face them in the ring, with (I hope) his assistance.

"Nah, she ain't so hot," he sneers. "You don't want to get all tense and shit." This makes me uncomfortable.

"Angel, she's really good. Did you *see* her fight?" I say.

"Sure, I did. Like I said, she ain't so hot."

I wonder about Angel sometimes. He trains me with that heavy concentration I admired from afar, but he also flirts his face off—all in fun, but the motif is often how useless we women are at this. I give it right back, but never touching on one incendiary theme—the subject of Angel's own boxing career. He didn't have one. I'm protecting him from knowing that I know because, like your shrink telling you all about himself, it could ruin the relationship. Today I want to lean on Angel, but I can't lean on him if he's being a baby, and a baby is exactly what he's accusing me of being.

The cameras are all set up now, the time to spar draws close, and I'm feeling the cool shadow of the gallows, my heart thumping. I wrap my hands and start to shadowbox, waiting for Angel. Mr. Minor is watching. Mr. M. is rarely seen. He is more oracle than trainer, a dapper, white-haired gent with a cane and several national amateur titles, from the fifties, I think, though the number is vague. (I never ask a guy about his record unless I know it's flawless, in case he's ashamed of his number, like me with my weight.)

"You're getting in with that girl, right?"

"Yep."

"Well, she's good. I seen her on the Tyson card. But she ain't going to hurt you."

I stop moving and peer at Mr. Minor.

"How do you know?"

"Because I spar how you spar."

"Huh?"

"I spar how you spar. I feint, jab, double jab, a little this, a little that. I ain't showing you nothin', what you gonna do? Punch my lights out? No. You gonna take it easy."

"Yeah, but what about her?"

"I spar how you spar. You start beatin' up on her, then it's gonna turn out different. She ain't gonna let you hit her, but she ain't gonna hit you first. Remember. I spar how you spar."

I stare at Mr. Minor as this revelation sinks in, the best explanation of sparring rules I have ever heard; in fact, the only one. Christy's request for a sparring partner was baffling, seeing as she and her husband had told reporters how there aren't any female sparring partners out there. If she's good enough to spar, they said, she'd be better used as an opponent. They can't have known what they'd find at Gleason's, any more than I know what they'll find in me. I figure either I'll prove pathetic, in which case she'd look bad beating up on me, or I'll be good, in which case she'd show respect in order not to look bad getting beaten up by me. I honestly don't know which scenario will play out since I don't *know* how good or bad I am—an alarming measure of uncertainty—and having been overcautious in my only woman-to-woman experience to date, I don't know how different it can get with someone not just my own weight but my own sex. "I spar how you spar" gives me back some control. It seems to lower the chaos to a level I can live with.

"I spar how you spar" does not apply to sparring with men. Too often, if he sparred how I sparred, he would knock me out cold. One can never quite tell how much he is holding back or, conversely, how little; it's not as if he'd admit to being evenly matched with a woman. Judging myself harshly, I usually assume he's holding everything back, like *I* do with the psychic. I wonder if the others think that way or if everyone else knows exactly how good they are. My skills have seemed alarmingly protean lately, going from supersonic to abysmal overnight. I was far from comfortable waiting to find out which side of the scales my skills would weigh down today. Last Monday, I watched Patricia Alcivar go a few rounds with the small, smiling Domenico Menacho, still my favorite sparring partner. I'd heard of Alcivar, of her reputation as the best female boxer at Wall Street Gym, all of nineteen years old, already a veteran of several New York marathons and about to face her first Golden Gloves final. I thought that on the eve of your big fight you were supposed to do a light workout, no sparring, in case you "leave your fight in the gym," but Alcivar wasn't playing it like that. She went six rounds in constant motion, throwing perhaps eighty punches a round without breaking a sweat, her waist-length hair swinging in its ponytail. I was so impressed, I took an ego nosedive.

"Look at her," I said to Angel. "How quick she is, how much she moves." (How big and slow I am. How pretty she is.)

"Yeah," said Angel, "but look how she's got her head down. She's got no power there. And her legs are, like, two yards apart." He was right, but it didn't matter, I let my heart sink anyway.

"Don't be getting down on yourself," said Angel. "You're stronger than any of the girls in here." So what? I thought. What use is strength when you can't breathe, when you don't think right? Boxing is ninety percent mental.

By the time it was my turn with Domenico, I had become my teenage self at her most abject. Oh, here we go then, do I have to, do I have to, I hope they're not watching. I hope *she's* not watching. Oh, the shame of being boring. "Come on, Kate, git moving in there," said Angel, but I was locked into my uselessness, and was despising myself for that. Nowhere is more conducive to self-loathing than the boxing ring, where there is even more opportunity for shortfall than in the fog-free aerobics mirror—*that*, at least, is solely about appearance. Neither is there a better place than the ring to practice self-aggrandizement, but this was not one of those days. I am always this bad, I was thinking as I circled Domenico, throwing out pointless jabs, letting him catch me with the most telegraphed of his. "Come on, woman, hook off the jab, hook off the jab," he was saying, as he always does, but I had forgotten how. The more encouraging Domenico became, staying open so I could hit him, suggesting which punches to throw, the more humiliated I felt, until it was impossible to tell whether my clumsiness was caused by my negative thoughts or vice versa. My heart was set on nothing more than getting out of there.

The following evening I sat with Domenico at Madison Square Garden's Paramount Theater for the second night of the 1996 Golden Gloves finals—it was the second year for women, the sixty-ninth for men—and I felt relieved, after yesterday's experience, to be spectating. Just like last year, Gleason's had had some successes the night before. Veronica Simmons had stopped a mother of three from the Bronx in the first round; laid her out flat. Sky had won again, this year by fighting. Her opponent was an actress from Alcivar's gym who, the program says, is boxing because "it's the rawest there is and I go for it all." Then, two of the Judah brothers had fought two fighters from Michael Olajidé Sr.'s Kingsway gym—Sr. being the eyepatch-and-Aerobox Jr.'s estranged father and onetime trainer. Jr.'s young half brother, Tokunbo Olajidé, had beaten twelfth-grader Josiah Judah, while the latter's eighteen-year-old brother, Zabdiel, won his third pair of Golden Gloves.

Gleason's shares Zabdiel's kudos with its resident Judah Brothers Boxing Club, a remarkable organization run by Josiah and Zab's father, Yoel, universally known as Judah, who was the undisputed world kickboxing champion in his day, and who, unassisted, brings up Josiah, Zab, and their five brothers—all of whom box (even little Yoel, aged four, messes about in gloves). Bruce says he's watched Judah's boys grow into boxers "as long as I can remember." There is always an embarrassment of Judahs around here—Dad, offspring, Uncle Jimmy, they *live* in the gym.

"I fought the courts for a year and a half to keep us together," Judah tells me. "That's why we're so tight." And of the multitude of reasons to admire the family, my favorite is that this closeness is so sincere. Even though Zabdiel is shooting up through the ranks at the speed of e-mail—he is number one in the country and will now turn pro—there's not a scrap of jealousy among them.

"My brothers give me confidence, you know what I'm saying, to work harder and harder and harder," Zab says. "We inspire each other."

"We go to all the fights," Josiah adds. "We hang out together. We party together."

"I didn't plan this," says Judah. "After I seen how they fell in love with boxing, how they really love it, I say, 'Uh-huh. Hoh-kay ...' Then I got them so hooked, after a time I'd say, 'You don't do well at school, you don't train for a week.' It'd *kill* 'em. Especially this one"—he nods at Zab on the bag. "He would cry *tears*." In addition to training six champions, plus sixteen other (unrelated) fighters, Judah runs a successful construction business. He cooks, does the dishes and the laundry. "And we're definitely spiritual," he stresses. "We keep the laws of Moses."

If I were ever tempted to succumb to stereotype vision—to see boxing as certain commentators and movies paint it, as a noble ascent from the ghetto, or from a dog-eat-dog grimy life, or to imagine that gender roles were stuck in the fifties—the Judahs alone could knock it out of me. Even if there were no women at Gleason's, it would be impossible to hang around here and not rearrange tedious clichés I may once have entertained. Yet in the Garden, this second night of Gloves finals, it was the women who were making the packed crowd think twice. The five female bouts blew the men's away, even though of the ten women left out of forty-four entrants (twice as many as last year), only two had been boxing more than a year. First up, Maritza Arroyo vs. Tyrene Manson. Tyrene I knew. She'd been coming over from Bed-Stuy Gym a lot to spar with Jill Matthews—finally, two perfectly matched women working together. It was beautiful how they'd ratchet up the heat and cool it, fight and box, fight and box, the trust and respect and skill levels sky high. Well, turned out Arroyo was every bit as good as Manson, going toe-to-toe in a beautiful bout worthy of Balanchine, and decisioning Tyrene in the end. "That woman is good," thought Domenico. "Which one?" I asked. He beamed. "Both!"

Now it was Patricia Alcivar. She fought Eileen Lacy, a gymnastics instructor from the Nassau Police Athletic League. She lost. Although the weight of the punches don't matter in amateur scoring, Lacy won by sheer power. Alcivar ran a marathon inside the twenty-foot square but her shots were feathers and the guys around me were restless. Even in the polite amateurs, heavier weights are the crowd pleasers because that's where knockouts happen, and this was proving no different for women. As the weights rose, so did the volume.

The 132-pound class featured Denise Lutrick, a controlled, athletic fighter, and easily the most experienced female, who'd won the 139-pound title last year. "Watch this woman," said Domenico, who had sparred with her a great deal. "She the best of the *lot*." Well, surprise surprise, every round was taken by newcomer Melissa Salamone, a six-month veteran with the showy moves of a pro. It was the fight of the night. Her brothers are boxers, explained Domenico, impressed. Then my weight class, 147 pounds, was won by Aimee Berg, a Manhattan sportswriter. I watched in sad silence, feeling ineffectually competitive. Last and largest was Bridgette Robinson, who was facing last year's "super heavyweight" winner (by walkover), Helen Braxton. Later I was to hear how Bridgette had almost refused to enter the ring, so ragged were her nerves, but you'd never have known it watching her. The crowd went wild as she laid waste to Braxton, who claimed twelve years of fighting experience. If there were ever a barrier to legitimacy for the female division, tonight smashed through it. This caliber of amateurs meant the beginning of a feed system that would ensure the future of the sport. The chicks had landed.

———————

In the right place at the right time with the wrong birthday, I was deep in self-pity when the Christy challenge arrived, three days after the Gloves finals. It transformed me. For the first time since the fights-that-weren't-to-be, I had a purpose, and the fact that nobody wanted to stop me was a terrific boost—suddenly, one degree of separation between me and the top cat. I stopped being down on myself like *that* and thought I was good again. "Whatever happens, happens," said Angel, relieved I'd quit whining.

So, my day at last. Mr. Minor slinks off, replaced by Katya and her cameraman, who want my feelings on film before they shoot the sparring session. "I haven't a clue how it'll be," I say. "Yes, I'm nervous as hell. I may fall over before she hits me." Yes, I'm nervous, but, greedy for my limelight, these nerves are fun. There's something unreal about the day, with all those cameras in a wagon train around Christy shadowboxing, with Sky and Bridgette popping over with a cheer—*Go get her Kate, beat the shit out of her*—and all the guys' eyes on me—*Yeah, her, she's gettin' in with that girl from the Tyson fight*. Over there, Christy looks small and, as everyone keeps saying, a bit pudgy in a plain T-shirt and shorts, her curly feathercut hair loose. From the corner of my eye, I track her progress through her workout, knowing they'll come and get me whenever she's ready, no warning. It seems a long time. Angel and Domenico take turns going over to spy on her but discover precisely nothing. It is so strange to have a woman boxer (even one who acts half male boxer and half wifey) be the one covered in cameras, not Arturo Gatti or Junior Jones or Kevin Kelly as usual. I haven't seen her smile yet.

The wait goes on and the wait goes on. Doubts start, that familiar twang of anticlimax. Rumors fly. I find Bruce.

"She isn't going to spar, is she?" I say.

"Well," he says, "we don't know. Let's wait and see."

We wait. The publicist flies importantly by.

"She ain't gonna do it," ventures Sky. "What's she got to gain?"

"But she *asked*," I say. "It was their idea."

"What if you smoke her? She'd look ridiculous," Katya points out.

"Ah, she *scared* of you, woman," says Domenico.

"I like that, but I doubt it."

"Yeah, she's chickenshit. She don't like the look of you," Bridgette says.

"She probably thinks it's you," I say. "That *would* scare her."

I do like to think she's marked us, wondering which is the one, but I doubt it. She's too busy being the superstar, having a payday, not a workday. Angel goes off to give someone padwork; Sky and Bridgette also disappear. Katya collars the publicist to arrange an interview and reports that they won't talk about the sparring, but she's been granted two minutes' camera time. It is obvious this isn't going to happen.

The publicist is finally cornered. Christy has hurt her hand, she tells us, but she'd be happy to sign an autograph. We are permitted to approach. Christy shows no interest in us, in the fact that we box, too. I don't know why I don't ask her about the sparring, but I don't. I tear a page from my notebook and she writes: "Kate, Best Wishes! Christy Martin," with an elaborate curlicue underneath and a small circle over the *i*, then poses for a snapshot with Bridgette, Sky, the heavybag, and me.

"Come on, woman! Let's box!" Domenico yells, and he and I get in the corner ring and go eight rounds, two more than I've ever done, and I am better than I've ever been and it's the antidote to the other day because Domenico isn't holding back. I let out the aggression of being led on by the diva boxer and I feed off the relief of being let off the hook. The other day I hoped Alcivar wasn't watching me with Menacho; now I really hope Martin is watching. Five seconds of this makes it to the final cut of *Shadow Boxers*, but nothing of her and me. Not what I had in mind.

Before I step into the ring, Angel says, "Don't hold back," so I know he's been conferring with her trainer and that they've agreed we'll go all out. He's never said that before, and Terry never did. It is a few days after the Christy nonevent and I've finally been let off the leash. When the bell goes, I square up and march to meet her. She looks determinedly fierce and very nervous. I put a jab straight through her guard. She is startled. Then I circle a little, feeling not like the circus cat I was with Leslie but like a hell-eyed shark scenting meat. I know I'm the bad thing in here. I can strike anytime because she has no defense. To get the suspense over with, I answer a tickle of a jab with a good stiff one and a hard right. She nearly cries. Sort of draws breath and goes *omigod* and looks at her trainer to save her. I pause while she does that, then I release another combination and now she is terrified. I read her mind easily. It says, *I didn't know it was like this!*

She thinks I am not human and not like a woman should be, but the truth is, we're more dangerous than men. We're better at locating Achilles' heels.

She holds up a glove to stop and I go over to the ropes.

"Angel, she's scared," I say. "I can't hit her."

"So hold back, then, but quit standing up like that. You're all stood up. Keep down. Don't be jumping around every time you throw a jab."

Her trainer is explaining something, both of them looking over here, she is nodding. When we start in again, still round one, I tell her, "It's okay, I won't hit you," thinking she's earned that insult, and I continue not to strike, figuring I'll work on my defense. But this woman is not the middle-aged psychic, she is extremely athletic and strong—which is why they said "Don't hold back" in the first place—and now she has every intention of hitting me, partly out of fear and partly just to get me back. Her attitude is transformed. She's leaping wildly around the ring with saucer eyes, kangaroo punching while I sidestep away and roll around the ropes, la-di-dah. In the breaks, I watch her all serious with her trainer and realize they are hatching strategies. She gets bolder and bolder and I'm wondering whether she notices I'm being the heavybag, not hitting back at all. I guess I'm half asleep when, in the third round, she lands one square on my nose between the eyes, a ramrod solid right that rocks me back and shocks me. It is the hardest punch I've ever taken. I didn't see it coming because, simply, I wasn't looking.

O irony, O ignominy, that it should come like this, my first big hit. All along I've been thinking, Yes, this may be boxing but there is more to come. Louder and louder, the suspicion that I am playing in a toy ring, until this hit, this miserable blow, this changes everything. The punch comes without pain. Instead, apparently random emotions ricochet at warp speed—disbelief, shame, outrage, mirth, irritation, shock, panic, petulance. My strength snaps away from under me like in the tablecloth trick, leaving all these familiar childish feelings scattered, upended on the surface. It takes perhaps half a second, but I am catapulted into a zone of suspended time where I think a lot of things through, debating, for instance, whether I want to do this anymore. This one punch shows how nothing saves you in here. All those pieces of paraphernalia that seemed so cool—mouthguard, headgear, breast-plate, the Vaseline—they're not playthings after all. Now I understand the melodramatic boxing clichés: "Everybody has a plan . . . until they get hit." "This is a hurting game." I am in it for real now. I extrapolate from this strong girl's lucky heavy punch, and there's my nightmare: an opponent doesn't work with you, hold off for a second if you're winded, trade nicely in technique. An opponent will nail you, stalk you around the small enclosure, take advantage of every weakness; no compassion. There are no more gender privileges. No tomboy's schoolyard whining, playing the trump card, *But I'm a girl*. If I hit like a guy, I will be hit like a guy.

The sparring continues another round and nobody, least of all Angel or the girl, knows how that punch got to me. (I have an odd feeling, however, that her trainer knows. He looks triumphant.) I have changed inside. I'm angry and hurt. I took it personally. My promise not to hit her was not an invitation to take advantage but a call to lay down arms, so her shot was, metaphorically speaking, below the belt. Yet I deserved it, and, for all her jerky moves and bent-elbow jabs, it means that she is the better boxer. Instead of hitting back harder to prove I am, after all, better, I'm afraid I'm going to cry the humiliated tears of a child who's done wrong and can't admit it. Pride goes before a fall, my mother always said, but that very arrogance is the most necessary of all tools in the ring. I'm not here to be a good child. I'm supposed to hit out as madly and wildly as I wanted to at age six, albeit with the control I'm learning in the gym. The ring is the one and only place where you're allowed—no, encouraged—to toss out all your sophisticated rules of moral and social behavior, but I can't. I don't approve of that. It quarrels with my nice view of myself as a reasonable and compassionate person. "I spar how you spar" is the prophylactic against every practice fight becoming an all-out brawl, limiting each boxer's attempts to exert their dominion, but this beginner girl seems never to have heard of that. She went on hitting and I felt violated. I had the word "no" screaming in my head.

Occasionally, I'll go without sparring on sparsely populated days, when Angel vetoes the only possible guy there. "I don't want you in with him," he says. "He'll just fight." "But that's okay," I say. "No, he don't know how to hold back. He'll try and hurt you," he says. I see how that might be now. The beginner girl had been like one of those no-holding-back guys, but without their power. Her assault was fueled by fear. Fear made her good. It isn't fear of the opponent, but the Ur-fear that assails us all. Those guys—the ones Angel won't let me near—are called "punchers." My new pal, Peter Kahn, a big kidder who says he's the world's only Jewish boxing trainer and does a mountain of thinking about everything pugilistic, explains how trainers weep with joy when they find a puncher. He's training one now, he says, and mentions a kid with the nicest manners and sweetest smile in the gym. "No!" I say. "Tommy's a brute like that?" "Oh yeah. You see him out here and butter wouldn't melt, but, man, I have to scrape him off guys in the ring." Peter says a pure puncher is pretty rare. Most are boxer-punchers, fighters who temper the pure aggression with strategy. I wonder whether Christy Martin is a puncher and how it would have been with her, whether I would have felt more the warrior, vindicated in retaliating against her polished skills instead of digging in my heels out of some private code of honor? The more this girl hit me, the more I refused to hit back. It seemed at the time that her fear itself was my opponent. It seemed at the time that to hit would have been to capitulate to fear, and that this could lead nowhere good. I believe in fighting fear. I want to become more loving. So why am I boxing?

Answers are not readily available to the things that perplex me. No scientific study on gender roles satisfies. They are all generalized, and everyone I know is odd. It has always seemed that men are sometimes coy and may withhold sex and act scared of me, like women are supposed to do. Men tend to like me, but I can't find one I like back, unless I'm a couple of thousand miles away, or he is just passing through town. I have changed from being the one who never calls to being a complete sap. I am susceptible to imprinting on the least suitable of suitors after just a kiss, which is why I can now have only long-distance affairs. I used to scoff at girls like me. Where's your pride? Your *cojones?* Now my heart hurts with the desire to join the world of couples I've despised. But it's complicated. I'm still a tomboy, I still act tough. I wonder if I'm gay. I'm not. Femininity is ganging up on me. I am out of step. I am white, middle-class, bookish, and the gym, which ought to be an alien environment, is my most comfortable place. There are others like me here—Katya, Jill, Lisa, Dee, Sky, the girl who punched me, the psychic. Veronica and Bridgette, too, but they, being black, may think we don't have much in common; I don't fully comprehend the extent of the racial divide in New York because I'm not American. Sometimes I imagine Veronica seething at me and my ilk and I wouldn't fancy sparring with her in case she does have an axe to grind. Though if she did, I sure couldn't blame her.

Since all boxers come from peoples who have not, historically speaking, held the reins, whether racial or ethnic minorities or female, women don't disturb the Gleason's ecology, not even Yale grads Katya and Dee. The male boxers come in fewer varieties than the female: all black, Latino, Irish, working-class, low-income. Some guys can't read. On the other hand, there is Stephan Johnson, who writes short stories about this world of boxing. And Francisco Mariscal, known behind his back as "the human punching bag" for his daily habit of sparring twelve or fourteen rounds (very poorly), is a poet. Mexico, or "Mehico," is the name he answers to. He usually stands next to me while I jump rope, and sometimes recites something he wrote, but mostly I am his barometer.

"I like a animal," says Mexico. "Sunday, I run five hours. I not stop for five hours. I crazy. You think I crazy?"

"You just got too much energy," I tell him as I jump. "You're lucky. I wish I had."

"No, no. Is crazy." I keep jumping. He stands there and smiles. Like Domenico, he is usually smiling. Then he says, as if it's just occurred to him, "You think I an ugly man?"

"No, Francisco, you're very good-looking." He is pleased.

"You think I can get girlfriend?"

"I don't know why you don't have one."

"You be my girlfriend?"

"No." I'm laughing. "I told you. It would never work."

"We get married?"

"Yeah, okay. That would work."

I find this very soothing. In some ways I don't believe anyone could ever want me, despite (or because of) the dubious evidence of Sam and Co. In other ways I act imperious, and it has been said of me that I eat men for breakfast. Somewhere in the middle is a sanctuary I can't even imagine. I like it here in the gym because everyone's a bit damaged and is using that in a very concrete and practical way. Of course, most of their damage was itself pretty concrete. To be able to hit without compunction, it helps to have been hit yourself when you were too young to retaliate. Then you have the anger in the right place in your soul, ready to slip out at the first Pavlovian punch. Not every boxer was a beaten child, but it helps to have at least been raised where toughness is more of a virtue than, say, turning the other cheek or humility. Still, so many boxers are religious, asking the Lord for strength, thanking the Lord for victory. Evander Holyfield, for instance, prays fervently before every bout. George Foreman, who preached on street corners in Houston, has a gospel choir sing him into the ring. How they reconcile beating the shit out of someone with their stringent Christian morals is beyond me. If you are the Lord's assistant, fighting the good fight, does that make your opponent the devil? What if God is in *his* corner also? Does the more pious man win?

Angel provides only a muddy window into the boxing world. I can't discuss this kind of thing with him; he'd just laugh. That laugh, so appealing at first, sounds more and more like a wall. When he tells me I'm sparring with the psychic the day after I got hit, I demur. This morning I woke up sad, with a bruise like a smudge of ashes on the bridge of my nose and my left eye slightly blackened, my neck stiff like I slept in a draft on a transatlantic flight, in coach. My body doesn't know I was in cahoots with the damage; it's acting like a victim. But Angel insists. Don't be a baby, he says. Over four rounds several gentle jabs to my poor nose get through, and every one feels like an insult, a nose fatwa. It's weird how the middle of my face suddenly seems to contain my whole self. I feel five years old and permeable. Some tears fall.

"Whassup, Kate. Don't be crying in there," yells Angel.

"I'm not," I lie.

"You're too emotional, Kate," he says, laughing at me. He doesn't understand—I'm not emotional, I'm angry, but at whom? Not at the psychic, who is only doing as she is told and after the "sparring" insists on performing a healing on my nose, holding her palm over it. I'm angry with myself, but I'm giving me a break. This is about learning.

One thing I'm learning is that Angel doesn't take me seriously. For a couple of weeks he calls me Brook, the name of another girl he trains, another brunette, but unfriendly and a crap boxer. I suppose he finds us interchangeable. When I do something wrong, he pantomimes the mistake, mockingly. "Don't *do* that," I say. "You're reinforcing the wrong way. I learn by copying. Show me the *right* way." But he keeps parodying. Someone shows me how to turn my left shoulder in and up to shield from the right, like a bird with its head under its wing. I show Angel. "How about this, can I use this?" "Yeah, sure," he says. "Why didn't you show me that?" I say. He shrugs. "Not your style." But it *is* my style. What about all the other things that could join my repertoire that I don't know to ask about? Far from working with my style, he seems to be countering my natural rhythm.

"Tomorrow I'll get out the ten-ounce gloves and I'll whup you. I'll hit you so hard. Knock some sense into you," he says.

"I wish you would," I say. "I might learn some defense."

It makes me mad that he treats me as if I were being lazy or recalcitrant, when I am actually so eager and trusting that I feel a fool. I have to insult him back, when what I really want and need is someone to confide in. I keep leaving the gym drained instead of energized after another session of going through the motions. When I ask Angel when the Metros start, the New York amateur competition I'm hoping to enter despite turning thirty-five in August, he says, "Oh, August probably. But you won't do it. Something will come up."

Men switch trainers like cars. When they want to move on, they just do it. Being boxers, they have trained their emotions not to intrude on their work even more than other men. Angel isn't the only one in here afraid of emotions. I am afraid. I'm afraid I'm a bad workman blaming his tools. I'm afraid of change, and of upsetting him, and of him not caring whether I stay or go. I'm afraid of my own softness. In here I am no good unless I am hard. But I don't want to lose my softness, my valuable good heart. I want to be hard and soft simultaneously, but for this I need a trainer I can trust. So what if I cry? Crying isn't quitting.

I know there can be more to the trainer-fighter bond than Angel will allow. I have been studying pairs of them and I see it—Bridgette Robinson and Reggie Forde; Jill Matthews and Lennox Blackmore; Judah and his sons (especially Zab, that one's exceptional); Terry Southerland and Victor Valle. I watch Angel with Sechew Powell and I see it there, too, the silent intensity, the pride. He was like that with me at first. When the bond is strong, it is stronger for being unspoken. It reminds me of the parent who cuffs the child playfully or even a parent whose constant criticism conceals overwhelming pride in the child; love—or care anyway—held at one remove. The ministrations the trainer performs for you are, in fact, very parental, but not paternal—maternal. He wipes your face, roots around in your mouth, holds the spittoon, laces your gloves, buckles your headgear, feeds you water, smears you with Vaseline. Angel does these things for me, as Terry used to do them, and it is one of the sweetest things in the gym. This brusque tenderness from a man who is not my lover was startling at first, but easy to get used to since they all have such facility with the mouthguard insertion and the sweat mop, like a professional masseur with the towel. Apart from the athlete's rub-down, the boxing gym is the only place I can think of where macho men touch each other with such easy familiarity, even intimacy, and now, without fanfare or special training, they do the same for us women. There is no sexual content.

Between men, the trainer-fighter bond can be as intense as the mentor-daddy-genius-kid thing that Cus D'Amato had with Mike Tyson. His beloved trainer's death sent that fighter spinning out of control, and it's moot whether he has ever recovered. Or the relation-ship can be completely businesslike. A trainer can make his reputa-tion with a single good fighter, but a rising professional is usually a young, supremely confident, unsophisticated man who can be seduced by big bucks and the title-belt mirage. His arrogance won't save him when bad, greedy management has taken him too far too fast and he's lost his one shot at the big time, because a fight career is more fragile than it seems to the hungry contender, and the trainer-fighter rela-tionship is an open one. The trainer can't prevent "his" fighter straying; if the fighter wants to get into bed with another trainer, he will. He doesn't mind ditching the one who cares in favor of the one who views him as a fighting banknote. Anyhow, in this sport, that jackal might actually do him more good.

With women the bond is so new it has barely been tested. At Gleason's—my split with Terry having been more of a mutual drift-ing apart—only Katya Bankowsky has so far made a clean break with a trainer. It was Angel. She tells me that when she decided not to fight anymore after the Gloves and felt like a change, he shrugged it off as if it were no big deal. But she and I and Bridgette and Veronica in a locker-room conference decide that they do take it more person-ally when a woman leaves, they do get more possessive. Maybe a woman leaving him reminds him of some woman he has loved leaving, or simply of the concept of loving a woman.

I am still agonizing about whether to leave Angel when he puts me in to spar with Sky. Why this hasn't happened before I have no idea—I guess we just haven't coincided at the right time. Now, Sky, though she won the Gloves fair and square, is still no good. She can fight, she can win, but she can't box for toffee, and she is the first to admit it—which is why I am incensed when she, just like the strong-but-useless girl, gets a right hand in. She can't get near me at first; then her trainer starts instructing her exactly what to do. I can hear him—something like "After she double the jab she be open," pointing out some habit of mine that I can't break. It's the same guy who was telling that other girl how to nail me. I walk straight into Sky's right hand and I have no clue why.

"Angel," I ask, "why?"

"Quit standing up like that," he says.

"No, that's not it. She's taking advantage of something I do. What is it?"

"You just jumping around again."

That is the last straw. It boils down to this. I can't imagine going into battle with Angel in my corner. He might not be on my side.

I leave him.

6

I Spar How You Spar

Teeth of glass, tongue ripped. You bit down, the body is coming apart. Serves you right, you hated it you said, that body. Serves you right. That brain. They said if your mouth is loose, your chin will smash, your jaw come undone. Cool, you thought. The bone up through the brain. A flesh flap opens, blood everywhere. They say, you go girl, you the toughest girl in here, they want that. You go. Do her bad. Bad is good. Stay in there, stay in there, suck it up, Kate, suck it up, they say. It's only just begun.

It is fear speaking. You may as well run hard at the dark because it's going to find you where you sit. After a while it is just funny. You see, Kathy Collins is coming to visit. Support your local team. She has been winning, fighting and winning, our pocket Christy. But something in the way she moves . . . She is an interesting fighter. She seems meaner than the creature of the Don King Show, the publicity-seeking coal miner's daughter, more complicated with her notorious hundred-pound weight loss and her attitude. I have never met her, only seen her that once when she seemed to beat

Leslie Howe and her world ended, temporarily, when they called it a draw.

Bruce sought me out one day. Kathy Collins is looking for work, he said. She's got a big bout coming. Do you want to do it? But of course I do. Not. Do. Not. "Yes" isn't so obvious now that I've been penetrated by blows, seen the skin of my own eye gray and violet, felt that sadness the morning after. Yes isn't obvious, but it is inevitable. Politely, I consult with my trainer and of course he is all enthusiasm— I would be upset at anything less—and Kathy Collins is called and we are all set, me and Lisa Long, who has recovered from her lion's-den Gloves trauma and is freshly martial. Both of us are the right size and ready.

My trainer? Naturally, I picked the guy who has been teaching other girls how to hit me. His name is Colin Morgan and he works in tandem with Reggie Forde because they are both from Guyana and knew each other back when. They hold court in their Guyanese corner, a table next to Johnny Rodz's Unpredictable School of Professional Wrestling, where they play the endless game of dominoes— more of a domino war really—cracking tiles on the table, insulting each other, gossiping. In addition to Reggie and Colin, the clique includes Patrick Forde (Reggie's cousin), Andrew Murray (Colin's middleweight, whose WBA ranking wavers between two and eight), and, when he's in town, Charles McGlaughlin, who scouts for promoters, splitting his time between Gleason's and, would you believe it, Isola Akay's Allstars in London.

When I left Angel, I hit on Reggie first, because he's done great things with Bridgette and because I thought he was the boss and Colin his second. Reggie took me seriously, made me work. Immediately he showed me what Angel never could, how it came about that I'd been getting hit by right hands. He'd been watching me.

"You know, I doan' say nottin' bad about nobody in the gym . . ." he said in that sweet singsong accent of the only English-speaking country in South America. The end of the sentence never came, it didn't have to. "You gotta protect yourself," he said, making me hold the left glove way up and in front, bending the body like a reed. "I *do*," I objected. I always argue with the experts before I comply. Most trainers were fighters (my first ones, Juan La Porte, Stephan Johnson, Lonnie Smith, Terry Southerland, still were); they teach you what they did, make you in their image. What they are used to are men who arrive complete with a stance, moves, a set of punches. But women are something quite different: fresh, keen, smart, ignorant. Bruce Silverglade says that women learn better because we don't think we know it all like men do. It's true. I was a deferential postulant, thirsty for knowledge, eager to please. Brand new and absorbent, I learned *this* thing from that one, and *this* thing from that one, and often the things would cancel each other out, namely: Juan La Porte's "Don't get on your toes like that" versus Isola Akay's "Don't be flat-footed, keep on your toes." My patch work induction.

I love how Reggie moves, fluid and insouciant even now, at a dozen pounds over his fighting weight, and many years past his excellent career. One year, he was the only amateur to fight in all the world's games up to and including the Montreal Olympics; as a professional he held light heavyweight titles; but my favorite of his accomplishments is his notice in the *Guinness Book of Records* as the only fighter to win two back-to-back bouts at London's Royal Albert Hall. He's gruff and irritable one day and chummy the next; he doesn't iron his moods. He has the face of a small boy incessantly forced to eat broccoli. Bridgette gets fed up with him. She works ten-hour shifts for Con Ed, fixing icy cables from six A.M. and she's exhausted by the time she gets here, but Reggie cuts her no slack, makes her go round after round on the bag while he plays dominoes. Still, during my problems with Angel she endorsed him strongly. When he's not around, she said, you get Colin: two for the price of one.

After two weeks with Reggie, I believe we've reached a deadlock. (So shoot me.) He will not shift his style an inch, and my questions meet incomprehension. I've got his signature move—drop down, hook to the body, almost simultaneous (that's key) short right to the chin—but now what? He has already lost interest. One day he's gone early, so Colin Morgan offers me padwork.

Only now does it click for me that it was Colin in the other girl's corner both those times, and how he's usually in the little crowd at the ropes watching me spar. He is familiar. He has a remarkably small nose, a mustache, cropped hair, and big, deep, thinking eyes, a face to trust; and apart from the bad knees that stalled his career at 17–1, he's still in fighting shape. We are the same height and age, though he looks about twenty-two.

"I fixed you be comin' to me in you orn time," he says after the padwork. "I don' say a t'ing." He grins, I grin. The padwork was the best ever: feet unglued, arms extended, wrists firmed, stiffness melted. Colin is really there with me. We have instant rapport. We joke that it's because we're both kind of British; we find this hilarious.

Colin's style is the opposite of Angel's. With Angel I boxed bent and still. Colin chases me round the whole ring; his mantra is: "Move!" My back had interpreted Angel's "You're all stood up" as an order to hunch; Colin straightens my back and twists my torso so my left hip bone is still pointing frontways but my upper body is more flat to the opponent instead of shoulder-in. This is counter-intuitive— the first thing I ever learned was how to lead with the shoulder, secreting my surface area behind my left side, keeping it all in a line to make as small a target as possible, the angle of my feet, the bend in my knees correcting the disequilibrium. Colin explains that bringing the body around gives you more speed with the right. Your *legs* move you away, your defense is to *move* more than to block, keeping every-thing in front of you. You can stay low, boxing from a crouch, or stand up. This is the British style, says Colin. You should like that. I don't, really, but I've decided to put myself in his hands. I can get accus-tomed to this, I can relearn.

Kathy Collins's upcoming bout will indeed be a big one. It is going to be the first-ever female professional boxing match at Madison Square Garden, and her opponent is Andrea "Sweet Feet" DeShong, an experienced, thirty-four-year-old brawler from Ohio whose claim to fame is that she is the only woman to have beaten Christy Martin—twice in the late eighties. The main event is Bronx heavyweight Lou Savarese versus Buster Mathis, Jr., with aging Puerto Rican showman Hector "Macho" Camacho and one of Gleason's champions, Junior Jones, on the undercard. Savarese, a very handsome boy who also trains at Gleason's, is slightly notorious for having never been beaten (in his next fight, he would lose a questionable decision to George Foreman) while never having fought anyone ranked in the top ten. Macho Camacho's infrequent outings are by now as serious as WWF spectacles, and this one is no different—he's facing a guy with a pitiful 10-19-1 record. Only Junior Jones (40–2, and currently between belts) is for real, but being a featherweight, and lacking the flash of Prince Naseem Hamed, he's not much of a draw. All in all, the August 20 card, to be televised on USA Network's *Tuesday Night Fights*, is a typically nineties lackluster affair. The women are the best reason to watch—at least for those few boxing fans who have so far acquired the taste—even if there is no female title at stake. The purse for each woman is a miserly $1,200 (Savarese's payday is $20,000).

In mid–1996, women's championship belts barely exist. In Florida, an organization called the Women's International Boxing Federation has been up and running for some time, staging its first six-pack of title fights in April 1995 in Las Vegas, and producing rankings ever since (DeShong is ranked second in the 147–pound class; Christy Martin is number two in the 135–pound class; Collins is nowhere). The WIBF is the brainchild of no less a personage than Battling Barbara Buttrick—"The Mighty Atom," the only female in the Boxing Hall of Fame, now in her fifties with a grown daughter of her own ("She doesn't box," Barbara tells me sadly, as if this were a major character flaw)—and a garrulous Irishman named Jimmy Finn, who might well be the world's chief proponent of women's boxing. Finn and Buttrick are doing the best they can; but the underfunded, overstretched, and unpublicized WIBF is hardly the WBA, or even the disgraceful IBF (International Boxing Federation). The two most powerful promoters, Don King (rumored to be scouting for more women to add to his stable of one) and Bob Arum (also rumored to be female-boxer shopping) do not acknowledge it. But it's all we've got.

Kathy Collins doesn't feature in the rankings because she hasn't been noticed yet. Since the Leslie Howe draw, she has fought two four-rounders, winning both by decision. The Garden bout is her big opportunity, the female-boxing equivalent of a title shot. Had there been a junior welterweight belt, Christy Martin would have been its first guardian and, since she had been beaten by DeShong, the latter is practically a champion. Collins is shooting for the top after three fights, and nobody is giving her a snowflake's chance in hell.

Am I nervous about sparring with Kathy? The day of her big bout, I will turn thirty-five. It is two years, almost to the day, since I arrived at Gleason's and three weeks since I started with Colin Morgan. I'm as comfortable with the new style as a ballerina dancing the dying swan in a wet fur coat. Twenty-four-year-old Kathy Collins does not let "the friendship and sisterhood thing" dilute her aggression. Six days away from her make-or-break bout, she needs to go all-out; maybe she asked for work at a foreign gym so she wouldn't have to batter her own teammates. I am bloody terrified. Also, I can't wait. After the Christy cancellation, I'm dying to acquire, finally, some notion of what stuff I've got.

Colin is patient; Colin is calm. When I hint at my fears, he doesn't laugh at me. He tells me how fear is normal and necessary. My boxing books confirm this, especially my favorite quote from the great light-heavyweight champion, chairman of the New York State Athletic Commission, and friend of Bruce Silverglade, José Torres. In Peter Heller's book *In This Corner*, he talks about what happens inside

the tough guy on the block the night before his first sparring session
at the gym:

> All of a sudden he starts developing diarrhea, he's very nervous,
> butterflies, can't sleep, and he feels that that's completely abnor-
> mal for a tough guy to feel that way. . . . So they don't go to the
> gym, and that's the end of the guy, because they don't under-
> stand that feeling, that having diarrhea, butterflies, and being
> afraid is so normal, it's not even funny. In other words, you go
> to the gym to learn how to control that feeling. . . . Fear is one
> quality that you need if you want to be a good fighter. That's the
> quality that makes you alert and makes you aware.

So instead of fighting fears, I'm *having* fighting fears. I find it paradoxically relaxing to have all my nameless, floating anxieties serried
together in one solid front of realistic dread. If the fear bombards
me too hard, I just remind myself, Hey, it's only sparring. Not that
I know how far this proper sparring will go, but Colin says I'll be fine.
He swears he wouldn't let me do it if he thought I couldn't handle it,
and it's not as if we haven't been sparring every day. I spar with
Domenico, who now hits hard where he used to hold off, with Hollis
Parris, a talented seventeen-year-old, and with Corey Jones, an
eighteen-year-old taciturn wiseass and four-time Junior Olympic
welterweight champ whom a lot of trainers avoid because he insults
their boys. Corey will pop up a string of jabs from waist level, or leap
in suddenly and *bap* the ears with both gloves as if clashing cymbals
with your head in between. "Corey vex me," says Colin. "He should
turn pro. He don' take it serious." I can't touch him until I learn to
capitalize on his scorn for the girls, going hard when he gets lazy—
then I can land some. I spar with Sandy Gutierrez, Colin's "big
daughter" (as opposed to his real daughter, eleven-year-old Cherita),
a super-heavyweight with a half-shaved head and a mallet punch.
Colin sometimes has to call her off me. I spar with Lisa Long, the one
who had such a bad time in the first Gloves. We are perfectly matched,

right down to our mutual reluctance to lay into each other severely. Lisa, in addition to holding a world title in escrima, has trained in kickboxing and tae kwon do, but boxing is "definitely the most gruelling physically and mentally," she tells me. "Boxing takes the most discipline and concentration." I am proud to be on a par with Lisa because she's such a fine athlete, but it's an uncomfortable pride because I think we tread too softly on each other's fears. We discuss the impending Kathy Collins challenge.

"What's the rules here? Are we supposed to go hard?" I wonder.

"I was gonna ask you that. I don't see the point. I mean we're doing her a favor. She's gotta know that."

"I don't want her practicing her death blows on me," I admit. "I'm going to keep it down. If she comes forward, I'm blocking." Lisa nods.

"You just don't know. When we go—me and you—we have a certain respect. It's clean. We can increase the intensity."

Lisa and I do increase the intensity, but only up to a point—a point somewhere below the big pain threshold. Cheating.

"Once I decide to go pro," Lisa told me once, "there's no more being nice. I'm there to make a name for myself. Unfortunately, I've got to be a mean bitch."

We both know that isn't quite true. Jill Matthews is not a mean bitch. And although her sparring sessions with Tyrene Manson are wars, they are now the best of friends. When I picture generic girlfriends, I think of hours on the phone, borrowing clothes, discussing boyfriends. I despise those clichés even as I take comfort and pleasure in them. We can be twee, a bit too cute. And when I picture generic male bonding (straight guys don't call each other "boyfriend"), the corresponding clichés are back-slapping, competitive bantering, impersonal conversations. Jill and Tyrene's friendship sits on neither pole. It is girl rap lyrics in action, male pattern bonding with a female twist, it is—I don't know what it is, but I like it. It seems new.

Jill says she loathes coffee klatches. She calls girls wimps. "The minute it's normal to box," she says, "I'm outta here." At the moment, she's having trouble getting *into* here, her career having hit a road-block since her debut last June against Anissa Zamarron.

"I got cut in the first ten seconds when I barreled into her head," she says cheerfully. "There I was, in the emergency room, going to David, 'Don't *ever* let me do this again. Don't you *ever* let me back in the ring.' Two days later, I was: 'I've *got* to do it again! When can I do it again?'" Since then, Jill has signed five contracts for her second bout. Every one has fallen through.

"I offered the second girl my purse, eight hundred dollars. She says, 'No, I want twelve hundred.' You know, I like getting the going rate. A hundred bucks per round is fine, but these girls, they say, 'I want more because I have *this*'"—she points at her crotch. "And they wonder why men are reluctant to take us seriously. If I was a guy fighter, *I'd* be pissed." Jill says she's thinking of listing all those five fights as victories.

"I'd be champ by default. But you know what? When you spar in the gym with a girl, that counts. If they're not gonna let us fight, then that's the best experience I can get. I'm looking at every sparring session as a bout." I like that thought. My fightlike nerves seem justi-fied now; or at least not "completely abnormal" as José Torres's hypo-thetical tough guy would think.

Kathy Collins has brought her trainer and a handsome man with slick black hair who, it turns out, owns her gym.

"Hi, I'm Frankie," he says. "This is Kathy." I thought so. I haven't a clue what to say. How was the traffic? That's a nice tracksuit?

"Kate," I say, hand outstretched, smiling on one side of my mouth.

"Hi," says Kathy, shaking with a power grip, friendly enough but not smiling. She is about five-foot-five, stocky, blond, hair braided in cornrows, pretty. She goes to change, the trainers huddle. Lisa and I will box alternate rounds, it's decided, three each, me first.

Eventually, she is ready and I take my corner. The absolute horror of this moment is delicious. I mean, here I am at the point of no return, a minute to go, thirty seconds to go, all my bleating, all my boasting, and now, the test. This is only a test. She feels different from Lisa or Sandy or Sky or any of the boys because she's made a one hundred-percent commitment to box, because I don't know her and she doesn't know me and there will be no consequences for her if she makes a mess of me. I fear she might. Kathy has the moves, she's stretching her neck side to side, shaking out her arms, doing deep knee bends at the ropes. She makes it clear this is her profession. I have decided to respect her. I've told Colin. "Thass cool," he said, "do what you do." The bell.

We are in the middle in no time. We circle, guard up. Damn, am I going to throw the first punch or is she? I seem to have a long time to think about this. Pap! There! I did. I jabbed to her headgear. I meant that. This is only a test. And instantaneously *pchooo!* She counters. Didn't hurt a bit. Didn't feel it. Some more of that, then I try something else, other angles, an uppercut, just to see if I can get in there. She blocks. Circling again, more jabs and so on and finally, bap-boom, a right. *That* I felt. It wasn't so bad. My heart is turning somersaults, I am deliriously happy. I know I'm going to be okay. She has a vocal accompaniment to her punches, like Monica Seles serving, only more sibilant: *pchooo-pchooo!* I think it sounds great and dangerous. I'm tempted to revert to my old hunch because this upright stance feels like a handicap, I feel like a doggie begging with his paws up, but I give it the benefit of the doubt. To tell the truth, I'm hiding behind it. This is yet another first, my first real-real sparring, and I am happy with her contender's status for now. Lisa can be the mean bitch today.

The round goes on and on and on. If ever you feel your life is accelerating too fast, step into the ring. Time shape-shifts in here; it has geophysical topography, does a little city planning, settles into epochs of glaciation, is prone to seismic events. In the ring you need concentration fit for the most convoluted endgame or Fair Isle knitting pattern, yet you must remain nonthinking, or nonverbal anyway. It's like meditation, a relief from my hectoring self-consciousness—or it would be, if I could only shut up, but I'm still issuing instructions to self, going in and out of the animal state. I love it. Every second is different and counts, but I'm suspending the payoff, storing information for later. It's okay for the first round, though. Every punch I throw, I measure the distance between us, and with every punch and block and move the geometry evolves like it does with every pitch in baseball. We are moving close, toe to toe, but we are both economical with the punches. It's what I'd hoped. Too many of the women's Gloves bouts I'd seen—as well as Kathy Collins's own pro debut—were marked by frenetic activity without pause. A phrase needs a caesura to be beautiful. Rhythm. She's probably thinking I'm boringly cautious, but I don't care, I like it like this. At the thirty-second bell, we close up. I am careful because she is dangerous on the inside—I've noted her left uppercut and this roundhouse right to the body that's her favorite shot—but I'm surprised how open I find her midsection. From the corner, Colin's going "Body, body!" and I'm pleased that I was ahead, instinctively knowing what to do in *this* pool of ring time, but reason overrides instinct. I wimp out. Then again, it's the first round. At the end of it, I'm a person who knows she can be good at this, a changed person. Mind you, I haven't had to eat any serious shots yet.

I climb out, Lisa climbs in. I find Kathy's done more work than I noticed; my ribs are sore. Lisa looks mean, verging on cruel. I know she has been agonizing over this day, refining her intentions, and now I can see what she decided. Her holster is loaded. At the bell, both boxers advance and this time there is no pause before the first exchange. Kathy's moved to round-two tactics. Lisa has also. I watch and learn. Lisa is at the top of her form. Where I left spaces, she fills them with combinations, and Kathy is having to work. Lisa isn't respecting her as I did, as I intend to continue doing. She looks for openings and seizes them. Yet as I admire Lisa, I have to resist comparing myself, judging; it's better to watch with curiosity and interest. (Oh boy, how often I have come up against that one?)

When it's my turn again, I remain cautious, but I crowd her more, barely knowing what I'm doing because I can't yet, as they say, "spell-fight." That is, I'm like a child who can read and comprehend but not yet construct a grammatical sentence. I move in on her, forcing the pace, and when that works and she is—oh my—on the ropes, I don't know what to do with her. I pummel her ribs with all the force of a cat pawing at the teat, then step out. It's the corollary to the other times when I thought I was a frightening shark attack and the other girl forgot to notice; this time I know that all the danger I'm embodying is only in my head. This is only a test. What I'm doing is aborting the fight. This is a door I'm not trying, not yet. Maybe next round. Well, Lisa goes in again and does the same again, exerting pressure, trading punches, trying doors. They look evenly matched. I shouldn't like that if I were Kathy. I'm dead proud of my sparring partner. And in the third—my third, Kathy's fifth—I let the brakes off at the thirty-second bell for the first time in my life. A diet of too much polite sparring has conditioned me to aim squarely for the headgear as if I were scoring points, as if I were allowed to fight amateur. Now I cross over onto the professional track and shoot for the nose, the throat, the temple, the jaw. She shoots back. Now she's warmed up and frightful and mighty, and though my defense is better than before, it's not good enough. I eat one huge right hand, but it doesn't stop me. *It doesn't stop me.* Man, I feel superhuman!

In the last, Kathy and Lisa go even harder. I have never seen Lisa look this good, fearless and strong. I can see clearly now that I'm off duty; I see the entire gym lining the ropes, I hear how they love it. (Were they this way for my rounds? Yes, they were.) I'm soaked in sweat, fulfilled and spent; this time I did come. My nose throbs. The crowd crescendos, Colin gets excitable, there is no blood, the bell rings, it is over. Frankie and Kathy thank us profusely, as if we had cooked them a fine dinner, and I realize how we have indeed done her a favor. Men get paid for this. Outside the ropes I'm shy with Kathy, although she is so much younger. She talks too loud, as if she'd been training her voice to fight too, and there is not a chink in her armor of machismo. I find that touching. I can't block this curious feeling of protectiveness toward her that I'm sure would offend her if she knew of it. Thanks to the sparring, I feel a bond that wasn't there before, even if it is only I who feel it. She is my fighter. I am slightly appalled at this sweetie niceness, the default coffee klatchness of me. Jill would throw up.

Now that the work is done we chat. Frankie is equal parts hearty dad, businesslike procurer, and emollient chat-show host. It turns out what he actually is, is Kathy's manager and paramour—they will be engaged within the year—and he has great plans for our sport, schemes that outstrip even Jimmy Finn and Battling Barbara's WIBF. He founded his gym, the Academy of Boxing for Women, in Huntington, Long Island, over four years ago and now is garnering support for his anagrammatical IWBF (International Women's Boxing Federation)—not a rival, he insists. There's room for more than one belt-granting body in women's professional boxing, he says. Never mind that none has so far been recognized, it's crucial to set them up right, with rules for the financial and physical protection of the athletes. The IWBF is not-for-profit; it will operate on a percentage of the fighters' purses, although Collins is the only one from the Academy who has seen a purse.

The next day, Bruce gets a call. Can Lisa spar again tomorrow?

"She wants you," I laugh. "You got the better of her. Now they're out for blood."

"I'll do it," she says. "But they'd better not try anything. I'm not in the market for a nose job."

I don't mind that they don't want me. I have no illusions. I can swallow my pride. I wish I'd fought.

I find Kathy Collins in the locker room in her skivvies, scowling at the scale.

"Man, I got five more pounds. I hate this shit."

"You got four days. You'll be fine."

"Yeah, yeah. I know. Sauna suit. Sweat. Same old."

I would like to ask many things. Does she have any doubts? What does she do with them? How are her nerves? But I chicken out because I'm posing as another blasé boxer, even though this is new to both of us and, though I'm off duty today, in the back of my mind sits the knowledge that we are two of a kind. We are welterweights. If I do compete, if I turn out to be any good, I may fight her.

We are welterweights. Colin, Terry, Oscar De La Hoya, Felix Trinidad, Sugar Ray Leonard, Thomas Hearns are also welterweights, though the last two were much admired for their successful metamorphosis into the heavier weight classes. Boxers are the most weight-obsessed men (apart, perhaps, from college wrestlers) you will ever meet, but it is a practical obsession, different from ours. Women's weight is taboo. Since I am heavy, the subject of weight has always felt heavy. Now that instead of fighting my weight I am fighting *at* my weight, it is delightful and horrible to be perpetually confronted with my number, to be actively checking my weight instead of avoiding the scale. Sometimes that's not easy. Men in the gym ask what I weigh in the tone usually reserved for "How are you?" As if it weren't an impertinent question. They already know what I weigh, anyhow. I can't lie about it. Men in the gym have caliper eyes, accustomed as they are to calculating their own or their charges' readiness for the weigh-in, where a half-pound extra means disqualification. The subject of weight is loaded differently in here. So many men at Gleason's are smaller and slighter than I am; there are many featherweights. How they admire me for my muscles and heft, how those string-beans envy me. I am used to men thinking I'm smaller and lighter than I actually am just because I'm female, but boxing people entertain no such charming delusions. So the insults I receive daily are compliments.

"What're you weighing, Kate? One-sixty?"

"Big LEGS!"

"You gain weight? You got big."

"My, you lookin' diesel."

Men outside the gym—but never women—also invariably ask me my weight. Sometimes I feel like saying, "One-forty-eight. And what's your salary?" but I understand how he's just making conversation and perhaps buying a few seconds while he reshuffles his weltanschauung. A woman boxer in 1996 is not yet a common sight. The other personal question nearly all men—but never women—ask is: "What about your breasts?" I explain how we have chest protectors, just like he wears testicle armor, whereupon he squirms and blanches as if this might lead to a breast shortage some day soon. The breast question usually comes before the weight question (one guy explained how he'd had it drummed into him as a child that if he hit his sister in the breasts, she would die), but both are inevitable.

I'm not always comfortable with being a walking experiment in outing weight, but it's better than dissembling about the number on the scale. There have been too many decades of calculating female body standards in ounces; too much pressure on our proxies in the movies and on TV to be not only gorgeous, but also skeletal (preferably with tits)—and let's not even mention models. It's a truism that womankind is sick of the pressure, and that the pressure makes us literally sick. Boxing is a cure. The "tale of the tape" before a bout is a whole new set of vital statistics—not bust, waist, hips, but height, weight, reach. This is the first locker room I've found where we discuss making weight instead of losing it, and even though that amounts to the same thing, it's a positive act with a practical purpose, not a passive obeisance to the idea that women should take up less space. In here it is understood how body types function and how to work with the material you've got. Fighting weight is your optimal functioning shape, not your hobby, and the weight you fight at is your natural size stripped down to its most refined version—probably about five pounds less than your "walking around weight." The categories, for both men and women, are:

Strawweight	105 lbs. and under
Junior Flyweight	to 108 lbs.
Flyweight	to 112 lbs.
Junior Bantamweight	to 115 lbs.
Bantamweight	to 118 lbs.
Junior Featherweight	to 122 lbs.
Featherweight	to 126 lbs.
Junior Lightweight	to 130 lbs.
Lightweight	to 135 lbs.
Junior Welterweight	to 140 lbs.
Welterweight	to 147 lbs.
Junior Middleweight	to 154 lbs.
Middleweight	to 160 lbs.
Super Middleweight	to 168 lbs.
Light Heavyweight	to 175 lbs.
Cruiserweight	to 190 lbs.
Heavyweight	unlimited

Men often go up one or more weight classes during their careers—like Hearns and Sugar Ray—but what women will do with our limited capacity for building muscle mass is not clear yet. So far, we are dropping down to lighter categories, as Veronica Simmons just did in her first Gloves, starving herself into the middleweight class, where she could find an opponent. When I got to Gleason's I didn't know what my natural weight was, so long had I been consciously manipulating it, ignoring it, lying about it, hating it. But after two years here my body was settling down and the impossible thin me in the back of my mind was finally dying. Yoga gurus say it takes seven years for every single cell in your body to be renewed, so that it takes seven years of daily yoga practice to reform your body completely. Well, three years of daily boxing and I'd metamorphosed into a pleasing version of me. Boxing is not an upper-body workout, it is a whole-body workout; it compacts the frame and chisels at you. Arms and the internal and external rotators of the shoulders are conduits for the body weight that you bring up through the legs, hips, and torso, so boxing is like doing multiple repetitions with light freeweights. Your abdominals must be hard enough to withstand blows. I was getting cut. My body fat was down to around 12 percent. Muscle is three times heavier than fat, so I looked leaner and weighed more. I enjoyed eavesdropping on the men talking about their weight problems; it was like a satire on my teenage years. In tiny towels, they hop on and off the scale by Bruce's office scowling and tutting. They yell in the showers, clearly audible on the women's side, "Oh, man. I got eight more pounds! I was down to sixty-five, I dunno wha' 'appen...." They do not cry about it. From them I was learning to transfer weight from body to fist, and also from problem to tool.

So bless Kathy for berating the scale instead of herself. They would have let her fight anyway, I bet—there aren't enough women in the pool to provide a last-minute substitute—but worrying about making weight must be light relief from grosser worries. Out there, Lisa awaits. Her attitude is different today, more resigned, I fear. We all know her role in this visit is as meat, so any amount of apprehension is justified, yet when they begin round one, Lisa looks quite as effective as the other day. In fact, the session is unfurling like an action replay, until suddenly Lisa reels back, blood streaming from her nose, and Colin jumps in the ring and everyone fusses around. I didn't see the punch because there hadn't been one. Kathy had straightened up abruptly and banged her head up into Lisa's nose: accidental head butt. Shall they stop? Frankie asks. No, Lisa's game to continue, but only if they keep off her face. She thinks her nose may be broken. (She knows the symptoms, because she's broken it four times before.)

Sure, they say, they'll keep off her face. But they don't. Kathy comes on as if nothing had happened, just like in a real fight, where three more rounds after a head butt is nothing unusual. Afterwards, they thank Lisa again and she goes "Sure" and we wait till they're gone to assess the damage. Lisa is not happy.

"I've never once got in the ring when they said they'd go light and they did," she complains. "I'm not doing that again."

"Why didn't you stop after the *incident*?" I ask.

"I dunno. Idiot. I thought they meant it about keeping off my face. You head butt someone helping you out, you give them some respect."

"Was it deliberate?"

"You don' know," says Colin. "You jus' don' know."

Four nights later, despite the fact that Buster Mathis, Jr., has been replaced at the eleventh hour with the underwhelming Tim "The Hebrew Hammer" Puller (13-4)—whom Lou Savarese will devastate, felling him in the second round—the Garden contains about 2,500 people, and thousands more tune into USA for the *Tuesday Night Fights*, an institution for as long as there's been cable, and on which Collins versus DeShong is the first female bout ever. Kathy's lack of remorse for what she did at Gleason's may have been egregious, but it's a good sign for her tonight. She must have zero doubts, since everything rides on this result. If she loses, she all but loses her chosen career. If she wins, she's on the map. Me, I'm the opposite of fighting tonight: champagne in hand, I'm watching with my twelve birthday dinner guests, wearing the black eye Kathy gave me the other day, a convergence of life with boxing life. Friends are bemused.

Well, Kathy wins. Not just barely, but by dominating every one of the six rounds, though DeShong is no slouch. It's an exciting fight, endorsed the next day by *The New York Times* in the headline: BRIGHTEST STARS AT GARDEN ARE THE WOMEN. Collins, writes the reporter, "energized an evening of very average theater." The piece goes on to relay her musings during the bout: "How nicely, she thought, Andrea DeShong's pink boxing gloves went with her red welts."

"She was real cocky the whole time," Kathy is quoted as saying, "sneering at me and saying, 'Hmm, that's good,' after I hit her. I'm thinking, 'Don't you know you're losing the fight?' I think I surprised her. I know I surprised myself."

Evidently, she also surprised the viewers at home. In a telephone poll, 51,000 of USA Network's *Tuesday Night Fights* viewers responded to the question "Do you want to see more women's boxing?" Eighty-one percent voted yes. Yet boxing at this moment was having one of its hours of disgrace: a bloodbath broke out ringside after the recent Riddick Bowe-Andrew Golota July 11 Madison Square Garden bout, sending half the audience home with worse bruises than the boxers. This was the first card at the Garden since then. The sport needed some good PR; maybe the women's bout did the trick. It looks like Collins's victory is a victory all round.

Six weeks later, USA gives the people what they want and carries another women's bout: a lightweight I'd never heard of named Kathleen Ridell versus the powerful Tracy Byrd. Tracy's brother, the respected heavyweight Chris Byrd, is the main event. Dad, her cutman, works her corner. So does God. Byrd, one of those Christian soldiers, has Romans 8:28 embroidered on her trunks: *And we know that all things work together for good to them that love God, to them who are called according to His purpose.* So much for my worries about this violence being a bad thing. God comes through for Tracy as she dispatches the ridiculously overmatched Ridell. It is so boring that even I, female boxing advocate number one, am beginning to doubt that our sport has legs. The talent pool must deepen, and fast. Promoters have to take the chick fight more seriously. Frankie G.'s got to get his WIBF in order. There are several great women in the ranks— flyweights Yvonne Trevino, Bridgette "Baby Doll" Riley, and Jolene Blackshear; featherweights Bonnie Canino and Nora Daigle; junior lightweights Laura Serrano and Fredia "The Cheetah" Gibbs; lightweights Daniella Somers and the twins Dora and Cora Webber; welterweights Mary Ann Almagar, Gina Guidi, the Frenchwoman Sandra Geiger, and the Brit Jane Couch—but there aren't enough in any one weight class to sustain the momentum, and currently there's nobody notable above welterweight. Jill Matthews is still begging for an opponent. I wish there were more fighters out there. I wish we had a star.

I am about to get my wish.

7

I Am a Contender

"Boxing is about love," says Colin, massaging my knotty shoulders with his green embrocation. I squint at him.

"Did you say boxing is about love?"

"I'm not being funny," he says.

"No, I know. But that's what I've been thinking lately."

"Not *love* love."

"I know."

"Not like that girl t'ink." Colin was accused of harassment a few months ago, such an absurdity. It hurt him. It pains me, too. Colin is my dream of dependability, the trainer I was hoping for. He feels like kin, which is odd seeing as we're from opposite worlds. He understands people without judging them; and his silly, eye-rolling sense of humor counteracts the melodrama of boxing. He checks up on me, like a teenager. "What you bin doin' last night? Let me see . . ." He searches my eyes theatrically for signs of substance abuse. "O-o-o-keeey, this time." He is known by some as the Professor for his Solomonic mien.

Boxing is about love. I am believing with Catholic passion in this

Pollyanna vision, all the more fervently since I have just signed a contract to fight. It is January 1997. I have taken one of Bruce's fights, and Bruce, let's not forget, books the opponents. Boxing, it seems from this corner, the opponent's corner, might just as easily be the opposite of love. The encouraging noises men make, the jolly gym camaraderie, the bonds between trainer and boxer, all this might be a disguise for a mean-spirited enterprise. It might be that each of us here tries to profit from the other, that everyone is out for himself, that everybody wants to do harm—after all, what are we doing here but learning to inflict and withstand harm? It is self-evident that the sport itself is founded on a corrupt power structure, in which boxers are good citizens toiling diligently, some rising to power through righteous bravery, but many more by selling their conscience for position. Around now, an FBI investigation into the IBF (no relation) is beginning. Two years hence it will disclose how a rise up the IBF rankings is guaranteed not by talent but by cash bribes. Prior to the actual indictments, one lunatic "decision" after another (e.g., Boxer A lands 40 percent more punches than Boxer B; Boxer B wins) will be derided in the press—yet remain inscribed in the record books. Boxing will be the laughingstock of the sports press.

Women's boxing, however, is another kind of laughingstock. *Women's* boxing, in early 1997, is roundly and routinely derided in the *boxing* press, if it's mentioned at all. The odd item in the newspapers, like that one in *The New York Times* about Kathy Collins's recent victory, is marked by a breathless, politically correct tone quite distinct from the normal sports-page item.

"Women need to stick together," Kathy Collins told me recently, rotating her attitude a few degrees after her epic bout. She is as much a contender as any of the girls, but just try getting paid like one.

"There has to be camaraderie," she says. "It's never gonna get done by one. The people who have a problem seeing it as a serious sport are the people in the sport. Don King uses it as a puppet show. Christy's bout didn't get the credibility it deserved."

Since women don't light the dollar signs in Don King's eyes, there is no buzzards-on-carrion reaction to a skilled girl boxer in the gym. If it is indeed true that everyone is out for profit, women may be safe from nefarious exploitation for now. This doesn't help me with my personal demons, the ones that have always been on my back, whispering, "Don't go thinking you're any good," or, succinctly, "You look a fool," and that work in many areas—my writing, career, figure, attractiveness, and, of course, athletic status. That is why I like Colin so much. He is my anchor in this place where I barely belong. Our symbiosis confirms I'm not here because I'm mentally ill. Colin has been in boxing since he was a teenager, and if he thinks boxing is about love, then I am not crazy to hope it's true. The evidence of my senses, our mutual project at the United Nations of Gleason's, makes me think it. Every day I sign in with Calvin—"How *you* doin' today, Miss Kate?"—I'm refreshed. All the boxers are here: Juan La Porte is thinking of making a comeback; Stephan Johnson is hoping for a title shot some day soon; Terry I see mornings. Those three are like beloved high school teachers who brought my favorite subject alive and keep tabs on my progress. Especially Stephan, who taught me my first punch, who is the sweetest heart of the lot—shy, earnest, hardworking. If I'm feeling sorry for myself, thinking nobody's in my corner in life, I come here and bask in the illusion of family for as long as we share the ring. Every boxing gym I've ever visited, except for the short-lived marble midtown palace, Strykers ("You don't *sweat* there," complained the boxers), shares this good spirit of dangerous people sending their power to work for the cause. Everyone here loves boxing.

"Anyone who like to box is great," said the famous trainer Hector Roca the other day as we watched a girl in leotards doing yoga by the heavybags. I was embarrassed by her, pointing her out to throw my own boxliness into relief, but Hector, who usually acts the curmudgeonly misogynist, just shrugged.

"I don't care if they no good. They try. She want to be here, that's great." He was right. I was grateful. Still, I thought of Terry claiming nobody here would talk to me if I were no good; I couldn't help noticing nobody talked to the yoga girl, least of all Hector. I think I'm here under sufferance, and I want to earn my keep. Sooner or later I must fight.

The women are not profitable, but we are beginning to be wanted, as the realization dawns among boxing promoters that we exist. A female fight on the undercard is a good gimmick. Small-time promoters don't care about the quality of this bout, and will get the chicks' fight any way they can as long as it doesn't cost much. If they can't make a match, there exists a—let's call him an impresario—in Ohio who will find an opponent at the eleventh hour. Phone this guy and he hits the streets, canvassing prostitutes, vagrants, crack addicts, junkies, until a girl who weighs about right agrees to an "easy" four hundred bucks. He flies her in, cleans her up, lends her a urine sample, and props her up in the blue corner.

"No—it's *disgusting*. They're showing her how to hold her hands at the weigh-in," says Jill Matthews, who finally fought again in November. Through no fault of her own, her opponent came from Ohio.

"Some of them are so out of it they can't even stand," she goes on. "You just—*poof*—throw a little jab and they're down." Many a female fighter has an early record papered by Ohio girls, but few are big enough to admit it. When I heard about the syndrome, I was quite interested in fighting one myself just to get some ring experience, but that was not the way the wind blew. As it turned out, Jill was the unwitting broker in scoring me my first opportunity.

"Opportunity" is indeed the correct term, but mine was a match made in Bedlam. It came about through a combination of impatience and pigheadedness, and it was Fox Network sports commentator

Tom McDonald's fault. Having noted the female division in the Gloves and at Gleason's, Tom decreed that the time was ripe for an amusing women's boxing report and brought the cameras down to Gleason's one morning. Jill was the only bona fide professional in the house. Then there was me. Would I, asked Tom, "move around a little in the ring" with Jill? No, that's absurd, I said, Jill being forty pounds lighter than me. You don't have to fight, he said, just move around a little. Katya Bankowsky had won a gratuitous cracked nose from a pre-Gloves photo opportunity just like this, yet I agreed.

As Colin laced on my sparring gloves, Jill's manager, Kip Elbaum, glared.

"What size are those gloves?" he asked.

"Twelve-ounce, but don't worry, we're not hitting her."

"Good," said Kip, "because we've got the fight next week, then we're on the Comacho undercard at the Garden on March fifth . . ."

"I won't hit her," I repeated.

"You'd better not," he warned.

"I won't."

"Well, don't."

"Okay, okay . . . I don't *want* to. She's my friend."

I didn't *want* to do it at all. Especially not when I thought of the ten extra TV pounds on top of my ten extra post-holiday pounds. Vanity is such a vampire.

Ah, well, the cameras set up, we climbed in, they started to roll, and the bell rang. It was so strange to be facing Jill, she felt so tiny, eight inches down. My shark illusion was back so I didn't even land on her headgear but stopped most of my punches short. Yet despite the mismatch, it was fun to move with her, my friend the Roadrunner, fastest boxer in the gym. It was fun until the pace rose and rose and, before I knew it, there was Jill in my face, laying into me full force. She was not hard to fend off and her defense was, as the gym critics liked to point out, nowhere. Still I felt the shots, and I couldn't help admiring.

But it did seem unfair. How come she got to hit me after I had promised not to hit her? I had been here before. From the ropes, Colin broke silence.

"Hit her harder!" he screamed. "Right uppercut, left hook! Hit her!"

I threw my voice over my shoulder. "No!"

I am nothing if not a woman of my word.

The round ended.

"Okay, I'm coming out, Colin," I said in the corner. "She's not remotely holding back. This is shit, I'm coming out."

"No, don't quit," he said, to my surprise. I thought he'd understand. "Don't quit now with the cameras and everything. Hit her, you've got to hit her. *They're* not holding back."

"No," I said. "I won't. What'm I going to do? She's forty pounds lighter. I can't."

"Yes you can," he said, urgently. *"Yes you can."* Then the bell went and again Jill was the bundle of fury and I was sticking to my guns, thinking over and over, *No, I will not hit her!* But now I was riled, my compassion at war with my irritation, and so it went till the bell, and again Colin hectored me, pointing out how bad I was looking, the big girl getting beat up by the little girl.

"I don't care," I said. And the third round was the same, and I felt I was very hard done by and probably a fool, but I would not hit her, I would not capitulate. The opposite of boxing. Then I remembered who it was in here with me.

"Hey, Jill," I lisped through the mouthguard. "I thought we were going light!"

"Yeah, me too," she said, hitting me.

"Back down," I hissed.

"Yeah," she said, stepping away. . . . "Hey! We're doing better now," said Jill, and we moved and feinted and I felt the air go out of the little crowd. They were enjoying that, the creeps. Well, they got more. Very soon I found Jill's glove in my ribs again and as I folded down to protect, I let in a gorgeous ferocious hook to my jaw.

Perfection. But she had gone too far. Now I wanted to hit her back, I really wanted to hit her, yet—and this scared the hell out of me—I couldn't. I was frozen. Even though she was ring-Jill, she was still Jill. Even though she'd whapped me with her best shot, my hands were tied. Maybe I can't do this, I was thinking. No killer instinct. Maybe I just don't have heart, which is ironic, seeing as it was precisely my heart that was stopping my glove.

When the bell rang, I left the ring, ignored Colin's raised eyebrow, and paced, fuming. I should have hit her, I should have. I did it again, I held back. Even when I got permission—no, *orders*—I didn't hit the girl. People came up to me to say I did good. I took it as insults. Tom McDonald collared me.

"That was great!" He couldn't help laughing. "Guess the little girl won. How's your jaw? She got quite a shot in there, didn't she? You'll be eating soup through a straw tonight!"

"Yeah, well, what am I gonna do, hit her? I'd flatten her. And now she gets to look good and I look stupid and . . ." I sputtered out, the butt of the joke. It was at this moment that my moral code crossed the road. Come what may, I would never not hit again.

By the time we got to the locker room, I was mad at Jill.

"So, what happened?" I snapped. "Your manager begged so hard, I couldn't do it."

"I think you just don't know your own strength," said Jill, "because you hit me *real* hard . . ."

"What, that jab? In the first?" I remembered thinking "Oops" when that slipped out and resolving to be more careful.

"Yeah. It was *real* hard. And then they were screaming at me— you know, Kip was going: 'You gonna stand there and get beaten up? Hit her! Go for it! You gonna get beaten up?' So I hit you."

That was the clearest information I'd ever got about the other end of my punches. No matter how much Colin told me I hit really hard, I didn't believe him, in case it was soft soap. But I remembered that jab and exactly how much it was pulled and how much power I had in reserve, so I took comfort in this backhanded compliment.

"It was good to hear that," I wrote in my journal later. "I felt better for that, though I went through the entire collection of negative emotions so far engendered by my boxing career. Sometimes I do wonder—why boxing?"

And I proceed to answer myself in histrionic prose:

Because it's crazy and unpredictable. Because the rules are only there precariously on trust. Because polite, corrupt, hypocritical society puts a veneer on the strangeness just below whereas in the world of boxing, what's below is tangible, and emotions are raw, because everyone here is in combat for no reason except choice. Because in here the whole equation is upside down. Because everyone in boxing is facing fears that most people don't even see coming. . . .

The consequence of the Jill episode was that Kip told the promoter about the big girl who was hit by the little girl and the promoter calls Bruce and Bruce comes up to me two days later.

"I've got a fight for you," he says. The phrase is familiar, but this time it sounds different.

"When?"

"Two weeks."

"Who?"

"Oh, it's some model. You'll beat her easy."

"What's her record?"

"She's had a few bouts. I know two of them were against the same girl. I'll find out more for you."

"Is she black?" (My spurious gym hierarchy—it still lives!)

"No, she's a white girl."

"What's her weight?"

"She's a bit heavier. I believe she's around one-sixty, but I'll have to check."

"She's really a model?"

"Well, the picture I saw of her looks like it. She's very pretty. Strange thing for a model to do, boxing. But, hey, it takes all sorts."

"I think I'm finally saying yes. I'm going to ask Colin."

The outline of the model gets colored in. Her name is Jen "Raging Belle" Childers. She is six-foot-three, 168 pounds, a righty, twenty-two years old; she won the Indiana Golden Gloves and her professional record is 6-0, three by way of knockout. Her contract allows her to fight in headgear. Bruce shows me her photo. She is putting up her dukes in a black jacket with the sleeves rolled up, dark lip pencil, heavy eyeliner, and mascara. She looks very eighties, like Duran Duran in drag—and I don't mean Roberto. I hate her. Well, at least, I scorn her. Soon I'll regret that, fearing the old hubristic set-up for the fall, but now I'm on the defensive and I think it's correct. Just before the Jill sparring, I'd been out of the gym for a month, I am thirteen years older than her, weigh twenty pounds less, and have no experience, but I'm a tough old bird.

Colin says I'm ready, but there's a caveat.

"You know Bruce's fights, Kadie. Happen the girl's a killer."

"Yeah, well, how tough can she be? She's a model."

It is true that Lisa Long nearly took a Bruce bout last month that looked fine on paper (since it would also be the other girl's pro debut). But rumors of this girl had preceded the offer (I guess someone saw her training) and I was among the contingent that advised Lisa, who was wavering anyhow, not to take this one, just in case. How right she was to turn it down. That girl knocked out one Melinda Robinson in the first minute of the first round. Then, in December, she scored a TKO over Kelly Jacobs, again in the first, followed eleven days later by another first-round TKO. Her name is Lucia Rijker, a Dutchwoman living in L.A., and she was the world kickboxing champion before she turned to boxing. Converted kickboxers and karate fighters comprise a sizable part of the female boxer population, and, being inured to combat and heavy training, they have a head start, but the buzz about Rijker far outstrips the buzz about any previous fighter. You should see this girl, they're saying. She's unbeatable. She makes Christy Martin look like Raggedy Ann. She's the real thing.

I put my money on Jen Childers not being the real thing, then I put my mouth where my money is and on the last day of January meet the promoter in Bruce's office to sign the contract. I'm not surprised to find Kip Elbaum there, all pally with the promoter, since it was he who scouted me—or reverse-scouted me—but I am a bit thrown to discover that he is the promoter's son. Kip has a regular-guy appearance, rather like a blue-eyed Paul Simon, but his dad, Don Elbaum, is straight out of central casting. He comes up to my eyebrows, has the bulbous, florid nose of a bruiser and brilliantined hair, and is dressed in a double-breasted black zoot suit, a black turtleneck, and pointy-toed shiny-black chelsea boots. He looks like a miniature Harvey Keitel—in *Bad Lieutenant*, not *The Piano*.

"That's a great outfit," he gushes. I'm wearing baggy black shorts, an old tank taped up in back, and wrecked boxing boots.

"Really," I say.

"I hear you're a famous journalist," continues Elbaum Sr.

"No," I say. "I write for magazines."

"This is gonna be great. We'll get them all down to the press conference. You can make it next Monday, right? We're gonna get terrific PR on this."

"I don't know about that. I'm kind of crazy with deadlines right now." This is no lie. I am beginning to doubt my sanity. "Anyway, where's the contract?" Elbaum hands me a pen.

"Hold on. I want to just make sure of a couple of things."

"Oh, right, yeah, you take your time."

"I see here the weight is listed at a hundred and sixty-five pounds. You know I'm fighting way under that, don't you?"

"Oh, yes, we are aware of that."

"Can she come down at all?"

Elbaum Sr. and Elbaum Jr. exchange glances.

"You know, I'll be perfectly honest with you. I doubt it. She already lost a lotta weight, it's quite a story. Came down from two hundred and twenty pounds. She's so tall, people made fun of her, but you should see her now—she's a knockout, really a knockout."

Resisting the obvious pun, I pretend I didn't hear the disturbing news that the model had a weight problem. It ruins my game plan of avenging crimes committed against average-looking women.

"Well, you should at least pay me a weight-handicap premium," I joke.

"We can do that. How 'bout six hundred? That's two hundred more than any of the guys on the undercard."

"Whoopee."

I am thoroughly enjoying this. It is very cinematic. I feel I should sign in blood, but I use the ballpoint, doing a double take at that phrase about understanding the risk of permanent injury or death. Kip pipes up from the corner.

"You know she wears headgear."

"Yes, I heard that. I hate headgear."

"You don't have to wear it. It's up to you," says Elbaum Sr. "Don't want to risk that pretty face," he adds to Kip, chortling, meaning her.

"If she hits her too hard," replies Kip, meaning me, "we take her out," meaning her. "First sign of blood." He makes the throat-cutting sign. Both Elbaums do a shifty laugh, the family resemblance is suddenly evident. Only now does it dawn on me that the girl is on Don Elbaum's payroll, that she is his fighter, and that this loads the dice in her favor to a most absurd degree. Well, it's too late now. I have signed.

"You write about restaurants, right?" says Elbaum Sr. when the business is done. "I know this great Italian in TriBeCa. Would you care to accompany me?"

"I have to train," I explain. Is he asking for a date? Or does the opponent always dine with the promoter after the contract signing? This protocol sure is peculiar.

———————————

As I box, I am aware of two pairs of Elbaum eyes watching critically. It is very off-putting, being scrutinized for mistakes, but it doesn't matter because I am doomed anyway to one of my hopelessly miserable gym days. I suck. I am depressed. This now poses as the absolute only state I am ever in, but at least I can unload it onto Colin: Are you sure I'm ready? Are you sure I can box? What are they thinking? What if they tell her I'm crap? What if they tell her I'm good?

"You look fine, Kadie. You be beating yourself up again," he soothes. "Don't pay them no mind. Let them t'ink what they t'ink."

It is torture, this self-judgment. Canvassing Colin and other boxers, I have concluded that everyone gets bad days in the gym ("Man, there's times I git tired after one round . . . "), but that the best boxers resist drawing conclusions from them. Katya and Jill, Veronica and Bridgette all admit to the same tendency of thinking they look bad, and it is heartening to reflect that those four never look bad to me. My very worst workouts sometimes elicit extravagant praise, like the other day, as I hit the heavybag and my inner soundtrack whined— *You're all stiff* (whap-whap-whap). *No power, Kate. When are you going to learn?* A Metro's champ I'd never met was watching me. "Hey," he piped up, "I wouldn't want to meet *you* in a dark alley. You got skills!" I wonder if my feminine propensity to fret about my physical appearance has infected me so that I care too much about how my performance *appears* instead of just accepting my limitations and working to overcome them. Colin says women are always worrying whether we're doing it right, whereas men just work. Men don't seem to take a bad sparring session so seriously. I want to learn from that. It's the same thing I glean from my basic but continuing yoga practice: "The mind makes a lousy master but an excellent servant." So teaches the Bhagavad Gita. The key to athletic prowess is to ignore the fickle bully of the mind altogether. The mind is not a good judge of reality.

On this note, the fact that Lucia Rijker is a practicing Buddhist astonishes me. Over the next two weeks, as I prepare for battle, this becomes more and more bothersome. How can she square the pacific live-and-let-live tenets of Buddhism with the efficient beatings she deals out? If it is true that she is so phenomenal, then her beliefs must be assisting her. How is this possible? Since Katya has entered nego- tiations with Rijker to film her fights and make hers the central story in *Shadow Boxers*, I hope to be able to find out from the horse's mouth sometime soon.

But that counseling is not available now when I need it. The pressure, the pressure is mounting so fast. Giant roller coasters and hurricane fronts of nerves take up residence, my thoughts boil, my heart plays bongos, it comes in waves. I am afraid of everything, of being wrong to fight at all because I am nice, of running out of breath mid-round, of losing, of brain damage. Colin gets me working extra hard on defense. "It take one punch," he keeps saying, an unhelpful phrase. A woman featured on one of the recent rash of TV specials about women's boxing—on ABC or *20-20* or *Sixty Minutes*—was the victim of that one punch. A bad trainer sent her into the ring prema- turely on one of those gratuitous undercard chick fights. She landed in a coma and now she will function at half-speed forever.

It's reassuring that at least half the crowd at Gleason's routinely sur- vives far bigger bouts than mine. They've all had a pro debut. Then again, their first fight came after they'd been training since boyhood, their first pro fight after many, many amateur bouts. I wish, oh how I wish, that the age restrictions could be relaxed and I could fight amateur, where the referees are still cautious with women, likely to stop the fight when somebody bleeds. My fight will not be stopped, not for *my* blood at least; especially not at the Blue Horizon, where blood is the Philly fans' favorite treat.

"Ooooeee!" whistles John Toliaferro delightedly, when I tell him my bout is at the Blue. "Git outta here! That place! I was there one time and this guy was takin' a *beatin'*, I mean he was out on his *feet*, and the ref don't stop the fight so his trainer, he throws in the towel, and the ref ignored it. He just ignored it."

"Gee thanks, John."

"Oh no, I don't mean—it ain't always so bad."

Word spreads fast. Whenever Colin steps away, I am showered with free advice.

"Ever fight a tall person? Oh boy. Gotta be smart."

"Stay inside."

"Stay low."

"Overhead rights."

"Go to the body . . . "

"Aren't you worried about her record?"

And the most common comment: "Giving away some weight there, aren't you?"

"Ignore them," says Colin. "You'll know what to do."

———————

This issue of weight is funny—funny ha-ha *and* funny peculiar. I have never before been tempted to gain weight deliberately but, boxing being all about transfer of weight, I am considering it now. Just as fractional adjustments in timing and angle allow you to connect with a punch or miss the target altogether, so a few pounds of body weight can make a huge difference in how hard that blow will be. It's physics; it's why Pierce Egan, the early-nineteenth-century chronicler of pugilism, writer, publisher of *Boxiana*, and hero of A. J. Liebling, called the sport "the sweet science of bruising." So I have learned that male secret I yearned to possess since the jazz-club incident.

Now I understand how throwing a punch is a question of converting weight to strength to power—power being the application of maximum force in minimum time—and how the secret that causes the weight to get into the fist is torque, a concert of twists at the hip, the waist, the shoulder, the wrist. There is only so much you can do with the secret, though, when you don't have the weight to back it up. This was illustrated beautifully by Jill, whose technique is sublime but whose hardest punch didn't sway me. Conversely, sparring with Sandy Guttierez, as I have been doing, lets me taste an extra sixty pounds. It hurts a whole lot, like a kick from a horse, and even though I'm in the run-up to the bout and ought to be sparring hard, Colin still calls her off me if I get cornered. Somewhere in between Jill and Sandy lies the model's twenty-pound advantage, which I could theoretically lessen, but I decide to leave it alone. I couldn't gain muscle fast enough; I would gain fat and self-loathing. So . . . yes, I am going to give her the weight.

After a few days' sparring with Sandy and Corey and Darius, a former pro about my height but heavier, Colin apparently decides I need stronger medicine. (Now, the night I signed the contract, my body started to disintegrate. I took this as a good sign. If I can get the rasping throat, blocked sinuses, raw lungs, shredded feet, period cramps, and narcolepsy over with now, I'll be in the pink *just* in time. On day four of this, ten days before the bout, I want to go into hibernation until it's all over, but, realizing that time is emphatically against me, I drag my pallid ass into the gym.)

"You're sparring with Veronica," announces Colin.

"Aw, not today, Colin. I was thinking I'd give sparring a miss, just today. I'm all weak."

"Nah, Veronica be cool. I seen her spar. She don't go hard. You just be moving around a little."

The phrase "moving around a little" is not one to trust, but I cannot beg off sparring simply because I'm feeling a bit poorly. I fit the breastplate, let Colin buckle on the headgear, smear my face with

Vaseline, slot in the mouthpiece, and wait. This year, Veronica isn't starving her way down to the middleweight class so as to meet fresh competition, but has entered the Golden Gloves as a heavy weight, although she weighs some eight pounds less than the 178-pound limit. I have only ever seen her spar with men, which is, of course, not unusual; still, of all the girls at Gleason's, she is the one I have the least desire to meet in the ring. I think she is the best of all of us.

At the bell, I see immediately how wrong Colin was. Veronica is not about to "move around a little," she is looking to fight. I have never felt out of my depth in a ring like I do now, and every weeping pore in my body is rebelling against the unfairness of this challenge. I would like to have had some lead-up; I would like to have known this was going to be war. I would have armed my defenses. There is no camaraderie here. At the bell, Veronica strides toward me, waits for my exploratory, rather reluctant jab and counters instantly. At one jab each I'm soothing myself, removing myself: *Hey, okay, take it easy, no need to go all out*—but when she doubles her next jab, bends and uppercuts, as if to test the fit of her glove in my floating rib, I see I'm not giving myself very good advice. From here on in, any punch of mine lights a fresh stick of dynamite in Veronica, until she seems to be composed of many fuses burning down: some slow, others fast. She's surging forward already, backing me up (hey, I'm the one who does that!) and I'm no good in reverse; I can't hit hard. To buy thinking time, I retract into defensive mode, which signals "let's cool the pace" as clearly as saying it out loud, but she is deaf to this. Her right hand finds a gap in my guard—one of those hammers I've admired from the ropes, wondered whether they're as hard as they look—and it's horrible, like being woken up at dawn by a fire truck. I snap out of my doze and switch on emergency overdrive even though the last thing I want is to fan the fire. I have no choice but to fight. I do not want to fight, not yet, not tonight.

I grapple with my conscience and my common sense, wishing I were lost in the moment but consumed instead by the useless ranting of my mind, the lousy master. The round is a blur. I am out-classed and I am outweighed. I feel overwhelmed. She is utilizing the full armory, up, down, hook, cross. It seems to last forever. I sense by peripheral vision how the whole gym has been drawn around, how the collective breath is being held, how we are furnishing an excellent spectacle. I have no anger. I feel sad that it's come to this. Finally, the bell.

"I thought you said she'd go light," I snap at Colin. "She's going all-out. I'm not into this." He mops me with the towel, squirts the water.

"I know, Kadie, I'm sorry. I t'ought she be cool. You jus' gonna have to fight."

"Okay, but how?"

"Like you do with Darry. Get your foot between her feet, push her back. Use your weight."

"What weight? She's so big, I can't move her."

"Jus' keep up the pressure, Kadie. You be fine."

I should have refused to go back, given my state today and the proximity to the big event, but there is no question that I will answer the bell. And the same thing happens, only more so. Veronica hits me like the apocalypse and all I can do is fend her off as best I can, absorbing blows, giving them back. I try to believe I am hitting hard, but the only sign that Veronica is feeling my punches at all is her relentless and increasing pressure on me. It is this I can't bear, not the pain; there isn't really any pain. I hate the confusion of having her always on top of me like a swarm of giant bees there and there and *there*, like she is pressing herself into my mind. No adrenaline rush is kicking in to help. I am resigned and weary and unhappy. Then, during one of her flurries, a realization hits me. This may feel like a fight, but it is not a fight. What if I quit? Colin would be mad at me, the crowd would be disgusted, Veronica would think I'm not for real, my friend Tom watching over there would see I'm not so good at this, I would probably wish I hadn't, but I could regroup. We could start again tomorrow. I'll be ready tomorrow. It takes one second to decide. I make a turn to my left, beginning to drop my hands and *bam*, Veronica, not knowing my intention—why would she?—takes instant advantage of the opening and slams her thirty-pound weight advantage neatly up my nose.

A flash of something like light in my vision, a river of blood, a great wail from the people, hands pulling me through the ropes, helping me down.

"Sorry, Colin," I say, mortified and cross, as he mops my nose, soaking my towel in red. "I didn't want to do that today. I was trying to leave."

Colin says nothing. There's a kerfuffle, people murmuring, "Hey, she didn't ought to do that." I'm the only one here not furious with Veronica. I am furious with myself. As soon as I can, I slip off to the toilet and shed tears of humiliation and then I feel oddly cleansed. Back out there everyone has a feel of my nose, which is swollen and red and cracked, but not smashed. Tom says he was really impressed by the action, as long as it lasted, which makes me feel better. I'm just glad it's over. And one thing's for sure: Raging Belle ain't going to hit like *that*. I figure I've had one too small and one too big, but third time lucky—she'll be just right.

Chances are, when people see a pair of black eyes on a woman, they're not thinking, "Ah, yes, of course, she's a boxer." No, they're thinking domestic violence. (Or, perhaps, like the salesgirl at the makeup counter at Henri Bendel's, whose gaze lingered on my white leather coat—which looks posh, though it cost me twenty-eight dollars—they think "rich bitch with a nose job.") Normally such evidence of physical trauma is the badge of a victim. Pain that descends unbidden makes a person pitiable, but a person who invites, endures, and gives back pain is thought heroic. Wearing my shiners around the streets of Manhattan, I am conscious that the day has not come where a battle-scarred hero (outside the virtual world of Lara Croft Tomb Raider games or the even less realistic one of Chyna and Lita of the WWF) can be a woman; the fact that my eyes hardly get a second glance tells me that New Yorkers have been inured to bruised women by the domestic-violence helpline ads on the subway trains. I know how I got them, though, and I hold my head high.

Gleason's is another matter. At the gym, my black eyes look stupid. "Thought your fight was *next* week," giggle the boxers. Ricky Frazier (no relation to Joe), a well-known light heavyweight whom I like a lot, collars me.

"Who's your trainer?" he asks. I tell him. "Uh, nothing against anyone, but how d'you get those?" I explain that I was trying to leave the ring, but it's no good. One thing leads to another and he's giving me tips, starting with my stance.

"What?" he exclaims. "Square on? You better be good at ducking and diving. That's why you got those. You'll get gun shy if you don't learn not to get hit." My doubts about Colin's "British" style reinforced, I thank Ricky and wish fleetingly he were my trainer. Angel comes over, which is rare these days, and palpates my nose.

"It's broken, isn't it?" he declares.

"Nah."

"It is. Thass why they're both black. Thass what happens."

"Nah. Look, I can do this!" I knock my nose.

"Well, it's broken. Just hope nobody hits you on the nose. So close to a fight, too. Shame."

I feel such a fool. The day after the "accident," I'd woken up depressed again, feeling beaten up. My nose is my Achilles' heel. Well, I'm just going to pass my nose karma onto her.

Something good is coming out of all this. I have declared war on the whiny voice, the one that goes, *Hey, you're not really an athlete. The guys here, they're from adversity, they have natural skills, they have the hunger. You, you're a nice girl. You're not even fit, you're a fat girl.*

And in the ring with Veronica, there it was: *Give up. You're out-classed, don't even try.* I will not take it anymore. I do not *like* being hit. Nobody goes into spar that heavily a week away from fighting; you do that earlier. (And, Colin, why hadn't I?) The week before, you go in with people who will work you hard, but not beat you up. I have been hard done by, but I have not been erased. My heart is stronger, coming through that fire. All you gym commentators, you trainers who don't get much respect and you never-contenders and you hangers-out who vaguely train—all of you know-it-alls. I don't need your bad advice, your backhanded well-wishing. I am not afraid.

Now Colin's trying to put me in with wimpy girls so I can beat them up. He thinks it'll make me feel better, but the prospect of bashing wimpy girls makes me angry on so many levels. No, I tell him, I will *not* hit Brook. No, I will not box Maria. Put me back in with Veronica.

But Veronica has not been in the gym since that day. Then, just before my fight, she appears. Having felt funny about her, as if she were my mugger, I'm glad for the chance to talk.

"Were you feeling bad about that?" I ask. "Because you didn't do anything wrong."

"Ah, no—I know," she says. "I jus' git so hyped up before sparring. You know."

"Not really. It was supposed to be light sparring."

"I git so nervous before sparring, I gotta do it. I'd been meditating half an hour on everything that gits me mad—you know, if a friend died, if a pet died—whatever gits you mad, and I couldn't go back down. The fear, it sits there in your stomach and the meditatin' pushes it down. Then you don't even feel the punches, you don't feel nothin', and your body just moves for you. The power's there, the moves are there, you're trained, you're strong, you got power. It's all in the mind. You gotta do that, too, Kate."

"I'm there," I say.

"You can't be afraid of being hit," Veronica goes on. "'Cause if you're standing back here afraid of trading punches, you'll be no good."

"I know," I say. "This was good," I point to my nose, "'cause she's not gonna hit as hard as you. No way."

Now, this is what I've got to do. Practice meanness. No apologies. Win.

8

Fight Time

"Who gave you the black eyes? Your boyfriend?"

Don Elbaum greets me at Philadelphia's Thirtieth Street Station for the press conference. It is Monday. On Thursday I'll be taking this train again to Philly for the St. Valentine's Day Massacre.

"Very funny."

"You look terrific," he backpedals. "Love the look." I'm wearing armor: my most posh jacket, black pants, and heels. In the car to the Front Street Gym, where I am to be filmed with the Raging Belle for Channel 6's morning show, I get Elbaum's story, how he had ten fights but was no good, and so turned to managing fighters, then promoting fights. He's a character, said Bruce Silverglade. Did you know he played a big role in getting Don King started? He's a great guy, said Peter Kahn. Peter is going to work my corner—that is, mop my sweat, swab away blood, expand on Colin's instructions. Peter, who has fighters on Elbaum's cards all the time, is one of the best in the business. Well, I refuse to like Elbaum. So defensively sarcastic am I, I've even alienated myself. I am terrified of meeting Jen Childers. I am terrified of liking her.

"You should wear lots of clothes at the weigh-in and she'll wear as little as possible," suggests Elbaum. "That'll bring the weights closer. How do you say your name again? Sea-kyools?"

"No. *Sek*-you-leez. Like Hercules."

"Right."

The neighborhoods of Philadelphia roll by, clapboard and brick rowhouses and boarded-up stores, stunted bare trees and billboards with flapping scraps of last year's movies, very *Rocky*, very East End of London. Not much has changed on these gritty, pretty streets in the twenty-one years since *Rocky* was released. At the Front Street Gym, in Kensington, nothing's changed since it opened, some twenty years before that. We climb a flight of steps and we could be entering Gleason's—the familiar atmosphere, the ammonia-mold-leather smell, one raised ring, a rank of bags on chains, a shuttered snack bar—except here every wall is papered with fight posters; there's even one of Kathy "Cat" Davis. "She was a fine little fighter," says Frank Kubach, the gym owner, a white-haired gent I warm to instantly. "There's a few ladies train here now. We're thinking of closing to men three nights a week." Now, Bruce got over the segregation phase, back when Charlie's Angels were a girl's only role models. This refreshes my plot of pouring scorn on the Raging Belle. I bet she won't have been sparring with Veronicas.

And here she is. My God, she's tall. I have to rock my head back to shake hands.

"Kate, this is Jen Childers. Jen, Kate Sea-kyools," says Elbaum, attempting to wrap an arm round her shoulder.

"*Sek*-you-leez," I say. "Pleased to meet you." Her eyes slide right off mine, so young and nervous is she, practically trembling, though the way she wears her height without stooping, doesn't fiddle with her long blond hair or shift on her feet or smile makes her seem reasonably tough. She is wearing a bright yellow nylon jacket and hoop earrings, and is surrounded by her trainer, Wesley Munzon, and his sidekick, and his sidekick's young son. I assiduously fail to charm them. They stare at my black eyes and fail to comment. I wish Colin were here, but he's back in New York at work.

The cameras set up and Karen, the Channel 6 presenter, starts planning the teasers to go out live before the report.

"How about both of you in the ring sparring?"

"I'm not dressed for it," I point out, relieved. We all know where "moving around a little" leads.

"Well, then, we'll have Jen in the ring shadowboxing, and Kate, you can lean on the ropes checking out the competition."

Fine. She moves better than I expected; nice straight jab, she's clearly athletic (it's not until after the fight that I learn she was a Division A basketball player), but I'm no good at the pantomime glaring. I hate this. Who am I?

"... one is known as the 'cover girl of women's boxing,'" says Karen's voice-over to the breakfast audience. "The other's an internationally known writer. They're going to match up in one of the biggest women's boxing matches ever...."

Garbage, but she has to dramatize. A couple more "teasers"—Jen hitting the speed bag (she's slow, but her form's good), Jen hitting the pads (that jab is really very impressive), me staring—before we get to the interview. By now I'm convinced Karen and everyone here despises me, except maybe Elbaum, who needs me.

"Love the look," he keeps going.

"Okay, you can stop saying that," I snap, getting into my bitch role. Truth is, I'm trying not to cry. Why did I come? I'm the foil to the cover girl, brains versus beauty, the dark opponent, my ridiculous panda eyes. My mean act just isn't me. She is so sweetly, blondly lovable, made for TV.

"So," says Karen, standing between us in the ring, a cute foot shorter than the Sears Tower of women's boxing, four inches down from me, "they don't look like your typical boxers, but these two ladies are preparing to face each other at the Legendary Blue Horizon on Thursday." She turns to Jen.

"The obvious question is ... model? Boxer? What if you get your face hurt?" ("Oh, and you're *going* to," I'm thinking, "you're *going* to." If I can only figure out how to reach it.)

"Well, I've got to face the possibility," she says in her gentle voice. "It's a hurting game. But I'm sure my manager will pay for a nose job." Big smile. ("We're gonna test that theory," I'm thinking.)

When it's my turn, I say it's my first time and I've no idea how it'll be. I hate how I come across, in my monotone, my accent, angling my eyes away from the lens, Mrs. Ugly.

"So," concludes chirpy Karen. "The big question: Who's going to win?" As if in class, with a little moue, Jen raises her hand.

"She raised her hand first," Karen tells me.

"Means nothing," I smirk.

And the show's over.

———————

Now we repair to—I must be tripping—a faux London pub called the Elephant and Castle in the downtown Holiday Inn for the press conference, where a blasé Philly sports press scoffs tuna salad and drools over the cover girl. Nobody talks to me. I spot a guy slumped in a booth, ignored also. He nods.

"She's tall," he says.

"Yeah," I grin, rueful.

"You fight someone like that before?"

"No. This'll be my first fight."

"Overhand rights every time," he says. "And body shots."

"I know. Everyone's saying that."

"Well. You'll be fine. Just do what you have to do."

"Yeah. Good luck to you, too."

He is the only boxer here.

Back home in New York I adopt the fetal position and try to die. I feel nauseous, I have a headache, I have the runs. I'm pinned to the amusement park wall-of-death thing where the floor slides out, and I can't stop, I can't scream, I can't cry. At the gym, I've never been so happy to see Colin.

"She's a giant," I wail. "I can't reach her face. I'm so, I'm so ... I've lost it."

Colin takes my hand and tells me a secret, about how Bridgette was before the Golden Gloves final, how she sat backstage with her head in her hands and refused to go in, how he held her hand, too, how he forced her into the ring.

"Bridgette? *Bridgette* was scared?"

"She was chickenshit. But Bridgette win." I want you hyped up, he says. You'll know what to do, he says. Fighting isn't like training. Fighting is easy.

Bruce appears.

"You'll feel so elated after you've won," he says. "You feel like hell now, but wait till you've won. You'll be on the most incredible high you've ever known."

"Yes, but I've got to win first."

"Oh, you'll win," says Bruce.

I find Jill in the locker room. What d'you do with the insane nerves? I ask. Is it right to be sitting on the edge of sanity?

"My first pro fight," she says, "I was too hyped up—it's why she won. She was real relaxed and I was all over the place. But whatever makes you feel better is good. I don't call it nerves, I call it excitement."

I try to feel excited, but I still feel sick. I go to yoga, to dinner with friends, rent the most sugary movie I can find (*Sabrina*). I call my karate-fighting friend, Cathy.

"You always do things this way," she laughs. "You can't just do it quietly in some little gym." I groan. Hoist with my own petard.

"Oh, it won't be as bad as you think," Cathy says. "Eight minutes of your life and you'll be out of it. However you do, I promise you'll be proud of it."

They're the first words in two weeks that have calmed me down.

"There's something about watching two women duking it out that causes a tingle in men's groins. . . . "

I'm in New York for the few days between the press conference and the fight, and a *Philadelphia Inquirer* columnist named Art Carey has called me at home (Elbaum has been generous with my number). It is Wednesday and though I leave for Philadelphia in a couple of hours and am in panic overdrive, I agree to talk in case it makes me usefully mad. He doesn't have much to ask me—he has an article I wrote about boxing that answers his questions—but has called me to listen to himself talk. Art says he's writing a book about "the epidemic of flat affect in America; how Americans are no longer capable of emotional spikes, enthusiasm, exuberance, have no élan or joie de vivre . . . " It's a sequel to his early-eighties work *Indefensive Marriage*. He has a lot to say about how things seem so shoddy and service so unreliable and about the decline of morals and education and what passes for art these days. Yesterday, says Art, he had the pleasure of meeting my opponent.

"Her sweetness and innocence appeal to me, I must admit. I think New York is the capital of insanity, illusions, and pretension. It's so rare on the jaded East Coast to get someone so good looking be so unaware of her gorgeousness. . . . "

Why, I'm wondering, might he believe I'd want to hear this? I'm going to fight her, not kiss her. And what are the odds that a female reporter would call, say, Lennox Lewis's opponent directly before a fight and ramble on about how cute she found Lennox and, my, isn't he sexy . . . ?

"She sure packs a punch," Art continues, oblivious to my audible heartbeat. "I was in the ring with her wearing those, you know, flat gloves, and I can tell you—I mean, I know nothing about boxing, but you're going to have your work cut out . . . "

. . . and Lennox hits like a freight train. No, I do not want to hear this. Though Art seems sad, deluded, and wrong, he has become the spokesman for this peculiar moment. Beneath his rant float unclean specters I don't want in my prefight neurosis gallery—specifically, the aspect of this game that plays into adolescent and unshareable male sexual fantasies.

"I love to see women mix it up and get muddy," Art continues. "It's all a matter of social convention. . . . "

Why doesn't he come right out and say it? He's titillated by cat-fighting, maybe even two women fighting over him. Or, alternatively, he could be romanticizing his dream girl's ability to protect him, presumably against the decadence of modern America. (The article he wrote after the fight seemed to confirm this, or both, attitudes. Childers, he wrote, is "a statuesque blonde Valkyrie with a face wholesome enough for a corn flakes box and a personality so sweet and innocent, so without affect or attitude, that it makes you rejoice for . . . midwestern wellsprings of old-fashioned courtesy, modesty and decency.") The apparent volte-face in traditional gender roles reminds me of how Sam eroticized my potential to beat him up. Have men really changed so much? They can't all be suddenly submissive; it's a hall-of-mirrors trick, and it traps me at this juncture. Whatever is going on, I'm feeling so vulnerable, this all hits me below the belt. My nausea redoubles. I do not want to be in a sexual arena when I thought I was in the gladiators' one.

For relief, I attend a British Tourist Authority press luncheon at the Four Seasons. I want to see how my big event is a tiny dot that has eclipsed the sun only in the spot where I stand. It works—like a Band-Aid over a bullet hole. The second it's over, the angry wound reopens and I'm back in the hurricane, fighting qualms, wishing for tomorrow, dreading tomorrow. So strong is my fear, it's like having another character inside, someone I can play with. I can edge up to the blackest scenarios of injury and humiliation and feel the violent surge of revulsion, and get a perverse enjoyment. It is larger than life. It is better than boredom. That's what I really fear: nothing. I mean the absence of feeling, of meaning.

Boxing is an injection of meaning. And I use the word "injection" deliberately—I do see a correlation between taking a hit and taking a hit. Both boxing and drugs are ways of avoiding pain. Both are all-consuming. "Getting out of your head" was what we used to call being high. I was trying then to medicate my way clear of anxiety into an alternate state, any state, the more extreme the better. All it did was obfuscate the issue that never goes away: life is hard. The ring offers a similar deal. Boxing connects cause and effect instantaneously, requisitioning every cell for its purposes, so that you can't concentrate on anything else. Bruises are satisfying; they're proof that it's working. *This* pain means I don't feel *that* pain. My black eyes can't currently see the empty acres of negativity, worry, old hurts. Feeling lonely and pathetic and static and pessimistic—*that* is pain. Getting hit is nothing. I can take that, I can take a punch, I am proud of that. I'm about to see whether I can really "take punishment," as they say about boxers—a curious term for a beating in the ring, because it implies that it's deserved, that a crime has been committed. Jake LaMotta wrote in his autobiography, *Raging Bull:* "I wanted to get punished and I took unnecessary punishment when I was fighting. I didn't realize it, but subconsciously I was trying to punish myself. Subconsciously ... I fought like I didn't deserve to live."

I used to live with an angry man. He would fly into insane rages for no reason, and I would shell up and cry and try to soothe, and that would make it worse. Only after the storm had passed would I feel the anger of injustice. He never hit me because he said he was afraid of what he might do. I wanted him to hit me. I wasn't afraid of that, I was afraid of the inchoate fury unleashed on me, undeserved by me, the twisted psychic torture. Physical violence would have been comprehensible, and a good reason to leave him, too. As long as he did the decent thing and held it in, I was obliged, I felt, to try to decode his fits, to try to understand him. After all, he was trying to be a good guy. One day, I'd had enough and I provoked him until he did it, he hit me. I didn't box yet. The blow sent me across the room, and I lay there in the corner and laughed. He was disgusted with himself and I laughed. I would rather eat glass than stay with an abuser, but at the time it seemed that the primal act was preferable to the emotional violence; it was satisfying to have his unmetabolized poison translated into just a fist. Now it is like that with boxing. My disturbances take on concrete form, rules, shapes, skills. Being hit is the shit in my life. Then I hit it back.

But the design is flawed. Hitting is an aberration. It temporarily deflects the pain of fear. Even the stylized hitting of the manly art, the sweet science, does this. Otherwise, why would some boxers, like Peter Kahn's Tommy Rodriguez, be punchers in the ring, while others are nothing but gym fighters, impressive in training, but lukewarm in combat? Jake LaMotta thought he didn't deserve to live—what inconsolable pain and fear fed that champion's triumph. Up to now it hasn't mattered, but the fear that consumes me on the eve of combat is that I made a mistake. I want to transcend fear, not feed it. It seems that boxing feeds it.

Colin's "one punch" idea has crystallized for me into one waking nightmare. My mother is involved in this. She is so unhappy about my boxing, I can't bring myself to tell her about the fight. When the London *Daily Express*, which is doing a story on the bout, called her for my number and she called me to ask about it, I told her some lie about an article I was writing. To protect her from worry. This makes me feel sad and alone and irrationally convinced I'm inviting the very thing that scares her. When I used to watch Muhammad Ali or John Conteh or Henry Cooper so long ago, Ma would quote Dr. Edith Summerskill, a Member of Parliament who spoke often on the radio excoriating pugilism—as if she knew she'd better start early to steer her daughter away from the ring. The fact that the British Medical Association remains, to this day, opposed to boxing has something to do with Dr. Summerskill's 1956 jeremiad *The Ignoble Art*. Reading it now, I see how my mother did manage to insert parts of it under my skin. Its psychology is laughably outdated, and its arguments are oversimplified and often specious, but there's a humanist voice there that, although I am loath to listen, speaks to me—as do some of its more disgusting medical descriptions of brain abuse:

> The brain weighs about three pounds; it is of the soft consistency of cold porridge; it is not tied down, and rests in a fluid in the bony skull. A blow causes it to wobble from side to side. . . . A severe blow which jolts the frontal lobes of the brain against the ridge will destroy the tissue, tearing through the fine membrane which covers the brain and the brain substance, and inducing bleeding. These injuries do not heal and the destruction of the brain cells is permanent. . . .

Secretly, I second Dr. Summerskill's assertion that "the first step to ensuring world peace is to control by example the destructive impulse." And I have to bow to the experience of the writer Paul Gallico, whose 1955 *Esquire* article Summerskill quotes. Gallico, who was in fact the founder of the Golden Gloves, can claim to have watched six thousand boxing matches in fourteen years of sportswriting.

"Boxing is the most selfish and self-centered sport there is," he came to believe.

> The rules, customs and usages of the game, as a boy rises from nonentity to fame, tend to make him cruel, vicious, lazy, irresponsible, unreliable, callous, untruthful, greedy, merciless and cynical. The profession may engender a certain stoicism, courage, stubbornness and endurance, but by and large boxing or ring fighting has never added an iota to the stature of anyone as a human being worth his salt.

This is exactly what I'm worried about.

I had grasped Colin's hand all the way to Philadelphia and asked him about his career, to color in the outline he's sketched between rounds at the gym. (Is this really the first time we've met outside?) All his opponents, Colin said, every one of them was a bad guy—a cheat, a thief, a killer. He had to stop them. How did you know they were, I asked? What if you just had to believe that in order to be righteous? Oh I knew, he said, I knew. I only took those kind of fights. He had eighteen of them, then his knees and his back went bad. The last one was in 1989, and he got to the ring straight off the red-eye, legs and back all seized up and in no state to fight. "I'm not mekking excuses. I lost, that was all." It was his first loss. He retired from the ring and started training kids, and the kids got older and some turned professional. "Everyone know me in Guyana," he sometimes says. And it may be so. Once a Guyanese cabdriver drove me to JFK. "You like boxing?" I asked him. "Sure, I like boxing. Boxing's huge back home." "D'you happen to know Colin Morgan?" I asked. "Oh, yeah," he said. "Everyone know him."

Now at least two of Colin's Guyanese kids train with him at Gleason's: Gary St. Clair and Andrew Murray. Andrew is awfully sexy. He wears a garnish of gold on his front teeth and moves like a big cat. He's ranked around number five in the WBA as a junior middleweight. Gary doesn't do any roadwork—that early-morning run I hate that lays down your cardiovascular foundation. Instead, he jumps rope and shadowboxes at least fifteen rounds before sparring and padwork and heavybag, dancing better than any MTV video to sounds audible only to him. I love to watch Gary. At 13-0 as a pro, he's on the cusp of a breakthrough, has just had a glowing write-up in *KO* magazine as the junior lightweight prospect to watch. This is a mixed blessing, since nobody wants his own rising fighter to risk another rising fighter. Everything depends on the next fight and the next; it could be stalemate, it could be glory. I take it as a good omen that I've borrowed Gary's robe, his name stripped out with coach tape. "My fighters don't lose," Colin says.

I am leaning on Colin so hard, it's amazing he stays perpendicular. It's unfamiliar and sweet. Usually I fight this sort of neediness, fearing the letdown, I suppose; but this, this is different, it has a purpose, it's for the result. I'm not risking my heart. After supper (I have no appetite) in a comfortless, fluorescent-lit diner, bedtime at the Best Western brings an illusion of relief, cozy like Christmas Eve. Nothing to do but lose consciousness and wake up and it'll be the big day.

In the morning, the weigh-in. As usual, under stress, I am constipated and, to my chagrin, weight in at 150 pounds, three more than yesterday with barely a bite of food. I wanted to be two decades lighter than she—she obediently wearing as little as possible, aloof in her special waiting room, Elbaum breathing down her neck (or lower back) as she signs in, saying, "Isn't she a knockout? Look at that outfit!" as the boxers scowl. HBO is filming her for *RealSports*, a women's boxing report that will be a triptych, including miniprofiles on Christy Martin, Lucia Rijker, and, yes, Jen Childers. In this show, Don Elbaum will relate how impressed he was when Jen split his forehead open while "auditioning" for him. Her trainer, Wesley Munzon, will state his belief that "women, deep down inside, they're vicious." Christy Martin will declare that she will fight Lucia Rijker, "but first they'll have to prove to me and the doctors that she's a woman." Lucia Rijker will be filmed clutching her sides with laughter at that. Bryant Gumbel will ask Larry Merchant, the dean of HBO boxing, "If I'm a fight fan, why would I want to plunk down twenty-five, thirty, forty dollars to go see what is essentially an inferior product?" And Merchant will respond: "If you go to a big tennis tournament and the women are playing, the women don't play as well as the men, but people enjoy watching the women on their own merits." (Just a few years later, fans enjoyed watching the Williams sisters, Hingis, Davenport, et al. a whole lot more than their male counterparts.)

Then it was lunch with Colin and his "big daughter," Sandy Gutierrez, here for the ride, and Peter Kahn and his puncher, Tommy Rodriguez, who's hoping to improve his record to 3-0, plus another Gleason's fighter, Francisco de Assia, the opponent for the headliner,

Vincent Thompson. Francisco eats plain macaroni. He speaks no English at all. Sandy, acting as interpreter, says he is the Brazilian junior middleweight champion and has no trainer. He doesn't even know yet who will work his corner. You don't mind that? I want to know. He shrugs. He will just fight, he says.

Back in my room, eight hours before the fight, the real nerves start. I swore not to do it, but I do, I call Colin, and he comes over. "Most of my fighters want me around at this time," he says. Really? The men do? "Sure. Some of them's big babies." It's a license to wilt, and I give in. Colin is great at massage, an innate skill of all trainers. I'm wearing sports bra and shorts, and I block my ears to echoes of other afternoons in other hotels with other men. The air is so thick with denial that anything here is unusual, we have to crack jokes about it so we can breathe easy. I know this about Colin, that he is afraid of being hurt, too. I know enough about his childhood, scenes that are secret. When, after the massage, we put on the TV and I try to sleep, I curl up with my head on his shoulder, and it is dear to do this, and safe, and we are both proud. I have not relied on a man for over ten years.

In the end, I do fall asleep and when the phone wakes me, I'm alone, and it's time to go. I pack my bag: clothes, boots (the beloved beat-up ones), Gary's robe, mouthguard, chest protector (I hate that thing; it's so wide I can't wrap my elbows in tight), headgear (hate that thing, too; it slips around), and, of course, pregnancy test. Every morning I have awoken too early and had the tape of the fight playing in my head, doing all the things I want to, hurting her, practicing wanting to hurt her, but I made myself stop watching. Too soon, too soon. I believe in visualization. In the rest of my life it works quite naturally, without effort, but for this, I've censored the pictures, and now it's too late.

Into my excuse of a dressing room pours a stream of visitors. Jill, Marysia, Nancy, Eric, Jody, and Janette have made the trek, the last two to cover my fight for an English paper. Also, I'm writing this up for a magazine, and two editors, the art director and a photographer have shown up. So what if she's got HBO in her corner? I've got Condé Nast and the *Evening Standard*. Very unpugilistic, but it makes me feel secure, and it helps to pass the time. For the entourage, this is a lark, a good night out, like going to see your friends' band, but more funky. Only Eric and, of course, Jill have ever seen a fight.

Eventually, I'm wrapped up and signed off and laced up and not pregnant, and the third bout goes in and Colin takes me to the Blue Corner Room to warm up and we bond with the opponents and they like my style and wish me luck, and there's a muffled cheer and the third bout is over. Tommy Rodriguez climbs the creaky stairs, triumphant, cradling the right hand he broke during the fight. (Though he will fight again, that injury will put an end to his career.) And now it is time and we take the stairs, and I am both sick and ready. Yes, I am ready.

In my corner, the blue corner, I meet my cutman, whom I hope I won't need, and Peter Kahn. They look like warped surgeons in short black satin cornermen's jackets. "Do good," Peter says. Colin is in a T-shirt and jeans. They tell him he can't talk to me during the rounds, only in the breaks. That's stupid, he says. Most of the places I went with fighters, you're allowed to say something. Oh shit, I think. When she climbs through the ropes in her red red gown, she's hidden inside her hood until we take the ref's instructions and then I see in her face the fear I am no longer feeling. I am feeling nothing at all now, nothing at all. DING!

Round One

One step, two steps, three, four and a half steps, BAM! I do what Colin told me to, throw that big right hand to "knock her thoughts out," and—look—she's shocked! I don't like her at all. I hate her. I want to hurt her. I want to get the face, the model's face. Model! What the fuck's she doing in here with me if she wants to be a model?

I'll show her. All I want is blood, that's all. Blood. I feel great. But that right hand. I'd never do that, never in a hundred years. I mean, lead with the right? No jab? No feeling out the distance, just bam? No, I wouldn't do it, but I did do it, and Colin was right. Women fight like this very often. He's seen it in the Gloves. You're doing all this fancy Gleason's footwork and then, *oof*, some vicious chick lays into you and you're circling, slipping, doing what you were taught, but she's all over you, winging and slamming, she came to fight, you came to box. We're not taking that chance. I'm the vicious chick tonight. I was so afraid I couldn't be, but it's easy. Man, it's great!

The right hand, I practically had to jump to reach her face. I only want the face, because that's where the blood is hiding. Overhand rights and body shots, overhand rights, body. In sparring, Colin has this knack, he yells out a combination at precisely the right moment. Whatever I hear, I do, and it makes me look amazing, because it always gets them. But where is he now when I need him? I'm all alone and, you know what? I realize something stupid. I don't know from overhand rights! How can a punch with a downward trajectory get to that face high up in the clouds? Six, ten, twelve seconds have passed. I follow the right with uppercuts to the body, but my gloves are bunches of bananas. In my dreams, I inflict a cracked floating rib, a wishbone snap, but here . . . it's a pillow fight. Body shots, though, they're about attrition. You don't feel them, but an ache exactly like menstrual cramps creeps up on you, then by round three you can't breathe and your legs have gone wobbly. But anyhow, I've cornered her. Her head's down and her hands are turned and she's pistoning her uppercuts into my sides. I can't feel them, but I'm worried about my sorry nose—her fist, my nose, they're the same height. Freak. Unfair. I step out—*Hey, this is not sparring, Kate, this is the fight, this is it*. Right. But now it's happening, it turns out I am still me. Colin's right, it's easy. I have the control, the shark illusion. When I back up, she doesn't follow. I swear she's afraid of me.

Oof. Shock of a jab, that snake arm lashing my hurt nose. Maybe forty seconds, maybe fifty. Damn, I felt that, it is *hard*, an infinitesimal blind spot, not pain, but my pride wails and I intuit that in real fights this is what you overcome, this desire to stop. No, no, wait, this is it, *this is the real fight.* Now she knows I can be checked. Damn. I wish I had not had that thought; it put a chink in my armor. No more thinking. Instantaneous decision my body makes now not to back down, and in a flash comes the full knowledge, the blessed conviction, that there is nothing she can do to stop me. I can fight through all her punches, it was my nose I was worried about, and now I have decided to sacrifice my nose. I know how she won six fights. When she hits, it's bad, but there are gaps. She is not Veronica.

"Move and jab, Jen, move and jab!" Shit. That's her trainer, loud and clear. How come *he* can yell? Why doesn't Colin come in now? I slip one and take one and I counter. Whenever I advance, she retreats. I'm forcing the pace here, I'm leading her around. Weird. I'm sure if I backed off, nothing would happen, there'd be no fight. It's really, really hard to move in on her, though, with that damn reach. Some of them I can see, but every, oh, fourth punch she throws I feel I'm running right into it, enhancing it. Colin! Why? I need to get under, get inside to the body, and I manage that and throw more bananas. Maybe halfway through the round and now she pipes up: "Low blow! Low blow!" Her voice, like Mike Tyson's, a silly high squeal. Come *on!* That wasn't *low,* the ref gives me a warning, though he doesn't take points away. "But her middle's up there," I yell and he says, "I know," sympathetic. I feel the crowd, I know they like me. I feel like a tiny missile. The spotlight's like the sun. It's a stage, that's all. We're the show.

"Pop that jab, Jen!" Her trainer's sergeant voice. Now she's heeding him, she's heating up, jabbing more, but most of them go sailing over my head, with my knee bends like little curtseys. I can't stop leading with the right, though, I've been reversed. I know it's wrong, but my interior trainer's saying, *Just do it and think later, just everything and to hell with how it looks. It's your first time.* It's my first round.

I get one beauty shot in that staggers her—a short straight right, of course—and there's a roar from out there; they're really on my side. And now here's the ten-second warning, going *knock-knock-knock*, like a clock on steroids. Oh. Oh no. Fantasy number one hits the deck, that I do it in the first, get that blood, but I'm still trying. Although she's so huge, I'm stalking her the whole way, I've had her in the corner three, four times. Now: *slam*. On the bell, she gets a right in, feels like the wall hit me, that's the first right she's connected. Ah, sod it, who cares. DING!

Here's my little stool. Wheee! I need it, though I know I'll get a second wind, that the first round is mere warm-up, like the first mile running. Colin's wearing white surgical gloves. Shock of the rubber smell, his fingers on my tongue pulling the mouthguard free.

"She's HUGE, she's fucking huge, Col."

"I know, Kadie. You doin' great." He squirts water in my mouth.

"What should I do?"

"Juss keep doin' what you're doin'. You doin' great. You won that round."

"Yeah?"

"Yeah."

The crowd emits a catcall, whistling, jeering. It's the ring card boy. He's wearing clothes, but at least they had the wit to use guys.

"I'm walking into her right. I'm doing that again."

"Keep watching."

I want to go back to the gym for a last session, to work on that. So many gaps in my knowledge. Can't spell-fight. Green as lettuce. *"Seconds out!"* Trainer, corner, cutman climb out. Too late. DING!

Round Two

I am iron. So what if I didn't draw blood in the first? I'll do it now. She throws two jabs, one I catch, the other I duck, then I move in and throw a right to the body that connects. Oh yeah, she is *mine*. I'm so relaxed, time looks like an open plain of opportunity. What shall I do? The Reggie move? Yesss. Jab to the body (I hardly need bend), right to the face, bam! Not only does her neck ricochet, but I turn her entirely; she's retreating. I follow, repeat the right jab but with less power, putting her briefly in the corner. That wasn't so smart. This is about confidence. I must trick myself into believing I'm experienced; an imperfect moment like that makes me feel uncertain again. Shake it off. Twenty, thirty seconds and she's on me now. She's mad now. I get a flurry of uppercuts in my face. Uppercuts are the most difficult punch to master; you have to snap them from the crouch, heaving the body weight up through your bent arm, the fist turned inward like you're flipping the bird. It takes a lot of practice to get any power in it. Tonight I have to push my uppercuts way high if I'm to avoid losing points for low blows—her waistband is where most women keep their ribs—and it's exhausting. Her upper-cuts, though, they strafe my face without effort. Not fair, not good. I back up.

In reverse, I throw another version of my new invention, the overhand right lead, and it clips her again. I do admit, I am landing a lot of my punches, not always with great force, but they're getting there. Nothing she's thrown has given me pause ... until now. One of her straight rights (she seems to have caught my bad right-lead habit) clocks my nose. I hate that, *hate* that. But my nose problem, it is actually helping. How *dare* she abuse my weakened state, the great big bully. Hasn't she enough advantages? I must avenge the nose. To gain an overview and test my theory about this being a fight only as long as I am exerting pressure, I move out of range and dance here a moment. It's the best thing I've done. She stands still and beckons me, as if to say, "Come on, chicken, stay and fight," an act so annoying that a lake of latent anger boils up in this geyser of energy. So you want me to come back, do you? Oh yes, we can arrange that, you fool. Oh yes, bitch.

And I stride in, batting away her rights like fat flies, not caring if one gets through, and bam-bam-bam, I throw a jab and—unorthodox again; thanks, Colin—double the right, and the second one cracks her so hard in the nose she loses her footing, drops her hands, and staggers back. I peer up to see what I've done and—rejoice! Rejoice for I have won! Blood is pouring out her nose, she looks horrible. There, model, that'll learn ya. And bam again, it's not over yet, she's in the corner, misses me. I want more of that, I'm wild on the case, waiting for the towel, surely they'll throw in the towel. Flash on John's story about the Blue and the ref's ignoring the towel, flash on the contract and the double Elbaum chortle and my elation drops to the canvas. *They're not stopping it.* I've got to go on. Energy drains. She's on the uppercuts again. Damn. I'll step out, to the side, jab, miss. Confusion.

Knock-knock-knock. I've got to keep it together, get to my corner, regroup. New tactics. My heart sinks. I have to go the distance. Only now do I realize I had no intention of doing that. No, eight minutes isn't long—but if all of life contained this slo-o-ow breed of minutes, we'd be immortal. My hands sink with my spirits. She saw that. I'm an idiot! I take two avoidable punches, the last one—DING!—bang on the bell.

Stool. Rubber hands, two pair. Cutman palpates the nasal cartilage. Colin pries out the mouthpiece. Water. Towel.

"Col, they were going to stop it, remember?"

"I fixed they be jokin'."

"You never said. I thought it was over."

"But you winnin', Kadie. You hurt her real good."

I'd better screw my head back on, better capitalize on what I've done.

"Yeah," I grin. "Blood all over."

"You really are doing great, babe," Peter adds. "Keep up the pressure. She's scared of you."

The ring-boy jeer goes up again, wolf whistles, baying. They're animals. I do not want to go back, I do not want to go back. *"Seconds out!"* Snap out of it, Kate. DING!

Round Three

I come in low, channeling Joe Frazier, the inside king, weaving down-round-up, side-to-side, and here I am, sticking her midsection with bananas, only I'm taking some back, too, as she extends octopus arms over the top of the action and socks me two times, maybe three. So I figure this isn't the way to start a round and out I get, but now she finally chases me down, and—hey, sod this—I'm in the corner. I eat a feeble jab and swivel out, like I've done so often in sparring but never before to save my skin. And it's maybe half a minute in and *whoosh*, here it comes, adrenaline. My free gift from fear. I had blocked fear and denied it and been afraid of it, yes, and finally I felt it, this true horror that I can't go on, can't breathe, can't find the energy. Revivified, I loom in, I'm inevitable, Boom Boom Boom, left-right-left-right, and the right finds the mark on her face, all cleaned up (they did a good job), and, whoa, I've got her cornered again. Bloody enormous cheer. And she slinks along the ropes to the other corner, tries to hold me off with her giraffe arm straight out, so I slip it and slam out another combination high into her face, left right hook.

Sadly, this is where experience tells. I've dropped my left glove, and her fist shoots surreptitiously into my nose, my poor nose-let, and I taste the salty metal seeping over my lip and it's suddenly bothersome to breathe, but I don't care. I only want to get *her* blood back, why can't I? First, I rest a moment, putting her in the clinch against the ropes, the first time I've done this, too, for real. And the ref comes in with his arms in a V, lifts and separates, and we go to the middle, stand off, bounce bounce. I am tired and I couldn't care less. We both jab. Hers, eight inches longer, wins. *Oof* I bundle in to retaliate, they love it, someone's chanting a rhythmic *hoo-hoo-hoo-hoo* like a gorilla in a cartoon, and I remove myself momentarily, to watch this surreal movie about how far I have come, remembrance of small bookworm Kate. Who is this creature, entertaining the crowd with her own blood? I hate the crowd for loving me for this. I want out.

That takes an eighteenth of a second, or an age, depending how you look at it. I snap the fighter back in, and we trade punches again, this section being, I think at the time, quite classic. I hit her, she hits me. I'm bleeding, but aside from embarrassment—I feel exposed having my insides out—it makes no difference. What matters more is that with that punch, my headgear slipped over my eyes and suddenly it's hard to see up to where she is. Only one thing for it, attack. Attack is my defense, Jill said once. Jill's here. Jill will understand why I'm not being classic anymore.

Knock-knock-knock ... I back her onto the ropes, the way I've learned I can. She will counter. She won't attack first. She seems to enjoy having something at her back, more leverage perhaps. I roll under her jab and execute a perfect Reggie—left uppercut and a right—that slams her, really slams, and there's the roar for reward, it buoys me. But now comes her retaliation, from the corner, damn, this is bad now this is hard, I'm kind of blind, but I swing out to the body, getting socked at the same time, the crowd is hysterical. DING!

Sit. Rubber hands, wiping, mouthguard out, water, ugh, what's this? I slap away the hands, still fighting, but Mr. Cutman sticks his Brobdingnagian Q-tips up my nostrils, a parody of my mother wiping chocolate off my face with spit. I hate this. This is the worst thing yet. They're all over my face like spiders. Can't hear Colin. "WHAT?" He's very very far away. All there is, is baying, whistling, jeers, *hoo-hoo-hoo-hoo*. Mayhem, bedlam. Only one round, only one more. "Keep your hands in front, Kadie, everything in front of you. Be smart. You got it." I can't get no rest here. I need a break. *"Seconds out!"* DING!

Final Round

And I am weary, so damn weary. I've run out of ideas. Do the Frazier thing, stay low, avoid those jabs. I swing at her midriff, head down, so wrong, I come out of that crouch. Now what? It's only ten seconds in.

In again. These body shots of mine, are they doing anything at all? Man, I hate this so much. Remind me never never to do this again. Remember this moment. Every second I have to pick myself up by the scruff of the neck and hurl myself back at her. My defense has gone to shit. Luckily, she's tired, too (maybe the body thing worked), and most of her punches miss, whether or not I'm slipping them correctly. My headgear is now firmly lodged over my eyes—is it the sweat? The fury has deserted me and I have to be very stern with myself; if I don't fight to the death, I will always regret it, though it feels pointless right now. It's halfway through the round, I'd say. The crowd is my friend. Every attack by me, it erupts. (It called me "Shorty," my friends inform me afterwards.)

It takes double the energy to strike higher than your head, and her monstrous size has worn me down. I'm connecting a lot less than in the other rounds, but so's she. One time, her jab stops short and she leaps back like a frightened bunny. I get a kick from that. Only now that I truly hate this do I know the thing I came to find out: I will never quit. If I had to, I could climb a mountain without oxygen, run a marathon in the desert, watch my own open heart surgery. Heart is what I'm finding now, but not heart as I know it. The boxer's heart gives and gives and gives, but not love like the civilian heart aims to give. The boxer's heart is not an open heart, but hard as steel.

Knock-knock-knock. This is music, but this is horrible. It hits me that, whatever they say in my corner, I am not going to win any decision here, not from the promoter's golden girl. I have to knock her out. Like Sisyphus, I heave my carcass one last time at the giantess, who backs onto the ropes once more, and I swing my lumpen arms up and up into the face I'll always remember and I connect and she misses, and this time she does not manage her final punch. I get mine, though. I punch the model's face one last time. DING!

I have never, ever been so happy in all my life.

"You did *great*, Kadie!" Colin unbuckles the headgear, picks out the mouthpiece, yelling at me. "I'm so-o-o proud of you. You did *great!*" Here's Mr. Cutman scraping my left eye socket with his bizarre appliance, the metal thing that pushes blood.

"Don't, whatever you do, blow your nose," he warns. "Your eye will swell up the size of a melon."

And Peter Kahn is unlacing the gloves, wielding the crooked scissors, freeing my hands, bowing to me in mock obeisance, like I'm Cleopatra.

"I am not worthy," he's gushing. "You were magnificent! So much better than I thought! Competitive!" This he will continue for at least a month. And I stand still for Dr. Death at the ropes feeling my nose with his rubber hands.

"I don't suspect a fracture, but you might get an X ray. You were hurt before the fight, weren't you?"

I pull a face and nod. Colin is just beaming.

The ring announcer takes the mike. Yes, of course she has won. As he raises her glove, there is a weak cheer and a lot of booing and hissing.

" . . . And let's hear it for Kate Sekules!"

"RAAAAAAAAAAH!"

My God, they like me, they really like me. Colin prods me and I step out and wave like a rock star. Raging Belle is hugging bouquets. I run over to embrace her.

"Well done," I say. "You're a brute." She looks alarmed. And here's Jill, bouncing up through the ropes to give me a bear hug.

"You were *amazing*, Kate! You fucking won that! You wuz robbed. You fucking won that."

That is the best compliment of all. That and the crowd, all these fierce Philly fight fans reaching for my hand, saying how great I was, how I really won—and the blue corner boys who have lined up along the creaky stairs to give me a standing ovation. My friends storm the dressing room, overexcited like children on sugar rushes, hysterical with pride. Sportswriter and lawyer Jacqui Frazier "of the boxing Fraziers" visits. "I'm writing my column about you, not her," she says.

"You're an inspiration to women." Cornermen, Blue Horizon staff, boxers, Dr. Death, Tommy are all congratulating me. If this is losing, who needs to win? The only person without a smile or a word of praise is Don Elbaum. Perhaps this is because, as I later learn, I broke Raging Belle's nose.

9

Big Belts

It's not exactly a hero's welcome at the gym—there's a hero a week—
but being the second professional girl here counts for something.
Peter Kahn performs his "I am not worthy" shtick daily. Hector Roca,
impossible to impress, tells his guys admiringly, "Hey, she fought
pro." Bruce congratulates me like I won. My first ever teacher,
Stephan, says he's very proud. Luke "Mad Dog" Massey from SoHo
Training calls me up: "Hats off to you, girl. I didn't think you'd do it."
Colin informs me that Roberto Duran lost his first two fights and
that I'll get offers from promoters because I fought so hard. I am part
of it now. I don't feel like a loser. I'm glad it's over.

Three days later the horror has faded and, just like Jill, I know I
must do it again. The doctor X-rays my nose. It's not broken, though
I have a new dent in the bridge—Veronica's donation, I'm sure. A
week later, the euphoria has faded. I am nostalgic for the nerves. I was
vivid. Now I'm dreary. "Don't want the anxiety," my journal says. "Do
want the concentration, the speed. All those things I didn't bother
thinking about—deadlines, background calorie counting, men, sex."
None of that feels as big as fighting.

Four weeks later, HBO sends me the tape of the bout and I crash.
"Colin, why didn't you tell me—I looked *horrible!*"

"Kadie, you were great. Everyone t'ink that. Watch it again.
You'll see."

I do so, substituting compassion for judgment, detaching my
ego, and Colin is right. Okay, so "Shorty" doesn't have perfect form,
but she's not so bad. I see ferocity, tenacity, power; I see a lot of clean
shots; I see her winning. Playing the tape over and over again, I count
the punches, and sure enough ... Round One, Raging landed a
mere fifteen percent of the punches she threw, while Shorty landed
sixty percent. Round Two (when I bled her), she landed thirty-one
percent, I landed fifty-six percent. Round Three (my blood), she
landed forty-three percent, I landed fifty-nine percent. And even in
my worst round, the last, she landed forty-one to my forty-eight percent. There were only two judges instead of the usual three; they
scored it 40-37 and 40-36. I was, indeed, robbed.

My moment in the sun over, April rolls around and it's time for the
Golden Gloves finals again. In its third year, the female division across
the country has trebled in size, and there are twice as many women's
bouts at Madison Square Garden in 1997 as there were in 1995. I'm
in L.A. at the time and don't see any of the fights. This rise of women's
amateur boxing is bearing more and bigger fruit, and by the time
I return to Gleason's, everyone's excited at the prospect of another historic first later this year—the as yet unconfirmed Women's National
Championships. As for the Gloves finals, I live them vicariously through
the blow-by-blow, admiring many a pair of little gold gloves. Gleason's
did great: Sandy won her first-ever fight and took home the super
heavyweight gloves; Sky, back in the welterweight division, scored her
third pair; and Veronica, fighting at 178 pounds, her second. She and
Tanya Dean, whom Veronica beat in 1996 in what she says to this day
was her only tough bout, had agreed to fight in separate divisions this
year, leaving the coast clear for Tanya's victory over a formidable
first-timer, Susan Gadomski, at 168 pounds. (Tanya's 1995 performance, said Gadomski, was her inspiration for taking up boxing in the

first place.) Like Veronica, Denise Lutrick—Domenico Menacho's favorite—went up a weight class this year, and she won the 139-pound gloves. Her 1996 vanquisher, the amazing Melissa Salamone, scored her second pair of gloves at 132 pounds, while Alicia Ashley, a frequent visitor to Gleason's, also got her second title, in the 125-pound division. The new girl in the gym, Evelyn Rodriguez, won her second-ever fight to clinch the 156-pound title. All the champions—except Tanya, whose workload caused her to (reluctantly) hang up the gloves—would be going on to the nationals, if, indeed, there would be nationals.

———————

I was in L.A. on business, but the best thing I did there was meet Lucia Rijker. Since the Dutch phenomenon first hit the scene, the rumors that she is the best female boxer in the world have only strengthened. In her kickboxing career, Rijker's record was 38-1, the sole loss having been to a Muay Thai fighter ... a man. So far, as a conventional boxer (so to speak), she has fought four women. After the first three bouts, Katya Bankowsky called her up and asked if she could feature her in *Shadow Boxers*—and, lo, the movie's central story is now Rijker's rise. With her tiny crew she flew to Rotterdam in February to shoot Rijker's homecoming (as a kickboxer, she's already a celebrity in Holland) and fourth bout, in which the European champion, Irma Verhoef, oddly attired in a pale gray leotard, was rescued by the referee in the fourth round. Next, in late March, Bankowsky's crew traveled to Corpus Christi, Texas, for Lucia's fifth fight, an eight-rounder against Chevelle Hallback.

"It was terrifying," relates Katya on encountering Hallback. "This woman disrobed at the weigh-in and she was huge. I mean, she looked exactly like a man." A few months later, Lucia will describe her feelings on Hallback to *Boxing Monthly*:

> I sat down with myself after the weigh-in and I said: "OK, they say it's a woman," although they didn't do a public examination

so I wasn't sure about that, so I said: "OK—so it's a man. So what? I'll fight a man." I just thought they should pay me more. I'd fought a man before. I don't mind fighting a man. Whoever's in front of me is an obstacle to where I want to go, so I don't care whether it's a man or a woman, I have to just be strong.

On watching Katya's footage of the fight, I had to agree that this fifth opponent looked terrifying. On the bell, Hallback, completely bald and wearing muscles on her muscles, stormed out of the corner and pounced on Rijker, who is not exactly a midget (and who's ripped enough to have been herself accused by Christy Martin of clandestine masculinity). Although I'd seen Lucia in action only for the few minutes Irma Verhoef remained upright, that was enough to be sure of her dominion. Her economy of movement is especially pleasing—the way she expands time to suit her intentions, her fist hovering like a hummingbird over the jaw or temple or chin before alighting on it and retreating, bereaving its owner of her senses, then disappearing out of reach to select the next target. Once glimpsed, she's impossible to imagine in peril. Then again, this is the way with any boxer on top of their game. They look invincible ... until they're not. Think of Liston quitting in his corner after the seventh with Ali in February 1964, Duran whispering *No mas* in the eighth against Sugar Ray Leonard in November 1980. The most infamous capitulations will always be remembered because they had once seemed impossible.

So when Chevelle Hallback steamed out in that way female amateurs have of casting all caution aside, using attack as defense— though Hallback certainly looked more coordinated, more, well, professional than those amateurs—it looked like Lucia might have met her match in the early dawn of her career. You could see it in her expression; the poker face was calculating odds, speed-thinking as she employed emergency evasive tactics to slip and block, retreating where she normally overwhelmed.

"At this point I was thinking, 'Okay, if she loses, what have I got?'" Katya remembers. "A story about another boxer with a 4-1 record isn't going to get the movie funded. It's not going to do much for women's boxing, either, when the supposedly best in the world loses her fifth bout."

The entire first round, Hallback maintained the pressure while Rijker played for time. In the break, Rijker's trainer, Freddie Roach, bent over Lucia and talked into her face as she nodded. Roach is a laid-back gent with oversized specs whose career as a featherweight was notable, but whose postseason record is even better: he has trained six world champions. But the second round went the same way, the fiendish energy of the challenger seeming capable of fueling infinite attacks, the pace relentless. Nothing Hallback threw was staggering Rijker, but there was no doubt that the bald one was ahead on the scorecards. In the break, Freddie leaned into his fighter again, relaying what he had noticed, developing a strategy—or so Katya hoped. And after another round of struggle, when Lucia's ideas were looking thin, and it was beginning to seem hopeless, Katya's crew crept the microphone into the huddle and eavesdropped on the corner talk.

"One-two-three and step to the side," Freddie was saying, "three-punch combinations, then step to the side, you got that?" And Lucia nodded and answered the bell for the fourth and, like an obedient actor taking direction, immediately put into operation the new plan: jab-right-hook, then swivel ninety degrees; jab-to-body, jab-to-head, hook, then whoosh around to the side. Every time she did that, Hallback was left facing thin air, unable to parse the new pattern, exposing momentarily her right side, which Rijker abused mercilessly—a textbook illustration of "ring generalship." Still, Hallback was far from through. If anything, this frustrating tactic was redoubling her aggression, although it was now possible to imagine her fatigued.

At the bell, Rijker looked worried as Freddie Roach coached. What new scheme would work? But in the fifth, instead of trying something else, she continued plan A, the three-punch, step-around trick, and now, finally, Hallback was clearly tired, hurling her rock-solid jab and missing, rushing at Lucia, aggression deteriorating into agitation until, halfway through the round ... touché. A Rijker right found its mark, as it normally does in the first round. Hallback stumbled back and Rijker stepped after her, loosing combinations to the head, demolishing the remainder of Hallback's defense, and in six seconds, this huge, bald, muscle-bound woman was destroyed. Rijker's final attack knocked her not to the canvas, but entirely through the ropes. Chevelle Hallback lost the fight prone on the ring apron.

Freddie Roach's one-ring gym sits above a laundromat at Vine Street and Santa Monica Boulevard in West Hollywood, its name, Wild Card Boxing, spray-painted graffiti-style on the white wall. Behind the desk, a photo gallery illustrates the flyweight careers of Freddie Roach and his father, plus the golden highlights of Freddie the trainer. It takes me a minute to realize that this diffident, jokey guy in the Andy Warhol specs and hoodie is Freddie himself. "She's over there," he says, nodding toward a motionless figure bundled up in sweats, holding a medicine ball above its head, like Atlas with the world, elbows crooked (try this at home; it hurts). When after ten minutes she sets down the globe, I sidle up. "Oh yeah, hi, Kate," says the world's best female boxer. "Let me change."

After training, Lucia always heads straight to the juice bar (she consumes nothing artificial, drinks no alcohol), and that's where we go. Lucia is one of those catalyst people, someone whose presence can't help but produce a reaction. She's an instant hit of joie de vivre, conspiratorial, concentrated, calm, kind, and, above all, fun. It would be impossible for her to prevaricate. The daughter of a white mother and a black father, she has big, happy lips, frizzy dark-blond hair under a baseball cap, and, in white jeans and sweatshirt, her famous physique gives the illusion of slightness. "Pshh. I am like a heavyweight now," she jests, patting a stomach flat as paper. Today is her first gym session since a rare Dutch post-Hallback vacation. We gossip for an hour, and after we part, her image fades slowly as if I'd been blinded by a flashbulb.

Next day, lunch at A Votre Santé, an organic café, is like meeting an old friend who happens to have become a movie star. I keep forgetting that she's the one who devours girls in the ring, partly because she asks as many questions as she answers—our shared status as boxers (even though I'm a beginner) is a bonding mechanism, similar to running into someone from the office in the Himalayan foothills. Fresh from my ring debut, my qualms about harming and karma are still perplexing me, and this is what I most want to know: How does Lucia Rijker reconcile being lethal with being peaceful? What is a Buddhist boxer? For Lucia, I soon realize, the dichotomy does not exist.

"I used to fight with a lot of anger," she begins. "I was vicious. It came up, so it was good. I thought it was healthy. Every fight for me was an adrenaline shot. It was an addiction, like heroin."

Then three years ago, Lucia adopted Nichiren Daishonin Buddhism, which she heard about from a friend in England.

"Something changed in me. It made me stronger, brought out my psychic part. Now I respect my opponents, I respect their courage, their hard work, because without them, there's no fight. Now I don't hit harder than I have to."

Nichiren Daishonin, a 750-year-old Japanese tradition, entails daily chanting that focuses not only on general peace but also on specific personal benefits. I knew about it, having briefly espoused it myself a few years back. Such a vogue was there in the U.K. for the "new" craze that it was much derided in the press as "yuppie Buddhism, chanting for a new car." Of course, the aquisition of consumer goods was not the point, though I did like to play with the power (we were encouraged to test it out), chanting *Nam myoho renge kyo* for, say, a taxi to appear on a deserted street at two A.M. It worked. It works even better for Lucia, who chants for hours a day. She is quite the mystic. Before every fight she receives a vision of the result during a three-day trancelike retreat from the world.

"I center myself. I make my body and spirit pure—though I don't want to be too high, or I'm afraid I can't come down. It can cost you your fight."

One time, she says, her customary vision of the last round was accompanied by an unfamiliar sensation, a feeling of light and peace.

"I didn't know what it meant. It was before the Muay Thai fighter, the guy, and he knocked me out. *Then* I understood what it was. I didn't understand it before because I'd never felt it."

"What was it like?" I prompt.

"It feels real good. It's a beautiful feeling, you just float away. But then, of course, I had a headache for two weeks."

The reason Lucia met a man in the ring at all was not to settle any scores in the war of the sexes, but was merely an effort to find a good match, having run out of kickboxing opponents of her own gender—the very state of affairs that would eventually convert her to boxing. But even that two-week headache does not make Rijker worry about the effects on her health of cumulative head trauma, despite the fact that (unlike Christy Martin) she welcomes the very toughest of opponents. Failure is not a concept that figures in Lucia's world. She needs to keep winning.

"I always was the best—at judo, fencing, kickboxing. Unconciously, I suppose I never got attention from my parents. From everyone else I did. But the ego boost is nothing. If you take it seriously, you also take it seriously when they say you suck. You need to be competitive in a healthy way; you can't start to think you're special. I never underestimate who's out there. In boxing, you can get knocked out on a bad day."

It seems so simple. Hit as hard as you have to. Be humble in the face of competition. But how to cope with the fear, the nerves?

"Do *you* get nerves?" I want to know.

"Oh yeah. Before the fight you're just chickenshit. You want to pee in your pants! But fear is a good tool. I focus on the positive. Not 'What if I get hit?'—that's negative."

"How do you do that?"

"You know, I reason with the negative voice. I sit down before the fight and say, 'Listen, I don't need you right now. Wait till I'm done with the fight and we'll talk.'"

Lucia is a walking self-help book. Everything she says sounds wise, lit by that radiant personality, colored by her self-deprecating sense of humor, animated by the example she sets in the ring, even if that example seems on the surface to be at odds with her clemency. She describes the boxer's hidden motivations.

"Most fighters want to be liked. They're looking for affection and love. They have trouble expressing emotions, they don't cry, there's no anger. Boxing is an excuse not to face that. In training, you're numb. Stop and you're sad and angry."

Is she including herself here, I wonder? Lucia doesn't seem numb; she is vital. She lacks the disconnection I've noticed in many boxers, whose gaze never quite meets yours, who fight their fears without understanding them. She is different, both because and in spite of being a woman. Gender aside, she is a superior athlete, with all the suspension of commonplace behaviors that entails. As a woman, she is grounded—as a building is grounded by a lightning rod. Women are born with a lightning rod, and whether we honor it or not, it is the feminine principle, a subcutaneous awareness of connectedness; it is why we are cast as the nurturers. Most of us bring this awareness to quotidian human relationships rather than the quasi-symbolic boxing kind. Until she's achieved her goals, says Lucia, she is concentrating all her forces on the latter.

"I've made it so far without a steady relationship. I see the picture of where it can go and I work with excitement toward the title fight. The more I work on myself, the more it'll come back to me— I apply this to anything I do. Relationships have got that in the past. Two more years, then I'll move on."

"To what?"

"I dunno. I have many ideas. I want to use this to create something for others, because people listen to you when you've done something with your life, when you have a name."

As always in Los Angeles, it is a sunny afternoon. We have finished our chicken breast and steamed vegetables. The Blue Horizon is worlds away, and it is right here at the table. I think of what Jill Matthews said—"The minute it's normal to box, I'm outta here"—and I see how it isn't normal yet. Lucia and I are perched on a frontier: ladies who lunch, and box. But she . . . she is way out there, she is the pioneer on the horizon, she has sacrificed for now the normal usages of femininity and has brought those female traits—intuition, courage, nurturing—to new territories, into boxing, where they have never been before. Consequently, she boxes better than many men. Yet here in April 1997, there are few women who fight fully conscious, without averting their eyes from the sinister. It is what I am attempting, but with the minutest fraction of Lucia's skills. She is probably the only woman in the world who can answer my real question.

"As you know, I'm a beginner," I begin. "But I worry about hurting. How do you, who believe in karma, in doing no harm, how do you get around that?"

This makes her smile—maybe I'm the only one who would ask the question—and instead of a pat answer, she begins to ask questions of me.

"Why do you box?"

"I don't completely know. But I have to," I reply.

"What do you love about boxing?"

"Well, a lot, but the challenge, I guess. The way it brings up my fears and forces me through."

"Does the challenge come from training?"

"Training's hard, yes, and it keeps getting harder the further I push myself."

"Why do you do that?"

Nobody's asked me these things before, not even me.

"Um . . . I push myself because I always have to overcome something."

"How does that make you feel?"

Good question. I see where this is going.

"Well, amazing! Sort of capable, more myself."

"So how do you feel after fighting?"

Scraping out the memory of my sole experience, obscured by the ignominy of not having been spectacular, I realize I felt pretty damn good.

"Same—amazing, but bigger," I respond. "Like I came through fire."

Now we are both laughing. She knows that I know that she knows we are both negotiating the same territory, regardless of how much better she is and how much further she's going.

"You see!" Lucia beams. "As soon as you draw the picture of why you're doing this big enough, you are able to hurt someone."

It would be a mere six months before Lucia Rijker achieved her ambition and won a world title, beating the German 136-pounder Jeanette Witte for the WIBF super lightweight belt. Barbara Buttrick and Jimmy Finn's WIBF was the first organization out of the gate to create bona fide girl champions, their inaugural crop having been sanctioned by the Nevada State Athletic Commission in an all-female card at the Aladdin Hotel and Casino, Las Vegas, back in April 1995. Prior to this, a couple of women's belt-granting organizations—the WWBA, or Women's World Boxing Association, and WBB, Women's Boxing Board—had come and gone (though not before staging a championship card in July 1979), but now, the nineties alphabet soup of women's belt-granting bodies was about to challenge the men's sport for confusion and illusion. How strange that Mexican super lightweight Maria Nieves Garcia had been allowed a title shot on March 29, 1997, when her record was only 1-1 (no KO). Then again, she took the belt, winning a split decision over the fine Belgian boxer Daniella Somers, who had, in turn, decisioned the excellent Russian fighter Zoulfia Koutdoussova a month before. There just aren't enough female professionals to go around.

Regardless of these developments, this month—April 1997—a third organization, the International Female Boxers Association (IFBA) sets up business. Its commissioner is a very glamorous woman named Jackie Kallen, a big-time boxing promoter (of Thomas "Hitman" Hearns, among others) and manager (of James "Lights Out" Toney, he of the amusing catchphrase: "He don't pay his bills, *the lights must go out!*") hailing from the famous Kronk Gym in Detroit. In July of this year, Frankie Globoschutz, who founded his IWBF in 1993, will finally grant his first belts. The IFBA, however, will pip everyone to the post with the first all-female pay-per-view card in . . . but I'm getting ahead.

Lucia beat three more girls before her title shot, the first even tougher than Hallback, and the only one to go the distance. That opponent was Dora Webber, the thirty-eight-year-old twin of light-weight contender Cora. A single mother of two teenage sons, Dora is a furniture mover and security guard by trade. Dora, you may remember, racked up eight wins in the 1980s, none of which was included in her "Fight Fax" record against Rijker, leaving her official pro record for the May 14 bout (at Foxwoods Resort, in Connecticut) at 0-0-2, with "draws" (remember the human frailty of judges) against Leah Mellinger over four rounds in February and our friend Kathy Collins over six rounds in March.

"[Rijker] has never faced anybody like me," claimed Webber in a press statement before the bout. "I'm gonna make her head spin like a Dutch windmill. I'm going fishing after I beat her. . . . When I'm done with Lucia and Christy, they'll be back playing with dolls!"

Maybe I should ask Dora how to enjoy hitting.

———————

The main event in Gleason's women's locker room, though, is the imminence of the amateur sport's grandest gesture, the first ever Women's Nationals, which really are taking place as promised, on July 16–19, 1997, in Augusta, Georgia. This is a very good thing all round, since fiercer amateur competition not only feeds those hungry professional ranks but also brings closer the day when a female division will appear in the Olympics. Once again, it is not without envy that I make the trek to witness—as Jill once put it—history in the making. (Now, of course, I am doubly debarred—by age and by professional status.) And when I get down south with my stable-mates, it proves impossible not to get caught up in the excitement.

The athletes are staying at the Augusta Sheraton, a hideous seventies concrete affair with negligible catering arrangements and a makeshift shop in the lobby, where Ringside is doing a roaring trade in "A Woman's Place Is In The Ring" T-shirts. Despite a respectably sized entry pool of sixty-seven women, who qualified by mere ownership of a USA Boxing licence, only two classes, 119 and 125 pounds, were popular enough to warrant a preliminary before the quarterfinal. This leaves one athlete in the unfortunate position of having to fight four bouts in four days. The unfairly burdened fighter is Leona Brown, the New York Golden Gloves champ, whose three decisions en route to the final have earned her the moniker "Baby Tyson" from the home team. Tonight she will square off against the ponytailed marathoner Patricia Alcivar, who has yet to win a title in her third year of competition.

The weigh-in for the finals resembles a professional one not at all. It's eight A.M. in the Sheraton ballroom and twenty-two finalists, ranging from eighteen to thirty-two years of age, from 106 to 201 pounds, and from twelve states, are gathered, plus trainers, referees, hangers-on like me, and the tournament organizer, Sandy Martinez Pino—freshly selected by the Amateur International Boxing Association (AIBA) to chair its new Women's World Committee. Since there are men in the room, the scale is secreted behind a screen, which is silly because it is the men who are conducting the weigh-in. There's coffee, doughnuts, and danish, which nobody touches. Women are grouped by states; I'm hanging in the New York corner with the eight hometown finalists, including the Gleason's trio: the 156-pound Gloves champ, Evelyn Rodriguez, Veronica Simmons, and, of course,

Sky Hosoya, who has evidently been appointed pep captain and official comedian. (Sandy Gutierrez has already gone home with the uncontested super heavyweight belt, and Dee Hamaguchi lost in the quarterfinal.) The noise level is library-like.

"It was scary at first because we had no idea who was out there at the national level in the rest of the country," Sky whispers. "But after the first round we sat down and said, 'Wow, the New York level's so much higher.' After that we were all: 'Pssst, don't *worry* about it, we're from New *York!*' We had each other."

"Each other" includes all the hometown Golden Gloves entrants—Alicia Ashley, Laura Kielczewski, Patricia Alcivar, Leona Brown, Denise Lutrick, and Melissa Salamone. Even the quartet that will be facing each other (Laura versus Melissa, Leona versus Patricia) are in the huddle. Outside the New York corner too, the general atmosphere here is more supportive than at the average weigh-in, albeit striated with seams of hostility. I intercept one of these periodically as it shoots across the room—usually from Evelyn. She is meeting LaTasha Washington, from Washington, D.C., tonight, after scoring the only knockout of the tournament (under Olympic Rules it's scored as RSC, "referee stops contest," but the girl was down), and is acting out a pay-per-view preview, standing alone by the wall, rigid with animosity.

"I can't talk, Kate. I'm staring her down," she says when I ask how she is. LaTasha scowls halfheartedly in our direction every now and again. Veronica, meanwhile, is being inscrutable. Tonight she will meet the only local hope left, Suzette Taylor, from Decatur, a first-timer who scored a split decision yesterday. I know Veronica's nervous only because she's told me so. Sky has already fought twice, and she is weary. Normally she relies heavily on the evil-eye approach.

"Scare tactics work to my advantage because of my physique and my face," she told me once. "Anyone who sees me fighting on videotape would go 'Ugh,' but put me in a lineup and looks work in my favor. The energy, the intensity, I put it in my eyes: 'I don't give a shit, I'm going to *kick your ass*, even if I have to *blink* you to death!' Put me next to Lutrick and Salamone and say, 'Who do you want to fight?' Nobody would pick me. They'd pick Lutrick or Salamone, because they look like candy, but they're the most dangerous."

Yesterday, Sky's customary intimidation tactic went awry.

"The whole time, I was staring down the wrong girl," she says. "When I found out, I went, 'You've been giving me dirty looks all this time—who the heck are you?' and she said, 'You're *lucky*. I'm under-aged.' Meanwhile, I was being nice with people and signing autographs, and one of my new friends was my real opponent's *mother*. It's like John Toliaferro said to me: 'Remember, these people are not from New York. They're friendly people.' It was strange."

Duly weighed, every fighter sits on the floor next to her opponent to receive her uniform (blue or red shorts and tank and a gorgeous pair of Adidas boots with matching stripe) and to hear Sandy Martinez Pino's briefing.

"I'm so proud of your behavior, the camaraderie. The men have a long way to come before they act as well as you did," she tells them. "I usually try not to stay on the same floor as the men during tournaments. Thanks for letting me get some sleep!" Big laugh. "You represent every woman in this country who wishes she could be here. Please encourage those who boxed against you to stay in this."

Sandy tells them that their uniforms must be immaculate, and to keep their headgear off before their bouts and take them off promptly afterward.

"We have some beautiful women here and we want you to be seen by the world."

Or ESPN2 watchers, anyhow.

Everyone I talk to is so proud of the athletes. Chris Filiberto, who is one of tonight's referees (and who informs me she was "the first lady ref" back in 1992), insists that the women's skills and their sportsmanship are better than the novice men's.

"It's incredible considering they've only had one or two bouts. They do less harm. There are fewer fouls and—no tears! They're fine athletes." Chris says she despises professional boxing because there is no concern for safety. It's not even a sport, she thinks. ("Some of us had no choice," I start. But I shut up.) If it took time for women to be allowed to take their corners, Chris's own story shows that becoming the "third woman" in the ring was just as hard a path.

"The Golden Gloves is a good-old-boy network. They never wanted women in there. At first, I'd get in the ring and there'd be dead silence. Or else they'd yell stuff."

"Like what?"

"Oh, like, 'Hey split tail! Whatja doin' in da ring?' Or, 'Nice rack, doe!' Charming, huh?"

We all repair to the lobby and mill about. I chat with various people and gather how outside New York women have had to fight hard in order to fight at all. Frank Murphy of the Somerville Boxing Club in Massachusetts recalls his first words to Raphaelle Johnson, the first New England female Golden Gloves champion and one of his two finalists here.

"I told her, 'You're never going to box in New England. It'll never happen in my lifetime.'" He laughs. "But she says, 'I wanna box. If you don't let me here I'm going somewhere else.' Then sparring, one of my boxers—a hundred seventy pounds—hit her in the nose and she seriously tried to destroy him. I said to Ralphie, 'Holy *shit*, we got a fighter!' When you can take a hard punch and your eyes water and you see the little dots and you come back . . . "

"I have a temper in the ring," explains Raphaelle, a 112-pounder. "My opponent pays for what I've been through. Women are up against a lot more in life in general. I feel like I've been fighting a lot before."

"There were times last night when I forgot whether it was men or women fighting," enthuses Dr. Joe Estwanik, the tournament doctor. A sports medicine physician and orthopedic surgeon, Estwanik is chair of the Sportsmedicine Committee of USA Boxing; he also organizes the annual Ringside Physician's Course at the U.S. Olympic Training Center and has just published a book, *Sportsmedicine for the Combat Arts*. I seek from him a definitive statement on the safety of boxing for women, a subject that can easily induce hysteria.

"There are no different injuries in women so far," is his pronouncement.

Then, over by the couches, I spot the Irishman Jimmy Finn of the IWBF with whom I've chatted regularly for three years on the phone, but have never actually met. I have always found him a flawless proponent of women's sports and have stolen his favorite illustration of our qualifications—the Irish Republican Army's instructions for their terrorists to "shoot the woman first. Shoot the mother. She's the most dangerous." But today he disturbs me. He is toting a large portfolio of glamour photos of female pro fighters—Laura Serrano, Dee Dufoe, Hannah Fox, Yvonne Trevino, Fredia Gibbs, Bridgette Riley (but not Lucia or Kathy or Jill). The women are all posed in revealing clothes, boxing gloves, shiny hair, and makeup. Occasionally they're fighting. Finn wants to start promoting, and this is his catalogue of contenders. He says he knows what boxing needs now.

"What, cheesecake?" I ask. "Cheesecake with ketchup?"

"No, no, no, not cheesecake," he says, "I'm just interested in great athletes. And if they're beautiful . . . " And as I flick through the book, he's saying, "Oh yes, that's Valerie, beautiful girl, beautiful girl," and "Oh yes, she's lovely that one, Sonia, really beautiful," then he turns to me. "You'll be wanting to get some photographs, then. Presentation, you know."

"No," I say.

"You know," says Jimmy, ignoring that, "men's boxing's dead."

"Well, it's in a bad way," I agree.

"You see, it's because—and excuse me, but—it's when these black guys started coming out with their attitude, you know, their big baggy shorts and all that stuff."

"Well, I don't think *that's* what went wrong with boxing. Big shorts."

Thoroughly depressed, I excuse myself, slink off to my room, and switch on the TV. And, blow me down, I'm just in time to catch a rerun of an infamous fight I had kicked myself for missing three weeks before: Holyfield-Tyson II, the ear-biting incident. Only it wasn't Tyson I cared about so much as the undercard featuring Christy Martin's long-awaited match-up with her old nemesis, Andrea DeShong. The fight, in which DeShong is knocked out in the seventh, is bloody, intense, vicious, mean-spirited. Identifying with my friends' imminent battles, not to mention my own next fight, I endure a wave of nausea. Chris Filiberto's judgment that "pro boxing is not even a sport," Jimmy Finn's cheesecake catalogue, and my own carnival mismatch troop mockingly through my head. The same things that appeal about this lark—that boxing exists outside regular society, that it is fueled by the dark impulses, that it is an extreme and naked exercise in control—have flipped over onto their backsides, and it all looks uncivilized, beastly. What's to admire in Tyson, that coward, chewing off chunks of ear? Or Christy Martin, who fights solely for fame and cash? And the amateurs on hand here are hardly the ladies' dance of honor that everyone in Augusta claims. It does seem that Paul Gallico, the founder of the Golden Gloves, and indirectly the father of this tournament, had a point: "Ring fighting," he said, "has never added an iota to the stature of anyone as a human being worth his salt." In the ring, after all, murder, though rare, is legal.

———————

The Bell Auditorium is filling up. I'm ringside in the press section, next to Steve Ross, director of media and PR for USA Boxing. Augusta is the first time Steve has witnessed women fighting and he's smiling with shock.

"They're amazing, quite different from the men—the lack of fear. They're staying in to trade punches. This one woman yesterday, she was like an animal out of the corner, lots of roundhouses, no defense. It was a vendetta. She looked like she took it personally."

Is Steve praising or mocking them? (*Us*, I should say. I, too, am taking this personally, the future of our sport being in the balance.) I think he is speaking admiringly—though, personally, I would rather see skills than all-action brawls. Tonight, it turns out, will be replete with both.

The first bout, however—165-pounders Brenda Derby from Maryland and D.C. girl Lakiea Cotter—has neither. The Marylander being hopelessly overmatched, the ref stops the bout midway through the second round. It is ugly and unfair, unfair that this beginner level should be witnessed by the public. I grit my teeth. Behind the press bench, so does the flock of athletes, all suited up in their blue or red shorts and tank tops, pacing. Sky, whose bout is the penultimate, is quite relaxed and sociable. There's a sort of wartime spirit backstage, she tells me, with everyone pulling together, probably because they're all exhausted, having fought at least one bout already. It's kinda weird, she observes, how much they're all rooting for each other; quite different from the Golden Gloves. Partisanship goes out the window after you've spent eighty hours getting acquainted. For her third fight in three days, Sky is not bothering to be nervous.

"I can't lose. I'm Japanese. It's the fear of humiliation, the shame of coming back to the gym a loser."

The next bout is all New York, the 119-pounders Patricia Alcivar and Leona "Baby Tyson" Brown, the latter stale from her three bouts in three days. They are both skilled, and the fight is close—the opposite of the first—but Brown, an inside fighter, has trouble finding her rhythm against the kinetic Alcivar, who has never looked so strong. In the end, the split decision goes to Alcivar. (On the strength of that performance she will be voted USA Boxing's first ever female "Athlete of the Month," in August, beating out all 21,577 registered male boxers.) Next up, Melissa Salamone versus Laura Kielczewski, another exemplary bout pairing two New Yorkers—though Salamone has recently moved to Miami. Of all the athletes tonight, Salamone is the star turn. She has all the flashy pro moves, the control to use them legally, and the show-womanship of the born champion. Laura spends every second of the three two-minute rounds efficiently fending her off. On being buckled into the inevitable belt, Melissa stares into the camera, dukes up, feints a rapid combination with her tongue out, draws a finger across her throat, then holds it up. Number one? Obviously. Arrogant? Certainly. But on her it looks fabulous.

I run into Laura in the ladies' room afterwards.

"I was praying I wouldn't draw Melissa," she grins. "I just boxed her, I'm happy I didn't get creamed."

To cut the report short, there are no surprises. Lutrick outboxes the girl from Pittsburgh. Evelyn Rodriguez makes meatloaf of LaTasha, though Ms. Washington from Washington fights a good fight. Alicia Ashley, in her balletic, stand-up-straight converted kick-boxer's style, wins a split decision. The girl from Decatur, green, very determined, and, needless to say, beloved of the crowd, manages to make Veronica go the distance for a change; but Veronica wins, as always. And Sky does her thing, rushing her hapless opponent—the other one from Frank Murphy's Massachusetts club—assaulting her with berserk punches, and winning by sheer willpower. The heavyweights, being the most entertainingly prone to damage each other, are always saved for last in amateur tournaments, but USA Boxing might consider rethinking this for the women. The final fight is a nasty one-sided brawl, which is stopped in the first round.

On the requisitioned school bus back to the Sheraton ("the cheese bus," as Sky has it), the mood is subdued—half the passengers lost, after all, and the New Yorkers have to get up in four hours for a dawn flight home. As it turned out, Sky was prescient about the dominance of our hometown: the only New Yorkers who lost, Laura Kielczewski and Leona Brown, lost to fellow New Yorkers. Leona is forlorn. "I was just too tired," she complains.

I am not the only imposter on the bus. Jimmy Finn is sitting up front, surrounded by a cache of winners. For him this is a recruiting drive. He leans into Patricia Alcivar, talking into her ear. I catch the odd word.

"You've got a great future," he's saying. "You know, you're a beautiful girl. You'll be wanting to get some photographs done. . . . "

———————

It soon becomes clear that referee Chris Filiberto's view of professional boxing was not shared by those she policed in Augusta, as champs and silver medalists merrily throw their hats in the ring for a purse. Leona Brown, Melissa Salamone, and Patty Martinez (who took the 106-pound belt on a walkover) all aced their pro debuts within weeks of the Nationals. Alicia Ashley, Denise Lutrick (or Moraetes, after marriage), and Laura Kielczewski followed within the year.

None of the national champs were quite ready in time to appear on Jackie Kallen's IFBA all-female card at Biloxi's Grand Hotel and Casino (casinos are a natural habitat for boxing) two weeks after the Nationals. Neither was I; but true to Colin's prediction, I was approached. When I saw the fights, boy was I glad not to have been half of one. Something had happened, a quantum leap in the standard. Suddenly everyone could *really* fight, with only a couple of the sixteen boxers anything less than polished, professional, and impressive. In a gratuitous throwback to "foxy boxing," the card was dubbed *Leather and Lace*, perhaps an effort to dupe porn surfers into paying the $39 pay-per-view charge. If the commentators were to be believed (and they weren't), the ruse was successful, since "thirty million homes" were reported to have ponied up to watch the prime-time bouts. Still, regardless of how many cable subscribers really tuned in, the hall was full to bursting, with every seat in the 1,750-capacity auditorium sold, so the atmosphere, even via the TV screen, was electric.

First up were the flyweights Anissa Zamarron, the Texan who, in her first fight, beat Jill Matthews, and Brenda Rouse, a mother of two from Oklahoma.

"She told me she can't keep her six-year-old out of the gym," said one of the two commentator guys, who kept oscillating between fight reporting and shallow incredulity. "Can't you just imagine him at school, Phil? 'My mother can beat up your father.'" Tonight, Anissa beat up Brenda in eight rounds of quality boxing. Phil and Steve were impressed, you could tell. The more impressed they were, the more their comments damned with faint praise.

Fredia "The Cheetah" Gibbs was next, up against a veteran—too veteran—Gail Grandchamp in the evening's worst mismatch. Gibbs was true to her nickname, and not just by virtue of her leopard-print loincloth. Bounding out of her corner, in ruthless attack-cat ring style, she pounced on the deer-caught-in-headlights Grandchamp, who looked to be in poor shape (though that can be deceptive: Andrea DeShong, Dora Webber, and Christy Martin can all appear flabby—until the first bell). Gibbs smothered her in punches, and the standing eight count arrived in perhaps thirty seconds, ending the fight when the ref spotted one of Grand-champ's teeth on the canvas. Phil thought that was hilarious.

The four title fights followed, for the featherweight, bantam-weight, lightweight, and welterweight belts, all of them as yet un-claimed. First, Bonnie "The Cobra" Canino, a converted kickboxer from Florida who used to train with Battling Barbara Buttrick, met Beverly Szymanski, from Detroit's Kronk. Though Canino was experi-enced, which won her the title, Szymanski was impressive, hitting hard, moving well. And that was the alarming and exhilarating part of it— that all these fantastic fighters had been secreted all over the place, quietly working away, now ready to climb onto the twenty-by-twenty stage in front of the cameras. It is what I had hoped to see. It was a vision of the future right here, professional fighters who happened to be women. Phil and Steve were beginning to come around.

"A cardio workout with a little leather bouncing off your head,

Phil?" joked Steve during the first round of the next bout, for the bantamweight belt, wherein the stunning, seasoned southpaw Yvonne Trevino (6-1-1, 5 KOs) met Susanne Riccio Major (3-1-1, 1 KO), who, Steve informed us, had a three-year-old named Evander Ali Major. By the late rounds, the commentators had been won over.

"Heart and soul and intestinal fortitude," Phil was saying. "This is where the miles of conditioning really pays off."

"They've shown they are professional at what they do," agreed Steve, as the huge and gaudy belt was strapped onto Yvonne Trevino, swamping her.

And so it went, eight brilliant bouts seen by maybe a million people.

"I want to give the Lord the glory of this fight," announced Tracy "Lady" Byrd (6-0, 4 KOs), sister of top-ranked heavyweight contender Chris, the fighter with Romans 8:28 embroidered on her trunks and the new owner of the IFBA lightweight belt. "I worked on bobbing and weaving with my brothers," Tracy explained for the cameras, "and if my dad wasn't an excellent cutman, I wouldn't have won."

Compared to all those ten-round battles, the main event was disappointing. It was Kathy Collins, looking to add the IFBA welterweight belt to her IWBF one, in the hope of becoming the first female fighter ever to become a sanctioned dual champion. This she achieved in the second round with an easy TKO over the inexperienced and barely conditioned Christina Berry (she'd been sparring three days a week for six weeks, said Phil, as if this were an acceptable regimen).

"I'd like to thank the Lord first of all for giving me the strength and the knowledge and the power," yelled Kathy to the audience watching at home. She was infectiously euphoric, and I hoped this might erase her desire to prove herself in gym sparring anytime soon. We were slated for another session in a couple of weeks, though whether it was the "moving around a bit for the cameras" kind or the real kind I wasn't sure. Because during all the spectator action, my own plans had been moving along. There was the card in Port Chester, New York, next month, then the Moscow (Russia, not Idaho) bout a week later, and having rashly said yes to both, I was busy deciding which one to drop. Boxing can be unhealthy like that. It encourages the illusion that you are in control.

10

My Heart

A snapshot of my glittering career: five smiling champions in street clothes, belts on their hips, Golden Gloves around their necks, Bruce the proud dad, and me in front, red nose to match my gloves— the official commemorative photo of the National Champs' party, complete with another Gleason's green-icing cake and soda pop. Bruce insisted I get in the picture with Veronica, Evie, Alicia, Patricia, and Sky.

"No, no, I didn't fight," I argued, blinking back tears (agh, I'm *pathetic*).

"But you have to be in it. You're my *professional*," said Bruce, kindly.

I mean to prove him right. The Moscow bout is the first of its kind, a post–Cold War eight-fight card featuring seven of the famous trainer Bob Jackson's boys and one female. Bruce doesn't know who the Russian girl is, but he thinks she's a 139-pound amateur. Soon this

will be amended to 132 pounds, two national amateur titles, and a 4-0
pro record—it's Zoulfia Koutdoussova. Since I am weighing 152,
I would not only have to drop twenty pounds in a month but I'd be
the grass-green girl again, struggling with the shock of the ring
while she called on her relatively vast experience. Now, much as
I enjoy the underdog status, I don't like it *that* much. After Philly,
I vowed my next bout would be against an equal. And as for losing
twenty pounds—once my permanent ambition—this now looks plain
stupid. I have faced it, I have embraced it, I am heavy, and, having
learned at NYU how to calculate my fat percentage, I no longer hate
myself for it. At 152, I'm carrying a mere fourteen percent fat and it's
probably impossible to hit 132 so fast without depleting my ammuni-
tion, my muscles. Reluctantly, I ask Bruce to find someone else, and
in a few days he's booked her. Dora Webber will go to Russia.

But all is not lost—there's still the bout in Port Chester, New
York, on one of John Beninati's cards. John B. is my new promoter
pal, who Bruce says has a huge crush on me. I have no idea about that
until he calls me on the Gleason's pay phones (every fight guy in
America has those pay phone numbers—you don't give out any information until you know who they are and why they're asking) to make
me the offer. He says we've met many a time.

"You know me," he says, laughing, and, the next day, when he
arrives at the gym with a contract, the penny drops.

"Why do you think I was always ringside?" he says. "You're sparring here, I'm here. You're sparring there, whoosh, I'm there. Did
you never wonder why? I've been watching you for a year!"

We drive out to Port Chester so I can make an appearance on the
local radio sports show and plug the card.

"Women's boxing's a gimmick," John declares in the car. "It'll
never catch on."

"So why promote it?"

"They like it. Anyway, it's an excuse to hang out with you." He
claims I've been disdainful of him. I insist I haven't been ignoring
him; I was just absorbed in training.

"Drop-dead gorgeous women like yourself shouldn't box," he says. "J.D., she can fight all she likes, but you shouldn't be allowed."

"So why did you sign me up?"

"Oh, I'm getting you a tomato can. I'll find someone who looks really tough but who you can chop up into little pieces."

"You mean you haven't found an opponent?"

"Not yet, but we'll get you some girl."

Oh no. I want to win, but even if everyone else has been papered, I want it real. Still, I do the broadcast with a fictional opponent in the putative other corner, another performance.

John B. is entertainingly eccentric. Turns out he was in music before boxing (and in wrestling—he promotes that, too); he used to be the Smiths' manager. He's really good looking, tall with pale green eyes, and this deferential mooning is therefore all the weirder. Extreme versions of this sort of admiration have been coming my way lately via the Internet, which is still a slightly subversive mode of communication, not yet the money minting machine it would be in five more minutes. For a trendy Web site, I'd just done an arty piece about boxing, including a women's section, and it has caused some lurid e-mails.

"Hi Kate, I am a 30 y.o. guy from Atlanta who just recently took up boxing. It is extremely strenuous as you know!" says one. "The women in my gym have shown very impressive skill. I would love to find out how well I would do against them in a fight. A few of the more experienced women could probably substitute my chin for a speed bag! Another would enjoy dominating me with her quick jabs and double or triple jabs. She would always target my eyes, making them puff up to the size of a couple of plump tomatoes with little slits. . . . "

Curious as to his response—will he dematerialize when confronted, like a flasher?—I reply. What's the appeal, I ask, in being beaten up by women?

"I am sexually submissive outside of boxing," he replies, "but it would be a turn-on to lose to a woman in the ring. It's not the pain

I enjoy as much as it is the fact that I am being dominated by a woman in a fair fight. Getting knocked out cold could be a little dangerous, so I think about getting my face rearranged by a woman and that also gets me off. The thing with the eyes was just a scenario. . . . "

I decline politely his invitation to spar in Atlanta, and, glad of his candor though I am, I'm perturbed because I simply cannot empathize. In my brothel-receptionist days, everyone seemed suddenly to be selling sex, buying it, faking it, mocking it, and the Atlanta e-mails bring that back. The soft end of S&M is very mainstream, long appropriated to impart edginess to liquor and fashion commercials and Madonna, but the proliferation of female fight Web sites my correspondent told me about, this is harder stuff. You should check them out, he said, especially the Ring Mistresses. Those girls are so sweet. *Sweet?* At the brothel, every other caller asked if we had wrestling mats, and lately, in Gleason's locker room I've been offered several private wrestling gigs, with guys in hotel rooms who want to lose. ("Two hundred bucks cash! Easy work!") Call me a prude, but I don't relish this any more than I wanted to spar with Dennis the masochist. The subtexts are unerotic, they make me long for an old-fashioned boyfriend, a desire that I am hazily aware of having been fighting through fighting—because I fear that if I invite a man in emotionally and physically, I'll be vulnerable in the ring. An open heart is not the boxer's kind, and, like Lucia Rijker, I'm not taking that risk. Unlike her, I suspect I may be using the ring as an excuse not to risk my heart. Instead of a relationship, I've got a thing with a totally unsuitable twenty-two-year-old boxer of breathtaking beauty, and now John B.'s unrequited crush on me. It's defensive.

I've come to believe that there is a fundamental difference in the way women fight versus the way men fight, and it is about our sexuality. Battle is the antithesis of female sexuality, whereas male sexuality is fused to it. Girl fights are a male turn-on because of the abandon, the passion they see displayed. It reminds them of women caught in flagrante delicto. Now, it is true that I must open up and let it all flow in order to fight well, but that opening up in the ring is the diametric opposite of letting go in bed—not the opposite of male-pattern emotionless sex-as-sport but of true body-and-soul lovemaking. I'm beginning to think boxing might mark the very crossroads of modern femininity and old-fashioned masculinity. Boxers in the forties, when even the word "sex" itself was risqué, were supreme sex symbols and movie stars' consorts. After the sixties and feminism, the sexual meta-phor of the ring became more overt. For instance, in his book *The Fight*, about the 1975 Ali-Foreman "Rumble in the Jungle," the bel-licose antifeminist Norman Mailer quotes a bit of training advice from Ali's sidekick, Bundini Brown: "You got to get the hard-on, and then you got to keep it. You want to be careful not to lose the hard-on, and cautious not to come."

So what about *my* hard-on? After *I* come, I experience a surge of energy (he falls asleep). Men, famously, swear off sex before a bout—or used to—so as not to weaken the legs, not to lose that hard-on, that virility. And the female word for virility is . . . what? Fertil-ity? Vampishness? Gusto, perhaps. A woman's sex drive is just as integral a part of her as a man's is to him; our hard-ons happen on the inside, and, when aroused, we are every bit as sexually aggressive as men. I'm not sure where that drive is located when we step in the ring, but I do suspect it sits in a separate compartment. Could it be that in fighting, men incorporate a drive that is normally external, whereas women detach that which is normally incorporated? Joyce Carol Oates in *On Boxing* cites Sugar Ray Leonard's desire to come out of retirement solely to beat Marvin Hagler—"I want Hagler, I need that man." "The Opponent," claims Oates, "is the rival for one's own masculinity. . . . " Was Jen Childers, then, the rival for my femininity? Absurd. I *donned* my aggression to fight her, lured it out of hiding places. Despite her "low blow" complaint, the only time I actually hit her below the belt was when I said, "Well done, you're a brute," after the decision. It was a vicious compliment. She had lost the femininity fight.

That fear of mine, that entering a relationship would deplete my forces, that I would be capitulating to a femininity that doesn't function in the ring, is spurious, I know. Lucia Rijker may share it in her fashion, but scores of boxers disprove it, and there exists an interesting subgroup of boxers who are intimate with, even married to, their corners—among them Kathy Collins, Christy Martin, Patty Martinez, Shakurah Witherspoon (heavyweight champ Tim Witherspoon's sister-in-law), Denise Moraetes (née Lutrick; it was love at first sight when she met Tom, Augusta Boxing Club's director, at the Nationals), and Jill Matthews, whose husband is now her manager. What a sweet thing to have your lover in your corner, literally, not just metaphorically. I see how this could come to pass when you work so closely together.

Since the fight, there have been subtle changes in my status around here. First, everyone at Gleason's tells me how much better I am now, so I know I'm getting dissed when my back is turned. This is an excellent compliment. Second, there is an extra bond between Colin and me. We talk more, trust more. His old friends from Guyana, he has told me, are dead, except for one, who betrayed him. He doesn't make real friends now, he says, because if a bunch of guys were kidding around and one of them happened to say something that got him angry, he thinks he could kill the man. It breaks my heart that he considers himself so dangerous. I only saw that side of him one time, when a brittle guy at the gym—one of those with yellowed clippings on his locker about the time he went the distance against Duran—got in some pointless argument with Colin's "big daughter," Sandy Gutierrez, which is almost impossible given her shy demeanor. She'd been provoking him playfully, but he got riled, started calling her names, pushing her, poking a finger at her. Sandy, quite capable of decking him, took the high road, but Colin saw red. It took everyone in the gym to restrain him.

Colin had suffered a loss recently that he dismissed as nothing. Gary St. Clair, his star prospect who never did roadwork, had been lured away by the Don King machine. Colin had started Gary as a teenager in Guyana and the kid had followed him to the famous Kronk in Detroit, then to Gleason's, where Colin got him his first American fights and got him noticed. As soon as Gary went to King's training camp in Miami, he stopped calling; he was there six months and Colin never heard from him—only through the grapevine, which informed him that the kid was being used as a sparring partner, often with bigger fighters, and was getting not a whiff of a bout.

"He shouldn't have ditched you," I said.

"I don't care," Colin said, with a shrug. "He can do what he want."

"But Gary's different," I said. "You were close."

"Nah," he spat. "That's boxing."

"I thought you said boxing was about love."

"I'm not going to help them anymore," he said, ignoring what I said. "Some of those boys, I knew them since they was little kids. I teach them everything. They don't have money, I still train them. Gary's stupid. I'm not going to help them anymore. I'm just going to train Americans. And women. You wouldn't do that, Kadie."

He was right, but this bothered me. I was not a twenty-three-year-old incredibly talented man; I was a thirty-five-year-old hard-working but deeply flawed female athlete. Colin had stars in his eyes about me since that fight. He thought I was set to soar. He also acquired a little gleam in the eye about me, which I treated as a running joke between us. I worried that he was serious and squashed the thought whenever it popped up. My emotions about boxing were complex enough all by themselves.

"When you ask me over to watch the Biloxi fights?" Colin would say, doing a Groucho Marx with the eyebrows.

"Ah, shuddup," I'd say and feint a jab to his chin. But he did come over to watch the fight tape, bringing a bag of grapes, and we sat on the sofa and discussed the bouts and ate grapes, and I heard him hoping and got uncomfortable and shooed him out. Much as I had grown to adore Colin, I wanted him to remain my trainer and my friend. He kept mentioning how sweet that afternoon in Philly before the fight had been, and I, without dissembling, would agree, ignoring what he really meant. The afterimage of that day had messed with our symbiosis. Lately, if I'd refuse to spar one day, or if I'd whine about how badly I thought I was performing, Colin would no longer just tell me to shut up and get on with it, or mock me ("You're being a *giiiirl*"—same taunt as with the guys); he'd let me get away with it. He admitted it was hard for him not to see me as "his girl" when I seemed vulnerable—or, I suppose, feminine.

"I'm not your girl," I'd snap.

"I know, I know."

"So don't make special rules. I'm here to box."

"You not like Corey or Gary. They vex me."

"Yeah, but I need bullying, too, sometimes."

"Kadie, if you don't feel like it, you don't pay me no heed."

"Oh, I guess you're right."

"You're smart. I don't want to see you get hurt. It take one punch."

"Well, that's for me to worry about."

"Maaay-be. But after boxing . . . "

"After boxing." I wished he wouldn't say that. What if he really did have his heart on the line? No, of course he didn't. It was just proximity, like an office crush. I mean, we saw each other all the time, three hours a day, six days a week. There were many aspects to our bond—coworkers, teacher and student, daddy (he could be more paternal with me than with his twelve-year-old daughter), couple of kids (he'd play tricks, tap my shoulder then disappear; he still does), friends, confidants (though we never discussed lovers), mom (I'd bully him about his health), but no sexual tension. That takes two. We trusted each other; he respected my space, and I needed my space.

———————

Kathy time comes around—as planned since before she became the dual champion. La Collins looks slick in the color-coordinated gear of Everlast Woman, her new sponsor. Myself, I am very hungover. In fact, I may still be drunk. Yesterday was my birthday, making it precisely a year and two weeks since Kathy and I last did business, though I've seen her regularly at the Gleason's Friday-night White Collar Sparring sessions. It turns out this is, after all, a "moving around for the camera" occasion—ABC, I think, is doing a feature on her—and I'm too tired to be nervous. Kathy demonstrates the use of the heavy-bag. She is killing that thing—being double champ seems to have doubled her power. I point out to Colin how I am in no fit state to invite a similar whumping. She's double champ; I'm seeing double. If she hits me too hard, I might hit the wrong one back. Colin raises his eyes to heaven. He's forever smelling my breath and checking my bloodshot gaze in a parody of the worried parent. This is the first time he'd have been justified in scolding, but he doesn't.

Kathy and I agree to make it look good at no risk to ourselves. She's forgotten her mouthguard.

"Huh," snorts Colin, "she doan forget it. She want you to take it easy, but she be going hard. Remember what they say to Lisa?"

But I trust her. It's like talking to an old friend you haven't seen for ages; it's as if we'd sparred yesterday. I'm comfortable. But the guys are bored, they want blood. I have her on the ropes, then in the corner—she went there like a pony, it was nothing—and I glimpse Hector, Menacho, Sinbad over her shoulder willing me to do damage, and Colin's right here: "Uppercut, uppercut, body. Come on! Bodeee!" and I'm ignoring them all. In the breaks, I preempt the harangue: "I know I know, I let her go. I told you, I'm not into it today. You think she'd just lay there and take it? This isn't a fight. Remember Veronica. . . . "

It is the least eventful, most enjoyable of sparring sessions. Though nobody says as much, I know Kathy was not "on" today either, and she is guiltily grateful afterwards, she and Frankie very friendly. This disgusts Gleason's. I let the gym down. I feel a bit guilty, too, because Colin lost face. "I understand," he says, crestfallen. "You doan want to go hard today, thass cool." It is not cool. Today I have trashed my place in the pecking order, lost the modicum of status I had won by fighting. To be honest, I'm more angry than remorseful— stupid little boys, wanting a war just for kicks and pride. They wanted to control my body, make it attack. How dare they tell me what to do! Boxing is all about that, though. You think you're an individual, fighting alone, but you're not your own boss. Others buy you, manage you, sell you, pull you out, send you in. If you're a fighter, you must fight. I don't realize it, but today I have begun to rebel.

———————

I got over the hangover, got serious—tomato can or not, I'm fighting in four weeks and I must spar. But with whom? There's Darius, the former pro about my height, and Charlie, a featherweight who wears a blue scuba-diving suit and spars at least twelve rounds a day.

"I have to," he tells me. "I have a lot of anger. See, I was messed up by my ex-wife. It's in there, and it's pain." Yet Charlie is a gentleman in the ring. He hits hard at innocuous targets like forehead, shoulder, biceps at worst, but pulls his punches to the face, temples, chin. He keeps denying this, but eventually he comes clean.

"So when you spar with me," I want to know, "that's not anger, is it?"

"That's more fun. That's exercise. With the guys, I get rid of the anger."

"Charlie," I say, "next time, will you go hard with me like you do with the guys? Could you do that?"

"I can try," he says, looking doubtful.

"No, really, because if you hold back, how will I ever learn?"

"Yeah, okay, we'll try it," he says. And he swears blind he's taken off the brakes, but I've seen him go for it, I know he's sparing me.

I spar with Zab Judah. He's 8-0 as a pro now, and recently won at the Garden—the big one, not the Theater. He's lost exactly one round since he turned professional, is number one on every fight magazine's hot list, and within a year will have won the USBA and IBF junior welterweight belts to cement things. Zab doesn't entirely hold back and I even get some shots in, so I'm pretty pleased with myself until I get to the locker room, where Evelyn is waiting.

"Zab making you look bad there," she declares, matter-of-factly. "Don't you *hate* that?" ("Good work, Kate" is what she'd said at the ring just now.)

"No, not really. I like that he went for it."

She looks at me, then erupts into grave concern.

"Ooh, how did you get that on your nose? He wasn't hitting hard."

"Well, he did pop me with a couple."

"Really? Didn't *look* like he was hitting hard."

Colin says I should spar with Evelyn. I know I should. She's the only woman the right size, but she scares me—more *outside* the ring than in it. Today, she greeted me like this:

"Hey, Kate! Looking flabby. What happened to your definition?"

Whenever a new girl appears, she gives her the lowdown on the boxing life. "If you work hard," she concludes, "maybe one day you'll be a great champion like me."

I think she'd try to kill me.

———————

I'm saved by the bell—of the phone, that is—when Dora Webber's people call Bruce seeking Kathy Collins for sparring. Kathy's not available, so they get the consolation prize: me. I love Dora's ring style. She's a wily fighter with tremendous power and a decade more experience than any woman I've encountered. She actually went the distance with Rijker. But I don't love her attitude: *I'm gonna make her head spin like a Dutch windmill* ... I can't sleep the night before her visit. It must seem as if the terrors are my constant companions in the gym, but almost the opposite is the case. Between highlights march hour upon hour of drudgery, instruction, pedestrian sparring, road-work, lots of fun and practice, practice, practice. It took a long time to reach this EKG period, long plateaus interspersed with red peaks, to have boxing stab me like a good horror movie with lovely dread.

Meanwhile I'm pestering Bruce for word on my Port Chester opponent. Get John to call me, please? I beg. It's odd. Normally, he's looking for excuses. I have a bad feeling. The imminence of Dora compounds it. She needs the work as much as I do—she is sparring for Russia—but what if she is a grudge holder, looking to avenge those evil draw decisions? What if she hates women? My bout is days away. I am ready, but it doesn't smell right. John B. won't even return calls disguised as innocent questions about the tickets I'm supposed to sell (most boxers do this, even famous ones). Bruce suggests I call the Athletic Commission to see when I'm down for the CAT scan. You don't fight in New York State without that. Even though I had a premonition, when I call and find there is not one single female on the list for that card, I can barely believe it. What a creep. Afraid to tell me. It feels like they canceled Christmas. Then again, it's like I passed the breath test after a pint of vodka.

Dora day. She's late. I watch Jill Matthews go a few rounds with former heavyweight champion Tim Witherspoon, half hoping Dora won't show and I can be next with him. But now here she comes with her trainer. Snub-nosed and square-shaped, blond hair in a seventies mullet, Dora is not a smiler. After some time, changed and warmed, she joins me in the ring and we await the next bell. It's the worst bell-waiting I've ever done, including the fight, and my dread persists, uncharacteristically, into the first minute. I'm on a hair trigger, catching jabs that aren't there, pulling my own, weedily aimed at her headgear. I drop my gaze to her throat, a Reggie Forde trick—he says it focuses you and disconcerts your opponent—but I still can't stop using my shoulders as earmuffs. Dora speaks.

"Hey, sweetheart, relax!" she says. I crack a smile. "There you go," she says. "See, this ain't so bad."

No, I guess it's not. I calm down, but only a little bit. After all, these exchanges are exploratory and I don't know what a heavier punch might buy. In the ring, Dora is quite the knockout artist, and I don't know how volatile she is, or how elastic the sparring protocol is when two women from different gyms are paired. She wanted Kathy for revenge, I assume, because of the recent dubious draw decision. Is she planning to take that out on me? Well, there's nothing to do but bite the bullet. I let my right connect with the middle of her face (what an asset that tiny nose is, dished at the bridge like black ones) at about seventy percent power, thinking, *Uh-oh, here we go*, and she accepts it, notes it; we circle, she catches a jab, slips one, sidesteps and—*wham!* There it is. A short, straight right. I think I let it in, I think I wanted it, to get it over. I'm gone; the black appears, but momentarily; a leg wobble. If she followed it with a hook, I'd be down. Wonder if she could have; yes, I bet she could have, but since she didn't, instinct throws a jab for me, so she knows I'm still here. And now it gets really good.

A superior opponent raises your tennis game, and so it is with boxing. Mind you, a fast rally may tax your skill, but a tennis ball won't break your teeth like a volley of punches can, and it just flies away when the pace beats you. Sparring makes me think not of tennis, however, or of the obvious analogy, dancing, but of riding a horse. You are harnessed to each other, moving in sync. You plus horse set the pace and the rhythm. Do we trot now? If I can ride, *I* decide; if I'm not in control, the animal carries me however it likes. Ideally, we work in tandem, moving together. That is how it is today. Dora is such a treat. She has figured out what I can and can't do, and she's pushing my limits. I learn and learn. I'm doing my utmost to best her, but she sees everything coming, does these great feints with her entire torso, not just arms.

"Colin, she's amazing," I keep saying in the breaks.

"She the best woman I seen," he agrees. "She fight like a guy." After me, another girl, a 105-pound novice Colin trains, asks for a round, and Dora nods okay. I figure she'll pull everything like I do with this girl, but Dora waits ten seconds, then knocks her down.

"Suck it up," she says, as the novice climbs back onto her feet, woozily. "Come on! Don't quit!" But she quits. This, too, is instructive. As the visitor, though she outweighs the novice by thirty-odd pounds and tons of experience, Dora did the right thing, but I wonder if I could be such a bully.

"Yeah, there was nobody to fight back in the eighties, nothing going on," Dora says after we're done training. "Now there's all these girls fighting. So I figured, 'Hey, get back in the ring, let's kick some ass.'"

"You getting a rematch with Lucia?" I ask.

"Rijker," she spits. "Hmm. She's the one I want."

"How about Kathy Collins?"

"She knows she lost that. I don't care."

I'm not scared of sparring with Dora anymore, but she is daunting in conversation—tough as a rock, keen on revenge. When Kathy Collins finally gets to spar with her a few months later, I'm gratified when she admits she was terrified at the prospect.

"But she's such a good girl," said Kathy after their second eight-round session. "You can really work with her. Fifteen years' experience! She's the only woman I've sparred I can really learn off."

———

Moscow, September 27, 1997—Dora Webber is the only American to win in eight bouts of U.S.-Russian matchups.

———

Kathy C. needs work again, but I have a deadline or something, and now no fight, so someone else gets her, and I arrive in time to catch the final seconds. A ripped blonde is leaning her full weight on Kathy, inelegantly shoving fists into her sides and occasionally up the middle. Who on earth is this? I follow them to the locker room.

"Man, we were really going for it at the end there," she's saying to Kathy, who I can tell disagrees by her frown and monosyllabic replies. Kathy addresses me instead.

"I'm sick of this shit," she drawls, slouching on the bench in her Everlast Woman. "Roadwork, roadwork, spar, spar, diet, diet …"

"You did get skinny. You dropping a division?"

"Nah, I just picked up my roadwork, to five miles a day. Makes a big difference. But I tell ya, I can't wait till I'm finished with this shit and get a life."

The blond brawler chimes in. "So what you doin'?" she asks me. "You fight in the Gloves?" She's very attitudinal, sort of Martina Hingis meets Latrell Sprewell.

"No—too old. Had one pro fight. How come I've never seen you here?"

"I train real early. Come in from Upstate."

Her name is Angela Reiss. We're the same weight, so we swap numbers to spar sometime.

———

Time passes. I'm fed up. I know what Kathy C. meant—and I'm not even sniffing another contract. Colin is fed up. He has stopped training new guys, plays a lot of dominoes, mentions "after boxing" often enough to be irritating. He gets me the same sparring partners every day, no new challenges—Darry, Charlie, that novice girl—and I'm just too lackadaisical to kick up a fuss. Life outside has trumped boxing. Then one day in late November, Bruce has news for me.

"You know your old friend Don Elbaum?"

"Er, yes."

"He wants to know if you'd like to fight on his card next month."

"Right. What is she this time? Seven foot, twelve-and-oh, all knockouts?"

"Well, no. This time, we'll get *you* the opponent."

"Huh? What happened to his golden girl?"

Turns out Jen Childers retired after our bout. Not only retired, but disappeared, shattering her management contract with Elbaum. Rumor has it, she ran off to California with her boyfriend, who's on the lam after being accused of murder. Elbaum is not happy.

"Jen Childers is over," sneers the small Don a few days later on his Gleason's visit. "She wasn't so hot anyway. Hey, now it's all Kate Sekules!" He is suddenly able to pronounce my name. Craving the closure I missed in September, I say yes to the December fifth card—that's two weeks away. It is an annual holiday charity affair in Scranton, Pennsylvania, a blue-collar town that, so Peter Kahn tells me, was once the mecca for fighters at the beginning of the road, famous for bottomless cards of hard-fought four-rounders. This will be a nostalgia trip, he says. I'll taste the days when everyone cared about boxing, when fights were fights. I'll also be the first woman to have fought pro there. Heading the card of four-and six-rounders is a gen-you-wine championship bout, twelve rounds for the junior middleweight belt—the IBC one. The IBC is the upstart organization whose ratings are not listed in the boxing magazines. The next day an opponent is confirmed at 147 pounds, and I add my signature to hers on the contract. Angela Reiss signed it early this morning.

Now that we have a purpose, Colin perks up, and so do I. Sparring every day, running every morning—like I've been doing all along, only now with gusto. Again, news spreads instantly. "Ah, you'll beat her easy," say the gym critics. "You're better technically, you're in better condition. She's gonna lose." A few hours earlier, they'll have said exactly the same to Angela.

I am delighted when Peter Kahn offers to work my corner. His irreverence is soothing, and he was there last time; he's good insurance. Colin, wanting another sweet Philly afternoon, is peeved, but pretends not to care. The special savor of anxiety is back. I know I'm not sparring hard enough. Colin isn't putting me in with Evelyn or Veronica, or calling up Dora or Kathy, and I'm not calling him on it.

The anticipation of hard sparring is much worse than the reality, and I've been feeling girly and weak before the gym. Then, sparring with Charlie, I manage to pop my left shoulder out of its socket. Bob Jackson, one of the world's best quik-fit body fixers, has a feel. He says it's badly bruised from the dislocation, but I'll be okay. Shelly, on the other hand, a genius physiotherapist whom Colin trains, says I've sprained my supraspinatus and may not be fit to fight. I discover the shoulder hardly hurts when I throw a good clean punch but screams during arm punches, twisted weak punches, wrong punches, and I figure I can work with that. The pain recedes.

———————

One week to go and Colin squints at me appraisingly.

"You weigh yourself?"

"Um, well not this week."

"You gotta weigh yourself, Kadie. You doan wanna be like Julio Cesar Green. He gotta lose ten pound overnight for that title shot. He was in here hours, jumping rope in four sweaters."

Certain I'm still 152 or less, I step on the scale and—oh shit! It claims I'm 158 pounds. My period is coming up. One of my great talents is menstrual edema, during which I can carry as much as ten pounds of extra fluid. It drops off just as suddenly, but, unfortunately, that stage is due after the weigh-in. When I report the tragedy to Colin, he shrugs.

"No problem. Ten pounds is nothing," he says.

"Oh sure, for men it's nothing. You can sweat it out overnight. But you've never seen a *girl* drop ten pounds in a week, have you? *Have* you?"

"Calm yourself. Ten pounds is nothing."

Ten pounds, of course, is the magic number, the amount that every woman, however skinny, thinks she ought to lose; the losing of ten pounds—we all think this—will usher in the new age and solve every problem. I thought I no longer minded the number on the scale, but having to lose that magic ten in a week heralds a regression. Sweat it out, says Colin, who has evidently ignored all my patient explanations about the science of sweating, how the weight loss is temporary; how it floods back the moment a sip of water passes your lips; how wringing out the last drops of moisture from tissues about to be pummeled is assisted suicide (if you dehydrate too fast, your skull will rattle your desiccated brain like a maraca); how over half a person's lean body mass is water and should remain so; how the sensation of thirst is no use as an indication you've dried out, since you've already gone too far when you feel it . . . Of course he hadn't been listening. He knew better.

Sweating and boxing have always been soulmates, because temporary weight loss, a mirage on the scale, is often all that is required. When you see an apparent discrepancy in size between opponents, you're not imagining it. One really is bigger—he's gained ten pounds since the weigh-in that morning. A man can easily lose ten pounds in the steam room or on a long summer run; more when wearing heavy clothes or a sauna suit. The fight gym is one of the last refuges of that crackly plastic top and pants clamped to your extremities by elastic. It isn't healthy to short-circuit your cooling system by preventing the evaporation of sweat, but it's effective, as the lake that collects around your ankles shows. Most boxers stay roughly at their fighting weight specifically to avoid the fatigue of emergency dehydration, but rare is the fighter who has never participated in the tradition of sweating at the last minute.

"I guess I was tired," one guy told me after a loss. "I was five pounds over, so I'd run fourteen miles the night before."

"The worst time," Terry Southerland told me once, "was when I'd taken laxatives and been in the steam room, and that stuff started working right about the fourth round. Man, that was the toughest fight I ever had."

"My own weight," wrote Jake LaMotta, somewhat hyperbolically, "could go from one fifty-five to one ninety-five in a matter of two, three days. . . . I figure that all through my career, I lost four thousand pounds of weight. Two tons." In fact, LaMotta's career was all but finished by sweating, when, weighing 187, he signed at 160 for his final meeting with Sugar Ray Robinson. Despite sweating and starving, he still had to drop the last five pounds in the steam room the night before. He ended up so weak, he described the Valentine's Day bout as a one-victim massacre.

Even though I'm a champion sweater, I don't believe that stupid sweat tricks will work for me, but with nothing to lose but the chance to fight, I decide to do it Colin's way . . . with a little modification. I would not follow his diet of dry toast and ice cream, nor did I believe his assertion that when pushed to the limits, your pores extrude actual fat; but I would try the trickle-and-spit hydration method of sloshing water in my mouth without ever swallowing, and I would train in a sauna suit. While New York is still believing the low-fat, high-carb gospel, I employ the body builders' method of getting ripped for a show, which involves cutting carbohydrates to the bone—the Atkins Diet method. It is a logical regime: carbohydrates are digested slowly, requiring four times their weight in fluid on their long passage through the small intestine; so dropping them restricts edema. Unfortunately, it also drops your blood-sugar level to the basement and makes you feel like a bear in winter. I compromise and eat cereal for breakfast. As for not drinking while training, I decide to ignore what I'd been taught, that about three eight-ounce cups of water per hour is advisable during exercise. Why do boxers take only a squirt from the bottle between rounds? Colin says you've got to get used to thirst, because you can't drink in the middle of a fight, and, anyhow, you don't want fluid sloshing around in your belly. You want it hard and empty, ready to deflect blows. Never mind that even two percent dehydration leads to a ten-to fifteen-percent reduction in stamina, and that two percent of my body weight—three pounds—translates into a mere six cups of water.

After the first workout using the traditional boxing dehydration system, I have lost three pounds.

"See!" crows Colin. "I told you. Ten pounds is nothing."

"It's just fluid," I screech. "It'll be back tomorrow."

But it is not. The next day—five more till weigh-in—I lose another two. This also stays away. I am living on grilled chicken and steamed vegetables. I am tired. I put it down to the gym work, not to mention my day job—a couple of travel articles are due before Scranton—but the fatigue is more than physical. I am weary, sad, and angry. Some chemical reaction has started with the diet, some reflux of hurt from the past, at being made to feel wrong in my body, of concentrating on it to the exclusion of more interesting subjects, of being alienated from it. The reason for the regime has escaped my subconscious ("The incentive to fight is always subconscious," says José Torres) and I'm feeling victimized and isolated, as if I were being forced to do this against my will and nobody understands. I fill an entire journal with self-pity. I feel like weeping but fear it would weaken me. Fear is back, as bad as before. I take it all out on Colin, who bickers right back, and on anyone who crosses my path in the gym, like the white-collar boxer who asks why I'm wearing sweat apparatus.

"Got to drop some pounds," I explain.

"I've never had a weight problem, luckily," he shares. "But you look fine."

"It's not *that*," I snap disdainfully. "It's that I'm fighting Friday."

How dare he assume this is vanity. How dare all men assume that all women care about is losing weight. Oh, this week I am made entirely of Achilles' heels.

A couple of days before Scranton, Patrick Forde, Reggie's cousin, is watching me doing ab work.

"You scared of your own anger," he declares.

I stare back. "In fact, I'm more scared of not having enough," I protest.

"No, you scared of it," he says, with a Mona Lisa smile. "It's the djinn. You know about the djinn?" He says how, back in Guyana, the djinn are malevolent spirits that jump in when your guard is down, when you're tired or angry or asleep, and cause mischief or wreak havoc. "You don't want to let go," says Patrick, "because the djinn will get in and you don't know what happen then."

What if Patrick's right? I think the djinn are the prescription I need. I never did learn to unleash the beast like the boys in the playground who fought for fun. Maybe I am afraid of what I might find if I lost control. I can't evade the truth that although there is much love in the boxing gym, fighting, even sparring, can feel like hate to me, that being hit feels personal. When I hit back, I can't help doing so without anger, through a retarding glue made of my cherished idea of me: that I am reasonable, compassionate, equitable. If I could only hit while feeling that fury I've refracted through tantrums about weight and feminism and injustices, I would be free. I wonder: If the djinn got in, would I still be me? But my defenses against that are impervious; it's not as if I had a choice in the matter.

Three days later I wake up in Scranton soaked in sweat. Out the Motel Six window, bloated snow clouds rest on low concrete block buildings, gray on gray on gray. We got lost in New Jersey, Colin and Peter and I, and finally arrived around midnight, whereupon Peter picked up the front desk phone and dialed Elbaum.

"She's not coming, Don . . . I dunno . . . No, she said she didn't feel like it . . . Well, right, go figure . . . More money? I dunno. Let me ask her . . . Ha-ha-ha . . . Yeah, we just got here. Eight-thirty at the hall? Right . . ." He's giggling like a schoolboy. "It always gets him. Every time. He never learns."

The entire trip was surreal, departing the gym after I'd jumped rope for eight rounds in the plastic suit, then lounging alone in the leather backseat of Peter's big car, like vacations in the parental vehicle, singing Flanders and Swann numbers—an obscure British duo big in the fifties whose entire oeuvre Peter knew—driving around and around industrial Jersey exurbs and down deserted Route 81, tortured by thirst and forbidden to drink a drop, finally feigning sleep while the guys talked boxing. There were so many crossed wires in my memory banks; it was more drug trip than road trip. At Scranton, they were off to the IHOP.

"No dinner for her."

"Hell, let's be gentlemen and see her to her room."

It was as expected: functional, ugly, musty, no towels, no soap, broken TV.

"Remember, Kadie," said Colin, "when you get lonely, one knock for me, two for Peter. No, change it to three, 'cause I might not hear juss one."

"We'll go in one by one," added Peter. "Only, we'll wait till after the fight, 'cause she'll be really tired then. She might beat us up before."

It's a strain and a relief to laugh at the clowns. They turn the thermostat up to full.

"Now, here's our blankets, too. Jump a few rounds of rope before bed." And that's why I wake in a puddle.

———————

My second professional weigh-in and I know the ropes, though the sense of occasion I felt last time is sadly absent, partly due to starvation. I haven't eaten a morsel or drunk a drop for twenty-two hours. Scranton's indoor stadium is indistinguishable from a school hall, with soda dispensing machines and granite staircases and scratched plank floors. We wait in a utility chamber full of molded plastic chairs, Formica tables, and a bunch of white boys, since at least half of every bout—except for mine and the title contenders'—is a local kid. Don Elbaum comes over. "This time you're winning, ha-ha," he says. I preferred him when he wasn't on my side; now he's all nervous— perhaps my snotty-sounding British accent is causing this, or maybe the fix is in. I don't want the fix. Then again, right now, I don't want the fight. *This is one of the worst days of my life, this and yesterday,* I wrote this morning, though I am trying very hard to look forward to it, trying to be like Jill and Lucia with their pre-bout excitement. There's Angela on the other side of the room. This is my first glimpse of her since we met in the locker room at Gleason's after she sparred with Kathy. Back then, I'd learned about her recent move from Brooklyn to the countryside upstate, how she'd decided to opt for a domestic life with her boyfriend, leaving city pressures behind. The nice spot of sparring we'd discussed then would have been entirely consistent with her bucolic plans, but this—this is something else entirely. Now, from opposite sides of the weigh-in room, we exchange hostile nods.

There's an interminable delay while Kenny Ellis (19-0-2), favorite for that IBC title, fails to make weight. The IBC commissioner, here to chaperone his belt, is engaged in Talmudic disputation with the Pennsylvania State Commissioner and Elbaum. Are they going to let him fight with an extra four pounds? It's a title shot after all. A half pound over normally disqualifies, as well he knows. "The scale's off," Kenny is protesting. "I was weighing fifty-two yesterday and I haven't eaten a thing." The IBC commissioner illustrates his organization's image problem by adjusting the equipment. When it's my turn, I hold my breath in case it's heavy, but I am fine. I hit the nail on the head, a perfect 147 pounds. You see, gloats Colin, ten pounds is nothing. And I have to admit, forever after, it does persist in seeming so. The medical is more perfunctory even than Philadelphia's—a blood-pressure check, a pregnancy test, and a question about recent headaches, then it's lunchtime.

A room has been set aside for our buffet in Scranton's finest sports bar, all gaudy carpets and video games, the Eagles and Biggy Smalls competing with the NFL. Boxers dive into the sloppy, oily lasagna the second it appears, vacuuming it all up. I order a chicken salad and soup, my hunger gone. Colin hits the pool table. The more I talk to Peter, the more Colin ignores me, and the more he ignores me, the more I talk to Peter. I'm mad at him for acting sarcastic, like a wronged boyfriend, when what I need is pre-fight succor. Our plan this time is another simple one: come forward, block and make her miss, tire her out, then throw bombs, all bombs, all on target. He's been assuring me I hit so damn hard that this is all I need, but lately, since he learned I'd got an extra corner, he's replaced our customary complicity with childish moodiness. Instead of patiently reiterating what I need to do, he just shrugs and says, "Whatever you like," denying anything's amiss when I call him on it, like he did about Gary: "I don't care." Padwork has been languorous, not urgent; sparring has been silent. I've given up on him. If he wants to be like that, let him. Peter can be my grown-up.

That afternoon is snapshots in my head: Peter and car left at the gas station; Colin and me crossing the icy wasteland back to the motel; me striding ahead, livid, savoring my conniption like a fresh piece of gum. Then: stinking room, I snap off the babbling black TV screen, rip *Vogue* to shreds, lie rigid on my back, eyes speeding, heart pounding, for hours. Then: I dial their room. "Col, would you come over?" A sinking of the heart. Colin, perched on the other bed, holds my hand. I say, "Sorry I've been shitty." He says, "No, that's okay. You be nervous." Making him count the ways I am a good boxer. Making him my comforter. My ire gone flat. Smiling him out the door, relieved that we were close again, perturbed because that is the wrong template. Fitful sleep. Pack.

———————

This dressing room is a giant sports locker containing rack upon rack of basketballs. The ceiling slopes to knee height in back where the couch is; rather homey. Peter, already wearing his cornerman's jacket, is in his element, darting in and out, reporting gossip from trainers and managers of his extensive acquaintance. He says she's down the other end of the hall, which means I must pass her en route to the bathroom downstairs. My neurotic bladder insists I do this immediately, and I nearly collide with her hovering outside what is literally a closet, holding forth to some cops in uniform, her pale hair braided like Heidi's, her eyes so hooded they're black, her gestures exaggerated for my benefit, though she pretends she hasn't seen me. They said she'd be strung out with stage fright, they said she's no good, they said I'll smoke her, but she is the strutting one, not I. Only now do I recall hearing (just after the contract-signing) that she has fought karate for years; she was runner-up in a world seido tournament. She is looking forward to this.

I'm slouched on the couch in my new black-and-blue Everlast robe and trunks. I chose these colors as a joke. Colin's compassion and solicitude continue, which I like and hate equally. Surely he wouldn't be mollifying his guys with one hour to go? When it's time to warm up, we go out to the corridor, punching our way into the opponents' dressing room just like last time, except that here the dressing room is the gents' toilet. Just like last time, we make extra noise on the pads to psych her out, though something tells me this gal isn't having a little cry but is more likely signing autographs for the Scranton Fire Department.

"Remember," says Colin, between combinations, "I'm with you, baby. You know when you get hit, I'm going to feel it too. You'll have my strength as well as yours."

"Ah, that's sweet," I say, but I hate that. Is my own strength not enough?

"No, I mean it, Kadie. I'll be in there with you. We'll kill the girl."

"Colin, I've got to fight. Don't baby me."

"No, no, I'm just saying I'll be feeling every punch."

"Well, let's not feel too many, eh?"

The front of the house is packed when I go for my final pee, and teenage girls in spray-on pants and spike heels don't bother disguising their drop-jaw stares. Suited up in my battle dress, I am part toxic alien species, part guy in drag, not much woman. Angela is so pumped, there's a testosterone fog in the corridor. As for me, on the eve of my period, I am all estrogen. I have told myself the PMS lunacy will work in my favor and am ignoring the weepy, sleepy, clumsy symptoms. There is no warning before the fifth bout, our bout, and now—right now—it is time.

"I have such a good feeling about this, it's ridiculous," says Peter as we stand at the doorway.

"Oh God," I reply.

———————

This time, it is she who takes her corner first, and she's bouncing in place, slapping both gloves together rhythmically. Boy, she's making a meal of this—seen too many fight flicks. "*I* told him that," giggles Peter when the ring announcer tells the crowd I'm from Philadelphia. "May as well get them on your side." Fine, but now I'm not me. The ref does his spiel, the seconds climb out, and here it is, the bell I've waited ten months to hear.

Her pair of jabs don't reach my face, my first stops short of hers, then—ugh, what is *that?*—she does some business around my waist level, then grabs me and spins. Look, let's start over. Plan: I come forward, stepping between her feet to push her back ("Always do that, Kadie, use your strength"), a jab and a right and she's at the ropes, three, four, five uppercuts by me. Good. She performs a U-shaped bob for no reason, and back again, really hammy ones, and then I make my first mistake. Showing the kindness of sparring, I let her off the ropes. Bad, bad idea. And I can't decipher Colin and Peter's yelling, and it's confusion as she—*she, not I*—comes forward, connecting twice with a double jab, missing another, then—YOWCH!—a right hand that pounds my temple like a battering ram, and on with this peculiar thing she does that's going to become very familiar. Her head drops like a charging bull and she walks, her fists going *bom-bom-bom*, one by one into my stomach, and, whoop, she's at my head again and I'm actually backing up—*Colin! Louder, goddammit! What the hell do I do with this creature?*—and now she's leaning her entire body weight on me. Where's the ref? Wish I'd watched her with Kathy.

We are about two-thirds through when I realize with horror that I've forgotten something important—been too distracted to throw a whole lot of punches. So I figure: get out from this gross hug, get after her, and—SLAM!—I eat another of those rights. They come from the side, loop around, really ugly, but, man, they're evil, heavy as anvils, I don't like them. I do not like them. Now I'm aiming for her face and I land some, but I can't taste my own power. Then I feel the ropes at my back and before I can swivel, there's another huge right—she leads with them and I'm not seeing how—and a jab and a leaning-on-me, and I stumble slightly and, horror of horrors, *now* the ref wakes up. He points her to a neutral corner and gives me the standing eight count. How *dare* he? I nod impatiently the whole time, arms akimbo; I want her back, but on the "eight," the bell rings. I hear the crowd burble and bleat—no Blue Horizon mayhem here.

Colin's got his rubber hands on again, extracts the mouth-guard, sponges the back of my neck.

"Okay, Kadie?"

"Yeah, yeah," I say, cross with myself. *Shit*, why didn't I spar harder? Then I'd know how to get around her mugger's tactics. "But she hits incredibly hard. This is not a good night to walk into rights."

"Keep her in front," he says. "When she come in with the right, get under and round with a hook."

The crowd comes to life in a wolf-whistle chorus as the ring girl ponysteps past in satin hotpants and a sports bra, grinning.

"Don't let her back you up like that," Peter chimes in.

"Yeah, what'm I s'posed to do? This bloody head butt thing ... Ah hell."

It's time again. Back again. Bell. The second round starts okay; I'm using my reach, clocking her with a selection of jabs and rights, but again, though she winces, I'm just not feeling my power tonight. She's irritating with this cocky loll, dangling her left arm like an elephant's trunk then swinging it up ineffectually. The ones that hurt come the other way—like this! Fifteen, twenty seconds in, smashing into my cheekbone, my nose, like Veronica's right, only this time I can't quit. It enfeebles me, but I'm okay. There is not a chance in hell I'm going down. And here's the bull act again, now she's not even punching, just clutching and stumbling me forward. *Why?* On the ref's blind side, she pins my right arm, illegally. I wrench it free and hook around her shoulder to the chin, but I'm off balance and it's weak. The rest is monotonous: she just keeps putting me in clinch after clinch and I step back to make space for uppercuts, but my leverage is off. I'm all ass-backward tonight, can't get untracked, treacle feet—oh, I knew it. *I've got to throw more punches!* So sick of this: clutch, separate, clutch, separate, clutch, separate. Bell.

Peter's wielding a cotton swab.

"Blood?" I say, surprised. No blood. I don't know what to say to them. I'm letting them down. I feel horrible. Can we come back tomorrow? I'll be more into it then.

"You okay, Kadie?"

"YES, I'm OKAY. Don't ask that! Don't I look okay? Don't answer that."

In the opposite corner, Angela is on her feet, apparently chatting with her trainer who's not even standing on the apron, but on the floor. Show off. Somehow, I can't absorb Colin's advice; it's sliding right out of my ears. It's halfway, I'm thinking—as the ring-card girl, now in green thong bikini, totters by to a high-decibel leer—halfway through, half done, glass half full. Seconds out, he says. Ding.

––––––––––––

I steam out, winging. Okay, let's get this over with, play her at her own game. I press her back into her corner, nice combinations; she shells up, then I take another slug in the face before allowing the dumb dance to commence again, more like wrestling than boxing at this point. She is so bad, they were right, I should be winning, but

I can't gain enough overview to unravel her, at least while I'm under this barrage of punches. Everyone, they say, has a plan until they get hit. Whenever *she* is in trouble, she ties me up, grabbing on to me like a raft in a storm—is that fair? Judges don't care. They're not scoring amateur, they don't mind a brawl. Here's the bull again. Pressing herself into me as close as a lover, I feel her rasping breath and even this I can't cash in on. I feel, so help me, bored. Look at me, Ma, a thousand total strangers baying while I hold this blond woman's head in my armpit and glumly rabbit-punch the crown. I don't see the point anymore. The punishment I'm taking is nothing, nothing. The bell. Release.

———

I have brought them here under false pretenses. I have stolen a thousand hours of Colin's life. They thought I came to fight but I came to finish fighting. I'm nodding intelligently as Colin explains the way out of her silly clinches, but he may as well be speaking Urdu. While I'm active inside it, the sweet science of bruising makes as much sense to me as particle physics makes to a neutron. My private plan: get out of here. Bell.

———

We are made to touch gloves before the final round, then in we go again and, as in Philly, my entire life has consisted of this idiotic conflict. Like they tell you, there is indeed plenty of time in the ring, time enough to slip a punch and forge a battle plan for the next exchange, or, in my case, plenty of time to ponder this year in boxing, how far I have come. I am, paradoxically, better now—none of her bombs has turned my head and I still have plenty of juice—but undermining my will is the spiritual malaise that drove me into here. I lack something I thought I could find in the ring, but it isn't here; there's nothing here for me. I do know I can throw a punch and take a punch. I have heart—I see the little black dots and keep on going—but I don't have enough to stop another's heart in its tracks. This shames me not at all.

Angela is looming laboriously, like Boris Karloff as Frankenstein's monster. She's run out of gas. Her rights don't sting anymore and her hands are so low, I'm clocking her jaw at will. The trouble is, I haven't any will. All that work and I just don't care. I do try to rouse my soldiers, assisted by a dim awareness of Colin and Peter's encouragement—"Dig! Bring it out!"—but it doesn't do much good. I am about to be made very happy, and not by the decision, which is bound to go against me. It will be some months before I can fully admit it, but what is coming up now really is the final bell.

POSTFIGHT

Stephan Johnson is dead. A routine right cross to the chin put him into a coma from which the man who taught me and thousands of New Yorkers how to punch never awoke. Stephan entered the November 20, 1999, Atlantic City bout knowing it was his final chance at a title shot. His record of 27-9-1 was that of a journeyman. After the gurney left for the emergency room, his trainer-manager spoke to the press.

"Stephan understood what his role was in boxing these days," he said. "He knew he was just the opponent, but he was trying hard to get back into contention, to make the big money. . . . He is such a gladiator. He was always one fight away from hitting the big time."

Stephan was Gleason's first fatality. Some thousand people crammed into the gym for his memorial gathering—family, fighters, friends, and fitness boxers from Equinox Health Club. I never did read the short stories he wrote about the boxing world. He would remember to bring them next time, he said. Now that Stephan is dead, it is harder to believe what the statistics tell us, that boxing, as dangerous sports go, is relatively safe. It lies at the bottom of the mortality league, below horse racing (which claims 128 lives per thousand participants), hang gliding (56 deaths per thousand), and scuba diving (11). Even college football (3 deaths per thousand players) is more likely to kill you than pugilism. A mere 1.3 boxers per thousand die in the ring, yet death by the glove is a horrifying prospect. A public execution.

Stephan died on December 5, 1999—two years to the day since my Scranton fight. The boxing scene has changed radically during those two years—the women's boxing scene, that is. The men have been slugging on: Oscar De La Hoya lost his crown; Roy Jones, Jr., is still unbeatable; Zab Judah looks to be joining him; sundry lawsuits are pending; and now there is this tragedy. With the men it is a case of *plus ça change*. But in the female ranks, events have been unrolling, some of them casting the infant sport in an unflattering Barnum and Bailey light, others garnering for it the legitimacy lacking in the masculine big-money ring.

In England, three months after my bout, the British-born welterweight champion Jane Couch won another fight—a sex-discrimination case at an industrial tribunal against the British Boxing Board of Control. The BBBC had hitherto turned down Couch's applications for a license to box on her home turf because it claimed she would be "emotionally unstable" during her periods and more prone to accidents. Women, said the BBBC, were more susceptible than men to bruising and therefore to brain damage. A woman, it worried, might also inadvertently box while pregnant.

The evidence was "incontrovertible," declared the tribunal, that Couch had suffered sex discrimination in the workplace, that she had been a victim of "gender-based stereotypes and assumptions." Since then, Britain—at least the beer-swilling segment of it—has clasped

Couch warmly to its bosom. Lippy and cheeky, she is a chat-show regular, has published her autobiography (titled *Jane Couch*), and pens a weekly advice column in *The Sunday Sport*, the tabloid with a higher nipple count than *Hustler*.

On the subject of nipples, the December 1997 *Playboy* won women's boxing some of its widest coverage yet (so to speak) in an excellent, thoughtful eight-page feature story by Amy Handelsman, who did her research at the 1997 inaugural Women's Nationals in Augusta and at two Brooklyn gyms, Gleason's and Bed-Stuy. Though not in the least bit prurient, the piece must have struck a chord with the magazine's teenage-boy readership, because two years later, in November 1999, *Playboy* reprised the subject. This time, however, the subtext had been exposed. On the cover stood a girl smiling broadly in red satin hotpants, holding her bare breasts with Everlast gloves. I.B.A. FEATHERWEIGHT CHAMPION MIA ST. JOHN NUDE, screamed the headline. Mia St. John had recently under-whelmed millions of pay-per-view fight fans as the warm-up act for Oscar De La Hoya's loss to Felix Trinidad on September 18. It depressed me to watch that bout, because it was boring and therefore bad PR for the sport, and because the commentators kept repeating how we would soon be seeing Mia St. John stripped.

"Most female boxers hate me," St. John claimed in her eight-page photo spread. "They're jealous, but I don't care. My posing can only help give women's boxing the recognition it deserves."

Whatever recognition women's boxing deserves, this is not it. Neither is it a *New York Times* story from June 1998, headlined: FIGHTER SCRATCHED FROM BOUT: SHE'S 21 WEEKS PREGNANT, about Maria Nieves Garcia (2-1), the WIBF lightweight champion, who was so non-plussed at the revelation she insisted on two further pregnancy tests: both positive. I mean, this is good comedy, but the belittling of female boxers is getting tiresome. Around now—in mid-1998—the excitement that accompanied the early women's bouts was running dry. Though female boxers were no longer a novelty, there still weren't enough to go around, and mismatches were legion. We needed a big bout. Christy Martin was still the only very famous female boxer, so it had to be Christy; Christy versus Kathy Collins; or, better still, Christy versus Lucia Rijker. Kathy muscled in on one of Christy's publicity jaunts before a Madison Square Garden undercard appearance. Hey, it's my hometown, said Kathy. I want her. She's just trying to steal my thunder, said Christy, refusing the challenge. Lucia's manager, Stan Hoffman, also attempted to make the match. Christy kept turning them down, as the purse got fatter and fatter. It grew to $750,000, but Christy still wasn't biting. Okay, said Lucia, you don't think it's enough? Then we'll make it winner-takes-all. Christy, her credibility flat on the canvas, sidestepped that one, too.

As for me, I left Colin. We never recovered from that bout. We stayed friends, though, and now among his trainees are the 2000 women's national amateur featherweight champion and a fitness boxer who's making quite a name for herself as the manager of fighters—Andrew Murray among them. I myself turned down a few fight offers, including one last-minute substitution with a big four-figure payday. That's when I noticed how unkeen I was to fight again. I trained alone. Then I switched to Baby—that's Victor Babilonia, from Colombia—then, when Baby disappeared, to Hector Roca. I got reinspired. New girls arrived, including several impressively skilled athletes: Yelena Binder, aged sixteen; Chika Nakamura; Jill Emery, now the *inter*national Jr Middleweight champ. We sparred; it was heaven. I took a job. I couldn't get to the gym as much.

———————

Two more Golden Gloves; two more Women's Nationals; the same winners—Veronica Simmons, Evelyn Rodriguez, Alicia Ashley, Patricia Alcivar. Just about everyone turned pro ... with varying success. Evelyn was knocked out by Vienna Williams in her debut. Denise Moraetes (née Lutrick), Leona Brown, Alicia Ashley, Laura Kielczewski, and Melissa Salamone are all doing well, especially Salamone (17-0), who has also been campaigning unsuccessfully for Christy.

Dee Hamaguchi and Bridgette Robinson fought their pro debuts (a draw and a win respectively). Veronica Simmons could not resist winning yet another pair of Golden Gloves and another national title (she has broken the record for amateur titles in different weight classes, male or female) but has now taken the irreversible step into the professional ring. Nobody wants to fight her. Kathy Collins (14-1-3) now has four belts—and a workout video. Jill Matthews at 8-3-0 has been a little less active lately. Lucia Rijker (14-0) has still been taken the distance by only one fighter, Dora Webber. Angela Reiss lost her second bout. She retired and switched to training others. (She got really mad when her first fighter was disqualified from the New York Metro Championships by failing the pregnancy test.) Then, in Seattle, October 1999, a boxer named Margaret MacGregor did the thing I once thought I wanted to do and took on a man. She defeated Loi Chow in a four-round unanimous decision.

And now it's fall 2000. *Shadow Boxers* won prizes at six film festivals and is a hit in theaters. *On the Ropes*, which features the story of Tyrene Manson, Jill Matthews's sparring partner, was nominated for an Oscar in 2000. (Tyrene, on work release from Riker's Island, attended the Oscar ceremony.) Sometime Gleason's habitué Karyn Kusama made a moving feature film debut about a female boxer, *Girlfight*, that won the Jury Prize at Sundance 2000 and made a huge splash on its September US release. Everywhere you turn, there's a pair of women in a ring—with the notable exception of the Sydney Olympics. However, the movement (led by Denise Moraetes) to achieve the critical mass of amateurs necessary for female boxers to reach the 2004 or 2008 games is growing. We are going to need teams from twenty countries. A preview will be available in 2001 at the Worlds Tournament to be held in the United States; the U.S. team will be drawn from a slightly widened net, as the age limit was raised by a year, to thirty-four, in October 1999, to bring it in line with an International Boxing Association ruling. At the same time, the medical requirements for the Masters (over thirty-four) were drastically relaxed, paving the way for any old girls who resisted the bait I took and remain eligible for the amateurs.

Still, in all this movement, it's the professional ranks that garner the most media coverage. The biggest news in women's boxing since Christy Martin first fought on TV has been the rise of the fighters' daughters: especially Laila Ali—eight wins—and Jacqui Frazier Lyde (the same Jacqui Frazier who congratulated me at the Blue Horizon). Frazier fought her debut in Scranton, Pennsylvania. Her manager: Don Elbaum. John Toliaferro was there. He said the reason they stopped the bout in the first round is that it was so embarrassingly awful. But of course it was; Frazier Lyde, a lawyer, mother of three, five-nine, 186 pounds, thirty-eight years old, was making her pro debut in public before she was ready, just like I did. Just like so many women still do. Laila Ali did the same thing. I met her in May 1999. She had just started to train and was not ready to spar; she couldn't even make the speed bag thunder yet. Her handlers swore they wouldn't let her step into the ring for a long, long time, that they'd do right by her, that she'd probably start with the amateurs. Five months later, she knocked out an overweight twenty-seven-year-old divorced mother of two in thirty-one seconds. KID GLOVES said the *New York Post* headline. BRING ON ALI'S KID, SAYS JOE FRAZIER'S DAUGH-TER. This is not what women's boxing deserves. Ali is beginning to fulfill her potential, though. She is training right, and, with seven wins to her credit at the time of writing, may soon be meeting some genuine boxers. Perhaps she will take the challenge from the one who lacks her notoriety but would upset her in the ring: Laila Ali versus Veronica Simmons is the match I want to see.

I still go to Gleason's; it's still my second home. Now I walk from the York Street F train station in the company of hip young artists who have colonized the neighborhood in the past few years, whose annual open studio is attended by the entire Manhattan art world. Should they wish to buy a place to live around here, they would need a Mary Boone endorsement and several dot-com billionaire patrons, since a loft in DUMBO costs, what, around $1 million minimum. The Between the Bridges bar is not broken-down now. It does a roaring trade, as does its neighbor, Superfine, a restaurant serving dishes like grilled sardines with baby bok choy. In summer, there is a permanent line for the sidewalk tables. There are 112 women registered at Gleason's—that's fourteen percent of the membership—many of whom fight, or intend to fight. It is time for Jill Matthews to be outta here. Boxing for women is normal.

AFTERWORD

Doesn't time fly? Eleven years later and, let's get this out of the way:
I'm not boxing much. I'm old! But that's not the reason. The awe-
some Australian writer Mischa Merz, for example, is about the same
age, and she's still fighting in the amateur Masters division, not to
mention teaching boxing classes in Brunswick (check out her books
"Bruising" and "The Sweetest Thing" –I'm mentioned!). No, age is
no barrier to boxing . . . but time is. Two or three hours out of my day
now that I'm a mother as well as a writer-editor and, these days, a web
entrepreneur, I can't really afford. I do miss the gym though. Gleason's is still going strong, packed with women these days, surrounded
by wanton gentrification—modern furniture downstairs, locavore gro-
ceries next door, avant garde theater down the block—with Bruce
Silverglade still at the helm. I miss the camaraderie, the discipline,
the training, the routine, the people. I don't miss fighting. Just in case
this hasn't been made abundantly clear: I am not a natural fighter. My
feeling that participating in any kind of violence, even a consensual,
controlled, all but choreographed kind, is not a useful contribution to
the evolution of humanity has only grown since I had those qualms

in the ring in Philadelphia. And, without the carrot of fighting, or at least sparring, training loses a great deal of its appeal.

But enough about me. What's happened to the sport of women's boxing? Did it, in fact, become "normal"? Well, yes and no. With the exception of one extremely headline-grabbing and overwhelmingly positive development, which we'll get to in a moment, plus an Oscar-winning moment in the spotlight, it chugged on at more or less the same level for the entire noughties. There were more female mismatches, more fighters' daughters bouts (sometimes those two were synonymous), and more neglect of women's bouts by mainstream media. On the other hand, there were yet more women taking up the sport, more boxercise classes in more gyms (it's probably illegal for a fitness gym not to offer boxing at this point), and more amateur competitions with more countries participating. There was also plenty of appropriation of the undeniably cool yet sanitized image of the female boxer in order to sell stuff. So the ladyboxer is certainly a familiar icon, and yet the real thing, the fighting female, remains out in left field.

This may be all about to change. Women's boxing is making its Olympic debut at the 2012 London Olympics—in my hometown, yet! As the U.K.'s Olympics minister Tessa Jowell put it, while announcing the news she called "historic": "London 2012 will now create the first-ever generation of boxing heroines and hopefully inspire even more women to take up the sport." In February, near Spokane, WA, at the first ever U.S. Olympic Women's Boxing Team Trials, 24 hopefuls in three weight classes will duke it out for the chance to go to the Women's World Championships in Qinhuang-dao, China, and thence to grab one of three possible spots to fight on by far the biggest stage women's boxing has ever enjoyed. This is of course, having knock-on effects in the wider world of amateur fighting. As I write, the International Amateur Boxing Association (AIBA) has just announced the inclusion of the sport at the Commonwealth Games. And this is only right: there were, at last count, 120 international boxing federations with female divisions. Even Afghanistan has a women's boxing team—Kabul-based teenage sisters Shabnam and Sadaf Rahimi have been getting a bunch of press lately, sparring in their long sleeves, with headscarves in place of protective leather headgear.

Protective headgear that doesn't always do what it says on the box . . . It hasn't all been a downhill coast for the women's amateur sport. In April 2005, geography teacher, triathlete, martial artist and regional Golden Gloves winner, Becky Zerlentes became the first woman to die in a sanctioned amateur boxing match when her opponent in a Colorado State amateur championship bout knocked her out with a "blunt-force trauma" to the head—through the regulation headgear—from which she never awoke. The horror seemed all the more acute to me at the time, because that was the year the Clint Eastwood film "Million Dollar Baby" was the big winner at the Oscars. The film, based on cutman-turned-writer F.X. Toole's short story of the same name, featured Hilary Swank's best-actress portrayal of a champion boxer (enjoying distinctly implausible worldwide fame, and an even less plausible eponymous six-figure payday) who suffers a knockout blow in the ring and ends up paralyzed. The movie hit close to home for me, not so much for its worst-case scenario—which I found egregiously melodramatic—but more for emphasizing how far out of the ring I'd fallen. Hilary Swank, you see, was trained entirely at Gleasons by my old pal Hector Roca—and I never managed to coincide with their Hollywoodish sessions once. Damn, but I missed the most glamour there had ever been at the gym! Also, the villain of the piece—the dirty-fighting Billie "The Blue Bear" who administers the blow—was played by our old friend Lucia Rijker. On account of the fresh dose of fame this bestowed on her, the promoter Bob Arum deemed it lucrative to revive the notion of a Lucia Rijker Christy Martin match up. Great idea! He'd call it "Million Dollar Lady" and the winner would net—thus disproving the abovementioned implausibility—a hitherto unheard-of six-figure purse. The bout was set for July 2005 in Las Vegas, and, though Christy by this time had been far surpassed in the most-famous-female-boxer stakes by Laila Ali, who had been steadily racking up wins (including a Christy Martin KO in 2003) and media hits, it was bound to be the biggest thing in women's boxing since Christy's breakout Tyson-undercard, Sports Illustrated cover-earning fight.

But it wasn't to be. Christy balked. That would have been her last notable bout. The seven she fought in the second half of the decade (three wins, three losses, one draw) were distinctly unexciting and against poor opponents. She hit the headlines (ish) again in late 2010 when she was stabbed and shot by her cornerman-husband Jim Martin. She survived, and now lives with her partner Sherry (yes, a lady) in Charlotte, where she's still, reportedly, training. Anyway, as that not-so-savory late career arc illustrates, it seems like business-as-usual in the unregulated world of the professionals.

Laila Ali, however, with her golden genes, has done her best to ennoble the sport. I met her again in January 2001, at which point she was eight wins—risibly easy ones mostly—into her new career. What I most wanted to know was: when was she going to fight Veronica Simmons? Oh yeah, said Laila, she keeps hearing about her. Sure she'll fight her, she said, but she—Laila—needed more experience to make it a good match. In other words, the Super Middleweight Brooklyn corrections officer who broke my nose remained too dangerous to fight. After her pro debut Veronica had waited a year for her second bout, which she won by TKO in 1 minute, 15 seconds, then another 18 months for her third, which she won by decision—at which point she gave up and exercised her athletic prowess by becoming a Linebacker with the IWFL New York Sharks. Laila Ali was not wrong to dodge Veronica at that stage in her development. She couldn't risk being beaten by an unknown, not only for the sake of her own career, but also for the sake of the entire sport. Ali was then, and remains, all too aware that she can practically single-handedly kill or cure women's boxing. She knew she'd be chum for media before she began, that she'd be helpless to prevent the world watching her for her name's sake. For a few years, it seemed that in one sense, she just couldn't win. No matter how seriously she trained, or

how much she improved (and she did, vastly), she kept being criticized for ducking difficult matches, when all she was doing was building her experience and record just the same as the rest of them, aided
by the odd guaranteed loser.

Because, yes, those Ohio girls recruited off street corners remained
as active as ever. The only difference now is that there are more of
them. Maybe it's the recession, but there are extra supplies flowing in
from Wisconsin, Indiana, and especially Georgia—home base of
Mezaughn Kemp, infamous Atlanta broker of opponents, who told
the *Miami Herald* he should be up for a Nobel Prize for all the desperate women he'd rescued from the streets. Whether humiliation in
shorts counts as being rescued is debatable, but the sour science of
tomato-can boxing has reached new depths thanks to the eternal
shortage of viable opponents and the persistent mirage of the purse
of gold for an unblemished record. Kemp has admitted to ruses such
as using fake blood for dramatic effect, and feeding strawberries to
an allergic girl just before the first bell to bring her face out in realistic welts. Sometimes he's pitted loser against loser to get a semi-
legitimate win on one record; more often he's padded the record of a
human punching bag—one Bethany Payne, for instance, was given
fifteen imaginary victories before she'd ever set foot in a ring to make
her look viable for a bout against Christy Martin. Payne also fought
ace fighters Isra Girgrah, Trina Ortegon, Chevelle Hallback, and
Daniella Somers—who, somehow, she took the six-round distance.
Payne "retired" in 1998, but there are plenty more where she came
from. Top contender Melissa del Valle (formerly Salamone) is one
who's been under fire for breezing through a few too many "Kemp
girl" bouts, even though this impressive boxer has admitted freely
that one or two stretches of her fine record were papered like a news-
stand. "A lot of my opponents come from topless bars," she once told
a women's boxing website, "sure they were mismatches, yes they
were. But I have to make a living."

Del Valle's candor about her use of certified losers is unusual.
After one of those first-minute TKOs you're more likely to hear the

victor going on about how she trained real hard for this one because you never know. But scratch the boxers' records and Kemp girls crawl out from all over the place. There is also the related syndrome whereby a rookie boxer gets overmatched at the last minute. Chevelle Hallback vs. Lucia Rijker was such an occasion. What I didn't know when I wrote about that March 1997 Corpus Christi fight was that Hallback, who had had precisely forty-seven seconds ring experience (she'd knocked the girl out), had been told Rijker was "not very good," so she took the match on a few days notice. The night before the bout, she happened to catch that HBO *RealSports* program—the one featuring Christy Martin accusing Rijker of being a man and a five-second shot of me fighting the giantess in red shorts. In that light, it's incredible that Hallback fought at all, let alone that she gave Rijker four rounds of trouble. This kind of thing goes on all the time, though it's probably true to say that the vast majority of contenders would prefer to fight only strong opponents. Or would they? Hell, I don't know. Since the vast majority of contenders fight virtually unseen, it's hard to tell.

As often as not, the female bout that kicks off big boys' bout undercards takes place before the TV cameras start rolling. Women who fight in cages—and I mean mixed martial arts, not some exotic club specialty act—are more likely to gain cable time, and You Tube hits. The only girl boxers deemed worthy of regular public scrutiny for most of the past decade remained the fighters' daughters. But the daughters did earn their keep. Jacquie Frazier Lyde improved no end, and the overhyped daughter-grudge match, the so-called Ali-Frazier IV (quickly dubbed the "Groaner in Verona") turned out to be far more competitive than everyone feared. Frazier Lyde also took on Suzette Taylor (10-6-1)—the same Decatur resident who took Veronica Simmons the distance at the first Women's Nationals, and was by then fighting pro out of Las Vegas—and beat her. Ali retired from boxing in 2007 with a 24-win record—unblemished except for the constant criticism that she dodged the serious competition (Ann Wolfe, Natascha Ragosina, Vonda Ward . . .)—and promptly became far more famous by almost winning the fourth season of *Dancing With The Stars.*

When I do make it to Gleason's, I find it both unchanged and radically different. Colin's moved on to another gym, but Reggie Forde, Bob Jackson, and Hector Roca are still around, joined by a score of new trainers, and Domenico Menacho is still exhorting women to hook off the jab. There are many to exhort. In DUMBO at least, women's boxing is so normal that there are periods when we outnumber the guys. It's great to hit the bags and not stand out in any way; I don't miss the limelight that being a pioneer brought. Okay, maybe a tiny bit. But no matter how many hordes of women insert the mouthguard, wrap their hands and step through the ropes to fight, I do have one quiet claim to fame. I'm pretty sure I'm Gleason's first *retired* female professional.

ABOUT THE AUTHOR

Kate Sekules recently founded Refashioner, a marketplace for pre-owned couture. She was editor in chief of *Culture + Travel*, travel editor of *Food & Wine*, consulting editor-in-chief at Conde Nast Digital (*Concierge*, *Gourmet Live*), and has written for *The New York Times, Travel + Leisure, Interior Design, Town & Country, The New Yorker, New York, Vogue, Harper's Bazaar*, and *O*, among others.

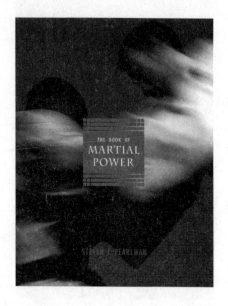

THE OVERLOOK MARTIAL ARTS HANDBOOK
by David Mitchell
978-0-87951-759-5 · $16.95 · PB

This is the most readable and complete martial arts survey available.
Covering Karate, Kendo, Kung Fu, Judo, and Aikido as well as the
lesser known disciplines of Budo, Hapkido, and the Thai martial
arts, it includes the history, basic moves, principles, equipment, and
terminology of each, illustrated with 150 superb line drawings.

THE OVERLOOK PRESS
New York, NY
www.overlookpress.com

A WOMAN'S GUIDE TO MARTIAL ARTS
How to Choose a Discipline and Get Started
by Monica McCabe Cardoza
978-0-87951-843-1 • $13.95 • PB

"With the information in this book, you have a foundation on which you can build as you explore the martial arts world." —CAROL WILEY, EDITOR OF *WOMEN IN THE MARTIAL ARTS* AND *MARTIAL ARTS TEACHERS ON TEACHING*

"Look out Jackie Chan! *A Woman's Guide to Martial Arts* teaches us to work through martial arts to shape the body." —*NEW YORK POST*

THE OVERLOOK PRESS
New York, NY
www.overlookpress.com